The Camden Expedition of 1864 and the
Opportunity Lost by the Confederacy
to Change the Civil War

The Camden Expedition of 1864 and the Opportunity Lost by the Confederacy to Change the Civil War

by MICHAEL J. FORSYTH

McFarland & Company, Inc., Publishers

Jefferson, North Carolina, and London

LIBRARY OF CONGRESS CATALOGUING-IN-PUBLICATION DATA

Forsyth, Michael J., 1966–
The Camden Expedition of 1864 and the opportunity lost
by the Confederacy to change the Civil War / by Michael J. Forsyth.
p.   cm.
Includes bibliographical references and index.

ISBN-13: 978-0-7864-3735-1
softcover : 50# alkaline paper ♾

1. Camden Expedition (1864)   2. Steele, Frederick, 1819–1868.
3. Arkansas— History — Civil War, 1861–1865 — Campaigns.
4. Louisiana — History — Civil War, 1861–1865 — Campaigns.
5. United States— History — Civil War, 1861–1865 — Campaigns.   I. Title.
E476.35.F67   2008   973.7'36 — dc21   2003004182

British Library cataloguing data are available

Cover photograph: Union Major General Frederick Steele,
commander of the Federal Department of Arkansas and the
VII Corps (Massachusetts Commandery Military Order of the
Loyal Legion and the U.S. Army Military History Institute)

Manufactured in the United States of America

*McFarland & Company, Inc., Publishers
Box 611, Jefferson, North Carolina 28640
www.mcfarlandpub.com*

For Nana

Acknowledgments

In writing this book I became indebted to a great number of people who provided me with assistance and encouragement. I would like to express my gratitude to the folks who did so much to enable my success.

First, I must thank God for blessing my life far beyond reasonable expectations. I would also like to thank my wife, Maryellen, and our children, Andrew and Ashley. I spent many long hours working away at completing my work and my family, as always, supported my work in spite of the inevitable papers and books I routinely left strewn around the house. They have always provided me with the foundation and steadiness I need to keep plugging away. For this and everything that you all do for me, I thank you.

Next, I want to express my thanks to Dr. Karl Roider of Louisiana State University. I first met 'Doc. R' five years ago as I began work on a master's degree at the university. Since then Dr. Roider has never hesitated to provide advice and suggestions to improve my writing. In spite of a heavy schedule, Dr. Roider graciously agreed to read the manuscript. His insight helped immensely in my formulation of the thesis and supporting ideas. Once again, thank you Dr. Roider for your support.

Ms. Sheila Duckworth is the librarian of the United States Field Artillery School's Morris Swett Technical Library. I met her while I was teaching at the school. As I began to work on this project, Ms. Duckworth enthusiastically found numerous sources for me, making my work infinitely easier. I cannot express how much I appreciate her selfless assistance in words, but I hope she will accept my heartfelt thanks. Without her the book would certainly have lacking.

Finally, I must thank my parents Jack and Edith Forsyth and grandmother, Jean Alviti. They provided me with the enduring tools to survive in a tough world and because of them I am a better person. Thank you.

Contents

List of Maps

Introduction

In 1864, a cornered and struggling Union force in Louisiana was saved from extinction by a federal offensive that has come to be known as the Camden Expedition. Though little remembered today, this expedition overcame the forces of the South's Red River Campaign and, in so doing, prevented the Rebels from turning the war in their favor.

The Camden Expedition even more than the Red River Campaign is a forgotten chapter of American Civil War historiography since it occurred in a region considered a backwater to both sides during the war: Arkansas. By 1864 Arkansas was cut off from the eastern Confederacy after the fall of Vicksburg and seemingly unimportant in the larger scheme for winning the war. Yet, a complicated turn of events thrust this unknown Federal offensive onto center stage in determining the eventual outcome of the war. The Camden Expedition is a story of personal conflicts, arduous marches, desperate battles, and the strength of the human spirit. Because of the efforts of a small Union army in Arkansas, a larger one in Louisiana escaped danger and eventually exerted great influence in momentous battles in the East later that year. As a result of the sacrifices of the men in this tiny army, they enabled—albeit indirectly—the Union to win the war and sealed the fate of the Confederacy.

Camden is an intriguing study because of the influence it had on the war and the "might-have-beens" had the key characters made some different decisions. Since the Camden Expedition is such an obscure episode in the record of the Civil War, I would like to set the stage with a brief introduction. It will provide a quick snapshot of the situation in 1864 and the role Camden would play in winning the Civil War, particularly with respect to the national election. In addition, this introduction will provide a glimpse of the intriguing personalities of the opposing commanders who decided the fate of the expedition and the now quiet Arkansas fields where the armies collided.

Optimism ran high in the North as the war entered its fourth year. For the Confederacy, 1863 had been a disaster as their armies met with resounding defeats at Gettysburg, Vicksburg, and Chattanooga. Rebeldom was suffering ever-increasing hardships as the Federal armies pressed in closer to the southern heartland and the blockade choked off trade with her ports. Now with a new general-in-chief, Ulysses S. Grant, at the helm it seemed only a matter of time before the Confederacy would collapse. This proved a hasty assumption as the tenacious Rebel commanders had other ideas.

Upon assuming command of all the Union armies, General Grant brought a war-winning strategy to the office. It involved a coordinated offensive by all Federal armies directed against the primary Confederate armies still in the field. By placing unstoppable pressure on the South's smaller armies, eventually they would collapse. The key to the strategy was to ensure that all of the North's vast resources focused on destroying the slowly withering southern capabilities. Here the strategy skewed. Before assuming command, Grant's predecessor, Major General Henry W. Halleck, set everything in motion for a campaign west of the Mississippi—away from the heartland. The effort, known as the Red River Campaign, represented a major diversion from Grant's program for 1864. A key component of Halleck's Red River invasion was to mount another smaller offensive from Arkansas in order to "co-operate" with the Federal troops moving through the Red River Valley. Grant allowed it to continue after taking command because he believed Federal forces in Louisiana and Arkansas could wrap up the campaign before the scheduled jump off date for his spring offensives and he did not want to embarrass his former boss, Halleck, by countermanding his previous orders. It did not work out as planned.

Confederate forces west of the Mississippi under General Edmund Kirby Smith and Richard Taylor quickly defeated and cornered a much larger Union army under Major General Nathaniel P. Banks. When it appeared the Rebels had Banks' army and a large Union fleet in the Red River on the ropes, the Confederates abruptly stopped. Why? Because the Federal army moving southward from Arkansas toward Louisiana threatened the hinterland of Smith's Trans-Mississippi Department confusing Smith as to which column represented the Federal main effort in the region. This Union force under Major General Frederick Steele was the Federal VII Army Corps—also known as the Department of Arkansas—moving down from Little Rock in accordance with Halleck's original scheme.

Kirby Smith, over the vociferous objections of Richard Taylor, stripped Taylor of most of his men in Louisiana and moved into Arkansas to join General Sterling Price's small army in defeating Steele. Sterling Price had successfully stopped Steele's column with his robust cavalry column and forced him into Camden in search of forage for the army. With Steele effectively stymied, Smith actually had no need to turn north for Arkansas. However, Price had successfully lobbied for a counter-offensive against Steele in preparation for an invasion of Missouri—Price's home state. Taylor, a Louisianan, failed to convince Smith of the need to press the advantage in *his* home state. Conflicts of personality figured prominently in the decisions made by Smith.

The Federals had handed the Confederates a golden opportunity to turn the war in their favor. The Union had diverted 50,000 men from the main effort in the east to an unnecessary sideshow west of the Mississippi. Capturing or destroying a large portion of the Union army could have had a detrimental effect on public morale in the North and, as a result, Lincoln's reelection bid. However, the Confederates failed because of a rigid strategic vision, infighting, and confusion created by the Camden Expedition.

Camden almost did not happen. Steele, commander of the Federal Department of Arkansas, had serious reservations about his role in supporting the Red River Campaign with a movement south. Many factors made an offensive in southern Arkansas prohibitive, and Steele attempted to find a way out of making the attempt. Correspondence streamed between Arkansas and Washington as Steele made his case to the Federal high command. Eventually, a direct order forced Steele's hand, and he lurched southward toward the Red River Valley. This saved the sizeable Union Army of the Gulf from destruction. What if Steele had won in his lobbying effort to avoid making the march?

I contend that had Steele not received the order to move, disaster would have stricken not only the Army of the Gulf, but the entire Union cause. This is because the army cornered by the Confederates in Louisiana later escaped and went on to make significant contributions to the final outcome of the war. Their efforts not only enabled the Union to win battles, it helped seal the fate of the Confederacy when Abraham Lincoln won reelection. With the series of disasters that befell the Union cause in early 1864 it is debatable whether Lincoln could have won without the men from the Army of the Gulf.

Therefore, the small Union army under General Frederick Steele that never numbered more than 15,000 men made a contribution to the war effort far beyond its small size. The minor and seemingly insignificant Camden Expedition helped extract a much larger army from danger and distract the attention of the Rebel high command. Steele's men braved quarter rations, torrential rains, mud, and horrific combat in a forlorn offensive. Though on the surface this expedition appeared a failure for the Union by immediately tangible measures, it actually proved fortuitous when considered in a strategic context. The evidence suggests that had Smith not turned north to Arkansas but pressed the advantage in Louisiana, the Confederates could have destroyed Banks and the Union fleet. Because Steele's men marched south from Little Rock as ordered, they saved an army and, more significantly, their cause.

1

"A mere demonstration will not be sufficient..."

At first examination the 1864 Camden Expedition appears as nothing more than a failed Union invasion in a backwater theater of the Civil War. Indeed, it is largely ignored by contemporary historians as most have chosen to write about the momentous events that occurred in the East. To date only one full-length account of the expedition exists and it is simply a narrative of the events.[1] However, on further investigation this minor Federal offensive had a great deal of influence, not only in the Trans-Mississippi region, but also in the larger context of the war as a whole. Probably the most interesting aspect of the expedition is the fact that it almost did not happen.

Major General Frederick Steele's Department of Arkansas, far removed from the major theaters of the war in 1864, seemed unimportant in the big scheme for winning the war. However, plans laid in Washington would thrust the department onto the larger stage. The high command in Washington planned the Camden Expedition as a secondary effort in support of the Red River Campaign slated for spring 1864. The campaign up the Red failed miserably, but could have been disastrous if not for Steele's thrust into southern Arkansas. The expedition forced the Rebel high command west of the Mississippi to choose how to allocate their meager resources to meet two simultaneous invasions into the heart of the region. As a result of the decisions made by the Confederate commanders, the Rebels lost one of their last significant opportunities to win the war. In short, the failed Camden Expedition saved Federal forces in the Red River Valley from certain destruction because the mere presence of Steele at Camden forced the Confederates to deal with the threat. Without Camden, the Rebels could destroy the Union Army of the Gulf on the Red and deprive the Federal war effort of 30,000-plus veteran soldiers and possibly win the war.

Though the Camden Expedition fades into obscurity when compared to the Overland and Atlanta Campaigns in the East, it represented one of the Confederacy's most successful defensive efforts. The small, austere Confederate District of Arkansas initially performed an admirable delaying action to prevent Steele's rapid advance through southern Arkansas. This retrograde movement forced Steele to slow his rate of march while effectively depleting his commissary stores in a barren country. As a result, Federal forces diverted to Camden to establish a base of supply and launch details to forage the countryside. Rebel Major General Sterling Price's vigilant cavalry successfully ambushed the scattered Federal detachments and created a crisis at the Union headquarters. After midnight deliberations, the Yankees decided to retreat back to their starting point at Little Rock. Following a final meaningless engagement at Jenkins' Ferry, the Federal army pulled into the Arkansas capital. The losses in the expedition paint a grim picture of the Union invasion while conversely demonstrating the still potent striking power of the Confederacy's Trans-Mississippi army.

The following chart contrasts the losses of the two armies in the Camden Expedition[2]:

Camden Expedition Comparative Loss Chart

	Union Losses	Confederate Losses
Men	2750	2300
Wagons	635	35
Animals	2500	under 100
Guns	8	3
Boats	*Adams* and *Chippewa*	Steamer *Homer*

The irony of the great success enjoyed by the Confederates is that the victory of Camden unwittingly allowed a more significant Union force in Louisiana to escape destruction. As previously noted the Camden Expedition was part of a larger military offensive, the Red River Campaign. Major General Henry Wager Halleck conceived the idea to conduct a two-pronged offensive into the heart of the Trans-Mississippi region. In late 1863 he set wheels in motion that would result in the offensive.

> [I]t is necessary ... that the flag be restored to *some one point* in Texas, that can be best and most safely effected by a combined military and naval movement up the Red River to Alexandria, Natchitoches, or Shreveport, and the military occupation of northern Texas.... By adopting the line of the Red river you retain your connexion with your own base and separate still more the two points of the rebel confederacy. Moreover, you cut northern Louisiana and southern Arkansas entirely off from supplies and reinforcements from Texas.... I write this simply as a suggestion, and not as a military instruction.[3]

The main effort centered in the vital Red River Valley where Major General Nathaniel P. Banks commanded over 30,000 combat veterans. Banks' objective was Shreveport, Louisiana, the de facto Confederate capital of the Trans-Mississippi Department. From here the Federal authorities could consolidate power over the entire region by controlling commerce on the Red and clearing out any remaining Confederates in Texas.[4]

As a part of the campaign, Halleck wrote Banks on January 4, 1864, outlining further details of a move southward by Steele from Little Rock to link up with Banks in the vicinity of Shreveport. In his dispatch he instructs that "as soon as you have sufficient water in the Atchafalaya and Red rivers, you operate in that direction [and] Steele's army ... should be directed to the same object." Once the two forces combined, Banks was to move back to New Orleans with a portion of his force for a planned assault on Mobile. Steele would then take over command of Union forces on the Red to clear the region of Confederates and reestablish Federal authority.[5] The plan, however, quickly fell apart as both Banks and Steele ran into trouble shortly after embarking on their separate courses.

As Shelby Foote points out in his *Narrative*, "the most difficult of all maneuvers was the combination of widely divided columns."[6] With this in mind it is easy to understand how the widely divided Union columns with a Rebel army interposed between them came to grief. One participant noted that "it was hardly possible [for Banks] to communicate with Steele." A quick glance at a map of the Trans-Mississippi Department shows that Banks and Steele would be separated by over 150 airline miles of hostile territory or twice that distance via river.

Major General Nathaniel P. Banks, commander of the Federal Army of the Gulf, escaped destruction of his force when the bulk of the pursuing Confederate army turned north to drive back the VII Corps in Arkansas. Courtesy Massachusetts Commandery Military Order of the Loyal Legion and the United States Army Military History Institute.

With communications as primitive as they were in 1864, cooperation between the two Federal commanders was impossible.[7] As a result, Steele did not have knowledge of the trouble Banks had run into on the Red.

Banks launched the Red River Campaign on March 12, 1864, at Simmesport, Louisiana. His Army of the Gulf made admirable progress in the initial stages of the campaign. Within five days his veterans had reduced the stout Fort DeRussy on the lower Red and moved on Alexandria halfway to the objective, Shreveport. Here circumstances began to conspire against the success of the offensive. First, the naval contingent under Rear Admiral David Dixon Porter had difficulty ascending the Red at Alexandria due to falling river levels and the infamous "rapids" opposite the city. After much cajoling the navy got above the dangerous and rocky rapids at Alexandria. However, if the river levels fell any further there was a chance the fleet would find itself trapped up the Red.

Second, the cool relationship between Banks and Porter deteriorated amid allegations of speculating for profits in cotton. Banks, a career politician, and Porter, a crusty naval "lifer," were required "to co-operate"[8] according to the correspondence from Halleck. With no command relationship established it would be challenging at best to make these divergent personalities work together. With recriminations about cotton flying and Porter's anxiety for the safety of his boats, it became next to impossible to achieve any semblance of "cooperation."

On March 27 Banks advanced northwest from Alexandria toward his objective less than ninety miles away. At the small hamlet of Grand Ecore, Banks made an ominous decision that would doom the outcome of the campaign. From Simmesport to Grand Ecore the army had used roads in close proximity to the river. This allowed the soldiers to draw logistical and fire support from the navy. However, at Grand Ecore the road northwest diverged from the river — or so Banks believed. Upon arrival at Grand Ecore Banks received a dispatch from the new Union commander-in-chief, Lieutenant General Ulysses S. Grant, ordering him to conclude the campaign by April 10. Since it was already April 3, Banks decided that conducting proper reconnaissance to confirm or deny the availability of a suitable road close to the river would take too much time.[9] He instead moved his army up the Mansfield Road away from the river. At Mansfield he could turn back toward the Red where he could again use a river road to handrail the rest of the way to Shreveport. This route, he reasoned, would allow him to move more quickly to his objective in accordance with Grant's directive.

This decision provided the smaller Confederate forces with the opportunity to strike the Federal army at a point of disadvantage in the "pine desert" of west Louisiana.[10] Lieutenant General Edmund Kirby Smith commanded the Confederate Trans-Mississippi Department. His primary subordinate in Louisiana was Major General Richard Taylor. Taylor, who had closely observed Banks' steady progress up the Red, recognized his opportunity and planned to strike Banks boldly at a country crossroad south of Mansfield. Taylor's District of West Louisiana had about 12,000 troops available for the assault. The Federal army had about 30,000 troops, but they would be strung out on a narrow dirt road bordered by a thick pine forest on both sides. Taylor laid a well-planned ambush across the Mansfield Road to hit the head of the Union column. Once the Yankees stopped and attempted to deploy into battle formation, he would strike into the flanks with an attack column. Finally, he would charge down the road upon the Federal retreat in a tightly packed column destroying each individual piece of the enemy army in detail. As an added incentive the Union army had an enormous 700-wagon field train accompanying the march that would prove a coveted prize for the ragged Rebel force.[11]

Taylor sprung the ambush in the early afternoon of April 8, 1864, destroying the lead division of Banks' army and pursued the flying column in a running fight for miles southward back toward Grand Ecore. This was the turning point in the campaign. Flushed with the euphoria of victory, Taylor brought up fresh troops that had not participated in the fight at Mansfield in order to press his advantage. Banks had drawn his army up in defensive positions around the small village of Pleasant Hill. Taylor pushed his army all night and into the early morning hours of the 9th. After a short rest, he attempted a flank march around the Federal left about three o'clock that afternoon.[12]

Taylor's attack miscarried as one of Banks' most competent subordinates, Brigadier General Andrew Jackson Smith, turned the tables on the Rebels and caught the flanking column by surprise in their own flank. The Confederate attack melted as Smith's veterans cut up the assault. That night Banks momentarily regained his composure calling a council of war to consider whether or not to reorient his forces and press on for Shreveport or retreat.

Lieutenant General Edmund Kirby Smith, commander of the Confederate Department of the Trans-Mississippi, made the fateful decision to pursue the Federal VII Corps in Arkansas allowing the Army of the Gulf to escape destruction in Louisiana. Courtesy Massachusetts Commandery Military Order of the Loyal Legion and the United States Army Military History Institute.

However, when most of the assemblage counseled for continued retreat Banks lost his nerve and consented to a retrograde movement that night.[13] Thus, Taylor had cowed Banks into retreat in a dominating performance of generalship. Banks turned a tactical victory at Pleasant Hill into a strategic defeat guaranteeing the Red River Campaign would fail. But, the magnitude of failure was yet to be decided. That decision rested in the hands of the Rebel command team meeting less than two miles from where Banks held his council of war.

Since the campaign began Rebel commanders Smith and Taylor had maintained a strained relationship. Taylor, a Louisianan, believed that the best way to defend the Trans-Mississippi Department was in his home state by an aggressive counter-campaign on the Red. In his view, the greatest threat to the department came from Banks moving through Louisiana, and therefore his District of West Louisiana should receive the bulk of departmental resources.[14] However, Smith had adopted what he styled a "Fabian" policy of defense for the region. Central to the policy involved the use of interior lines to mass the region's limited resources at threatened points. Smith would then use his concentrated assets to pounce on enemy thrusts, then quickly reorient to deal with additional threats in other quarters. The policy used the vast space of the Trans-Mississippi to draw the enemy in, buy time, reduce risk to the minimal Confederate forces, and prepare for the counter-stroke.[15]

When General Steele launched the Camden Expedition on March 23, 1864, it perplexed Kirby Smith as to which invasion column represented the Federal main effort. As a result of his indecision, Smith ordered Richard Taylor to withdraw his forward-deployed forces toward Shreveport. Smith believed this would give him time to identify the main thrust and make a plan for the Federals' discomfiture.[16]

Smith had formulated his plan by the end of March and described it in a postwar account as follows:

> As soon as I received intelligence ... I ordered General Price, who commanded in Arkansas, to dispatch his entire infantry, consisting of Churchill's and Parson's divisions, to Shreveport, and General Maxey to move toward General Price.... Price with his cavalry was instructed to delay the march of Steele's column whilst the concentration [of all the infantry with Taylor] was being made. Occupying a central position at Shreveport, with the enemy's columns approaching from opposite directions, I proposed drawing them within striking distance, when, by concentrating upon and striking them in detail, both columns might be crippled or destroyed.[17]

Taylor became enraged at what he perceived to be Smith's indecisiveness and began firing off a series of emotionally charged, insubordinate dispatches to his superior. When Smith retained reinforcements at Shreveport meant for the Louisiana army, Taylor exploded. "Two weeks have elapsed since the fall of Alexandria and I have cherished the hope from day to day that assistance would reach me before I was forced to give up the producing country," he complained. This, of course, was in accordance with Smith's Fabian defensive strategy and he replied:

> The battle must be decisive, whether with Steele or Banks. Our position is a good one. We occupy the interior line, and a concentration is being forced which otherwise could never have happened. While we retain our little army undefeated we have hopes. We occupy a largely superior force of the enemy, which east of the Mississippi would decide the fate of the campaign. When we fight it must be for victory. Defeat not only loses the department, but releases the armies employed against us here for operations beyond the Mississippi. The advantage of our position should not be given up by any movement which may jeopardize the loss of the command.[18]

Taylor fought the battle of Mansfield before Smith intended to commence the counter-offensive and the news came as a great surprise. Taylor announced his victory at Mansfield to Smith in a late night dispatch on the 8th. Upon receipt early the next morning Smith had his horse saddled and rode immediately southward to the battlefield. He arrived around ten o'clock P.M. on the 9th following the Battle of Pleasant Hill. Taylor's reception of Smith around his campfire that night was a cool one. In light of Taylor's string of acid-laden letters and his frustration with Smith, relations between the two commanders simmered beneath the surface. Matters would soon come to a head when Smith announced his latest plans.[19]

The meeting started on a bad note, as Smith believed Taylor had lost the battle at Pleasant Hill. He awoke Taylor from his repose and announced, "[B]ad business, bad business General." Puzzled, Taylor replied, "I don't know General, what is the trouble?" "Banks will be upon you tomorrow with his whole army," answered Smith. Taylor retorted, "Well, General, if you will listen, you will hear Banks' artillery moving out now on their retreat." The two commanders now gave full expression to their views. Taylor wanted to pursue Banks to Grand Ecore, believing he could now smash him against the Red and destroy or capture the fleet in the falling river. But, "Steele's column from Arkansas caused him [Smith] much uneasiness," Taylor said in his post-war memoir. Smith believed that it was unnecessary to go after Banks. He felt his Fabian strategy was working as planned and stated that he intended to turn and concentrate the infantry in Arkansas to crush Steele. Taylor countered that when Steele "must learn of Banks's misfortune" he would have no choice but to "retire to Little Rock."[20] The meeting adjourned with the commanders agreeing to reconvene in Shreveport within a couple of days.

Smith and Taylor met again on the 14th at departmental headquarters. Neither man had changed his opinion of how to deploy the meager forces. Therefore, Smith ordered Taylor to detach three divisions from his army for service in Arkansas. Taylor grudgingly assented and left the meeting believing that in the event "it was learned that Steele had commenced to retreat ... the Confederate infantry would stop, and he would be allowed to march against Banks."[21]

On the 15th Smith learned that Steele had in fact turned back due to failing logistics. Elated, Taylor returned to headquarters thinking the infantry detached the day before would soon countermarch and rejoin him to press Banks to destruction. Smith instead dropped a bombshell on him. The three infantry divisions would not return to Taylor, but would instead continue on to Arkansas where Smith hoped to personally overtake Steele and destroy his army away from its base.[22] This represented the end of even a veneer of cordial relations between the two men and correspondingly it forfeited a major opportunity for the Confederacy. One might ask two questions of Smith's decision. First, was it necessary for Smith to pursue Steele's already retreating column in Arkansas and second, what motivated this decision?

General Frederick Steele reluctantly started south from Little Rock toward the Red River Valley on the 23rd of March. Literally from the start his small army encountered significant problems. The very night the bluecoats stepped off, headquarters announced that the quartermaster would issue only half rations for the duration of the march.[23] Apparently the commissary of Steele's Department of Arkansas had failed or was unable to stockpile enough supplies for the expedition. Logistics proved to be the Achilles' heel of the Camden Expedition.[24]

Nineteenth century armies were unable to sustain themselves over long distances or for an inordinate amount of time away from their bases. To sustain itself away from a base an army had to have water or rail transportation or forage off the land. In barren country lacking in transportation, such as the picked over area of southern Arkansas, an army depended upon wagon trains. This solution, however, was inadequate at best because the draft animals pulling the train required most of the available space in the wagons for forage. Depending on the situation, nineteenth century armies would exhaust their supplies about 100 miles from their base without a water or rail connection. Further, if the country they moved through had significant partisan resistance, the operating distances shortened proportionately.[25]

Southern Arkansas by 1864 lacked most of the requirements for sustaining an army for an extended period of time. It had few railroads, poor roads, and one navigable river, the Ouachita. In addition, the country had been thoroughly picked over for three years to subsist the Confederate army. Finally, guerillas and thieves roamed the area stealing what they needed from anyone for survival.[26] This proved a recipe for disaster for a Federal force the size of Steele's army attempting to move through the area to the Red River.

Less than a month out of Little Rock the conditions in southern Arkansas and the actions of Rebel cavalry forced the Federals to change their course of action. Around April 12 the supply situation became so acute that Steele diverted from his intermediate objective, Washington, Arkansas. Instead, the Union commander changed direction in favor of establishing a forward base at Camden. He believed that he could use the town as a depot by using the Ouachita as a supply route. After a short respite he would then resume the march.[27] However, unbeknownst to the Union army, the advance would never continue. Turning toward Camden represented the turning point of the expedition and the initiative had passed to the Confederates. But, did they need to exercise it?

Soon after arrival at Camden, Federal forces heard nasty rumors that the column in Louisiana had received rough handling near Mansfield and commenced a retreat back to Alexandria. With the Federal main effort defeated and moving in the opposite direction from Shreveport, Steele had little choice but to retreat as well. There were two reasons for this. First, Steele knew that the country between Camden and Shreveport would not support his army moving through the area. Second, all Confederate forces west of the Mississippi could then mass against his small army. When Steele confirmed Banks' demise he held a council of war with his generals in Camden and decided to retreat back to Little Rock.[28]

This of course is what Richard Taylor expected the Federals to do. He had strenuously pleaded with Kirby Smith to keep Rebel forces in Louisiana in order to destroy Banks in the Red River Valley. In his own words Taylor states:

> I dismissed the idea that Steele should move on Shreveport — Steele, [who] has already retreated over one hundred miles and been completely foiled in his plans by General Price with his raw cavalry ... [while] The remainder of Banks' beaten army will now number double Steele's original strength, and he is accompanied by a fleet numbering more guns than any but a first-class naval power can put afloat. I cannot conceive what "political and military points of view" are to be obtained for the Confederacy by abandoning the certain destruction of an army of 30,000 men backed by a huge fleet, to chase after a force of 10,000 in full retreat with over one hundred miles the [head] start.[29]

Smith, however, frustrated Taylor by doing the opposite and taking most of Taylor's troops to chase Steele *after* the Federals had diverted. So, why did Smith insist on the foray into Arkansas when it appeared unnecessary?

Here is where the character of the individual commanders exerts an inexorable pressure on the decision-making process. Much of the credit for the decisions made is attributable to the personal and command relationships among the three principal Confederate commanders. Smith, the Rebel commander of the Trans-Mississippi Department, was a conscientious if somewhat self-righteous man. He had a great deal of patience in working with others—too much as it turns out. Richard Taylor, commander of the District of West Louisiana, was also a dedicated patriot of the Confederate cause. However, his temperament contrasted sharply with Smith's. His high-spirited and emotional outbursts made him intolerable to those he worked for or with. By the time Smith decided to move north to Arkansas, relations between Smith and Taylor had deteriorated to the breaking point.

Sterling Price, commander of the District of Arkansas, was similarly devoted to the Southern cause. Although an amiable character, he had a penchant for hard drinking and most of the senior commanders in the Confederacy lacked confidence in his abilities as a commander. Yet, Price's relationship with Smith differed from the Taylor-Smith association. While Taylor harangued and prodded his chief, Price seemed more amenable to Smith's suggestions and propositions. Therefore, in spite of misgivings about Price's competence, Smith came to support an incursion into Arkansas to drive Steele back to Little Rock.[30] Chasing Steele in Arkansas fit in neatly with Smith's Fabian strategy. Also, Smith could move into Arkansas and avoid additional ugly confrontations with Taylor and more easily keep an eye on Price.

Evidence suggests that Smith feared Steele's column from Arkansas more so than Banks' army. In a letter to Taylor Smith states emphatically that "[T]o win this campaign his [Steele's] column must be destroyed."[31] Perhaps this is because Steele was a professional soldier known for hard fighting while Banks suffered from a reputation of being a political general. Therefore, it is easy to see why Smith decided to pursue Steele rather than press Banks in Louisiana. In light of this decision, what did the Confederates lose in pursuing Steele?

Although the Camden Expedition represented a clear Confederate victory, it was a hollow one because the Rebels lost one of their last opportunities to influence the war in their favor. An understanding of the situation in 1864 is critical to evaluating the chance the Confederates in the Trans-Mississippi had in 1864. By the third year of the war the Confederacy's territory and military powers were receding at an alarming rate. Everywhere in 1863 Rebel armies suffered a series of major defeats. In the east, the Union Army of the Potomac defeated Robert E. Lee's venerable Army of Northern Virginia driving back the Confederate invasion of Pennsylvania at Gettysburg. In the west, the fall of Vicksburg split the Confederacy in two, isolating the eastern states from the Trans-Mississippi and losing the services of 30,000 irreplaceable troops with its surrender. In November at Chattanooga, the stout but hard-luck Army of Tennessee suffered a disheartening defeat while practically surrendering control of the state to the Federal authorities. The new Federal commander-in-chief,

Lieutenant General U. S. Grant, intended to maintain the momentum achieved with these victories in order to win the war in 1864.

Upon his accession to command, Grant immediately began to devise a plan to pit Federal strength against the primary Confederate armies. Grant believed that the reason the Confederacy had survived for so long lay in the fact that the Union "armies had acted separately and independently of each other." As a result, the Rebels had always been able to use their interior lines to shift their forces to deflect the Federal thrusts. "I determined to stop this," Grant stated. He aimed to correct this flawed approach by launching a simultaneous assault by all Union armies against the Army of Tennessee, Army of Northern Virginia, and the stronghold of Mobile. President Lincoln appreciated the plan and characterized the strategy in his western charm as only he could, exclaiming, "those not skinning can hold a leg."[32]

Grant's plan called for all the Union armies east of the Mississippi to advance on or about April 25, 1864, when roads would be in good condition for campaigning. Major General George G. Meade's Army of the Potomac would move against Lee's Army of Northern Virginia in a pounding overland campaign. In conjunction with Meade's advance the smaller Army of the James under Major General Benjamin Butler would lunge toward Richmond from a peninsula known as Bermuda Hundred south of the city. Also in Virginia, Franz Sigel's little army would march up the Shenandoah Valley in order to deprive Lee access to his "breadbasket."

West of the Appalachians, Major General William T. Sherman's combined Armies of the Cumberland, Tennessee, and Ohio would focus on Confederate General Joseph E. Johnston's Army of Tennessee. Finally, Grant wanted Banks to take Mobile, one of the last remaining Confederate ports. Grant explained the plan in his post-war memoirs by stating, "My general plan now was to concentrate all the force possible against the Confederate armies in the field.... Accordingly, I arranged for a simultaneous movement all along the line."[33] This brilliant yet simple scheme did not come to fruition as Grant intended, as the wheels were already in motion to derail his plans.

The man Grant succeeded in command of the Union armies was the indecisive Major General Henry Wager Halleck. Known as "Old Brains" in the old army, Halleck conceived the Red River Campaign. The campaign had its genesis in economics, politics, and Halleck's penchant for clearing his rear area before advancing forward. For some time northeastern textile interests placed pressure on the Lincoln Administration to open up the rich Red River Valley to extract its cotton. The starved textile mills of the north sought to alleviate their shortages by obtaining the commodity in Louisiana and east Texas.[34]

From a political perspective, the administration had three reasons for pursuing a campaign in the Trans-Mississippi. First, a large German population — known to be hostile to the Confederacy — farmed "Free-Soil" cotton plantations in east Texas. Northern politicians had clamored for some time to "free" these German-American citizens from the Rebel grip. Many German immigrants served in the Union armies and they felt a vested interest in helping their countrymen and the administration was inclined to listen to their pleas. Second, France had recently placed a puppet emperor on the throne in Mexico in violation of the long-standing Monroe Doctrine. This European infringement of affairs in the Western Hemisphere angered Lincoln and he and his advisors felt obliged to respond to French intransigence. Finally, with the national election looming in 1864 Lincoln hoped to readmit federally occupied southern states to the Union for the purpose of allowing loyal citizens to participate in the plebiscite. This, many Republicans believed, would deliver votes to their ticket in November enabling Lincoln to secure victory.[35]

As early as August 1863 General Halleck began suggesting to General Banks that "a combined military and naval movement up the Red River" would be desired. The purpose was to "restore the flag to *some one point* in Texas." Halleck's plan suggested[36] that Banks, reinforced by troops from Sherman, ascend the Red with about 30,000 men. In "cooperation" Admiral David D. Porter would sweep the river proper with a large naval contingent providing the army with logistical and fire support. Finally, Halleck wrote to General Steele stating, "[I]t is hoped that ... concerted [action] between yourself and General Sherman and General Banks to drive the enemy entirely out of Arkansas and occupy the line of Red River" will occur.[37] Banks' column would constitute the main effort while Steele's would serve as a secondary thrust to deceive the Rebels about the intention of the campaign. As already pointed out, this plan ran counter to Grant's intent for the 1864 campaign season. Grant, against his better judgment, allowed the campaign to proceed out of deference to Halleck and because Banks' men were already en route to their jump-off positions.[38]

General Steele began to have doubts about his capability to support Banks with a move southward from Little Rock. As a result, he expressed his reservations in correspondence with Halleck by tactfully attempting to avoid a full-scale expedition through southern Arkansas to the Red.

> General Banks, with 17,000 and 10,000 of Sherman's, will be at Alexandria on the 17th [of March] instant. This is more than equal for anything Kirby Smith can bring against him. Smith will run. By holding the line of Arkansas secure I can soon free this state from armed rebels. Sherman insists upon my moving upon Shreveport to co-operate with the above-mentioned forces with all my effective force. I have prepared to do so, against my own judgment.... The roads are most if not quite impracticable; the country is destitute of provisions on the route.... I made a proposition to General Banks to threaten the enemy's flank and rear with all my cavalry, and to make a feint with infantry on the Washington road.[39]

Steele wrapped up the dispatch by requesting permission to execute the cavalry raid and infantry feint. "I advise that you proceed to co-operate in the movement of Banks and Sherman on Shreveport, unless General Grant orders differently," Halleck responded, now acting as Grant's chief of staff. Halleck immediately forwarded the letter to Grant for his decision on Steele's proposal. Grant, having assumed command of the Union armies only days before, immediately realized the importance of Steele moving with his full force rather than a feint. Accordingly, he sent out a dispatch to Steele stating, "[M]ove your force in full co-operation with General N. P. Banks.... A mere demonstration will not be sufficient."[40]

Grant intuitively understood that Steele's movement would confuse the Confederate high command. Additionally, he wanted the Red River campaign wrapped up as soon as possible because he wanted the movement on Mobile to coincide with the movement of all other armies. He believed that Banks could take Shreveport by mid-April and then turn back to the Gulf to prepare to take Mobile by the end of the month. When Banks and Steele joined forces on the Red, Steele would assume command of that region while Banks would move east in accordance with Grant's program for the spring.[41]

Banks' bumbling put Grant's grand scheme in jeopardy. However, Grant's prescient decision to order Steele forward saved Banks from disaster and ultimately the entire Union war effort. Because Grant ordered Steele to conduct a full-scale campaign in Arkansas, it forced the Rebels to defend against two major threats to the Trans-Mississippi Department rather than one. Had Grant accepted Steele's argument "to make a feint" the Confederates would — with reasonable certainty — have destroyed Banks' army and Porter's fleet in the Red River Valley.[42]

Had Taylor retained the troops that Smith took to Arkansas he could have precipitated a disaster on Union arms. He had three distinct opportunities to do so with an appropriate force. When Kirby Smith left with three of Taylor's divisions the possibilities evaporated. The Army of the Gulf instead of heading off to prison camps, escaped back to their starting point. Grant then ordered these veterans to the main Federal armies in the East to participate, albeit belatedly, in the campaigns he planned for late April. An analysis of the impact the individual units had east of the Mississippi reveals the great contributions they made to the final outcome of the war. Without these veterans, the war with reasonable probability could have ended much differently.

By mid-June 1864 all the Federal offensives had stalled. In the east, the Army of the Potomac had suffered more than 50,000 casualties in its campaign against the Army of Northern Virginia. In spite of the bloodletting, Robert E. Lee had confounded the Federals at every turn. Not satisfied to remain on the defensive, Lee launched his 2nd Corps under Lieutenant General Jubal Early on a foray down the Shenandoah Valley in early June. Lee's purpose was to clear remaining Federals from the Valley to secure its fertile farms as a source of sustenance for his army. Also, he wanted to relieve pressure on the Army of Northern Virginia now holed up on a defensive belt covering Richmond and Petersburg. The opportunistic Early not only cleared the Valley in an aggressive drive, but he kept right on going across the Potomac into Maryland. After brushing aside a scratch force on the Monocacy, Early marched to the very gates of Washington panicking the Lincoln Administration.[43]

The government now demanded that Grant respond to this threat by sending troops to bolster the depleted Washington defenses. Grant dispatched the VI Corps from the Army of the Potomac and directed the XIX Corps arriving from New Orleans after taking part in the Red River Campaign. The XIX Corps helped save the capital and went on to play a prominent role in driving the Confederates out of the Shenandoah. In October, the XIX Corps proved pivotal to defeating and practically destroying Early's army at Cedar Creek.[44] The battle of Cedar Creek permanently closed off the Valley from Confederate control. Had the XIX Corps been captured or destroyed in Louisiana, Cedar Creek in all likelihood would not have happened.

In the west, Sherman's army found itself frustrated in its drive to Atlanta. The wily Joseph Johnston proved a master of defensive warfare always keeping one step ahead of his foe. Of greater concern, in Sherman's opinion, were the operations of the elusive Rebel general Nathan Bedford Forrest. "I was disturbed by a bold raid made by the rebel General Forrest," Sherman stated in his memoirs. Forrest spent his spring raiding through west Tennessee and was threatening to cut Sherman's tenuous supply line between Nashville and Chattanooga. Should Forrest enjoy success in this endeavor, Sherman feared he would have to abandon the Atlanta campaign. With this in mind he pressured Banks to return the 10,000 troops of the XVI and XVII Corps on loan for the Red River Campaign.[45]

Upon A. J. Smith's arrival at Memphis from the Red River Valley, Sherman dispatched him to keep Forrest busy and "off our roads"—the Nashville & Chattanooga Railroad. Smith, a tenacious fighter, did this in superb fashion by occupying all of Forrest's attention and fighting him to a draw at Tupelo in mid-July. Meanwhile, Sherman kept the pressure on Johnston by constantly forcing him back toward Atlanta. Smith's efforts against Forrest made Sherman's eventual capture of Atlanta in September possible.[46] However, if Sherman's veterans had been captured in Louisiana, where would Sherman have found the troops to occupy Forrest? The absence of these men could have caused a disheartening setback in the Atlanta campaign for Federal arms.

The XIII Corps formed the nucleus of the force that would finally make Grant's desired move to close Mobile. In August a combined army and naval force stormed the harbor forts and land face protecting the city. It was this battle that brought Admiral David G. Farragut lasting fame with his well-known quote, "Damn the torpedoes, full speed ahead." The XIII Corps stormed and took the fortifications protecting the mouth of the bay in support of the naval force.[47] Once again the question arises: Where would the Federals have scraped together enough troops to take Mobile if the Rebels had destroyed the XIII Corps in the Red River Valley?

Finally, the loss of the Army of the Gulf in Louisiana would have translated into the destruction or capture of a large chunk of Admiral Porter's Mississippi River Squadron. Low water in the Red had trapped the gunboats above the rapids at Alexandria. Therefore, without protection from the army the precious fleet would have been lost.[48] Infinite possibilities were available to the Rebels if they could have gotten their hands on a few good boats. At best they might have challenged Federal dominance of the Mississippi or at the very least the Confederates could have reopened communications with their brethren east of the Mississippi. This would have nullified the results of the great victory at Vicksburg the year before.

The key to success for the Union cause in 1864 lay in the minds of the Northern public because this was an election year. At the beginning of the year victory in the war effort appeared bright indeed. However, the combination of the stalled offensives in the east and west, high casualties, and near disaster in the Red River Valley sent morale reeling. In order to ensure the restoration of the Union, the Lincoln Administration needed victories on the battlefield to win at the polls in November.[49]

The Confederate strategy then should have focused on frustrating the Union war effort. If they could have made it appear that they could not be defeated in the near future by force of arms, the Rebels just might have achieved their goal of independence. As Shelby Foote points out, the Confederates simply had to hold the southern heartland by avoiding a large-scale defeat while launching limited offensives. "The object was to make each gain so costly in blood and tears that the expense would be clearly disproportionate to the profit," offers Foote. If by the second week of November, the Union appeared no closer to victory than they had been at the beginning of the year, the Lincoln Administration would have lost.[50]

The Red River Campaign offered the Confederates an unprecedented opportunity to exercise the winning strategy. Although the Rebels did enjoy success it did not achieve what it could have. A big reason for this is because the Camden Expedition perplexed Kirby Smith in Louisiana. His focus on defending the territorial integrity of the Trans-Mississippi rather than destroying the enemy resulted in his failure to reap the fortunes of the opportunity offered to him. The Fabian defensive policy merely fit neatly with Confederate war policy and with Smith's perceived need to maintain control of every inch of the region.[51]

In a twist of irony the little known Camden Expedition saved the large body of troops and naval forces in the Red River Valley for service on other fields. General Steele had attempted to avoid even making the effort. But, Grant's direct order to Steele forced him to support Banks. Had Grant not issued this order Banks would most certainly have lost his army and Porter the naval contingent. These troops went on to play important roles in the great campaigns in the east later in the year guaranteeing that Lincoln would win and the Union would survive. Although unknown to the men who took part in the Camden Expedition, their efforts helped save an army and thus contributed significantly to the success of the cause for which they fought.

═══════════

Notes

1. This account is the acclaimed historian Edwin C. Bearss' book titled *Steele's Retreat from Camden*.

2. Ludwell Johnson, *Red River Campaign*, 278; Bearss, *Steele's Retreat from Camden*, 178; *War of the Rebellion: The Official Records of the Union and Confederate Armies*, Vol. 34, Part 1, 680, 684, 692, 712, 714, 746, 767, 786–788 and Part 3, 147 (hereafter cited as *OR*); *Battles and Leaders of the Civil War*, "Opposing Forces in Arkansas," 368 (hereafter cited as *B&L*); Ira D. Richard, "Jenkins' Ferry," *Arkansas Historical Quarterly* (Spring 1961), 3–16 (hereafter cited as *AHQ*); Charles H. Lothrop, *History of the 1st Iowa Cavalry*, 158–159.

3. *Report of the Joint Congressional Committee on the Conduct of the War, Second Session 38th Congress*, XVIII, emphasis in original (hereafter cited as *Report of the Joint Committee*).

4. *Ibid.*, XVIII–XXVI.; *OR*, Part 1, Vol. 34, 683, 807; Johnson, *Red River Campaign*, 40.

5. *Ibid.*, 384.

6. Shelby Foote, *The Civil War: A Narrative*, Vol. 3, 29.

7. David D. Porter, *Naval History of the Civil War*, 520; *ORN*, Vol. 27, Part 1, 64. Letter from Banks to Navy Lt. Commander Thomas O. Selfridge. In this letter Banks discusses his difficulty in communicating with Steele and his belief that Steele "fails to cooperate" while unknown to him Steele had been campaigning for some three weeks.

8. *Report of the Joint Committee*, XXV.

9. *Ibid.*, 383–385.

10. John G. Walker, "War West of the Mississippi in the Years 1863-4 & 5," unpublished manuscript Myron Gwinner Collection, United States Army Military History Institute, 45.

11. Richard Taylor, *Destruction and Reconstruction*, 190–192 and *Report of the Joint Committee*, 58–61.

12. Taylor, *Destruction and Reconstruction*, 194–198.

13. *Report of the Joint Committee*, 13, 77, 195–196 and 326–327.

14. Robert L. Kerby, *Kirby Smith's Confederacy*, 246–248.

15. *Ibid.*; and Jeffrey S. Prushankin, "A Crisis in Command," M.A. thesis, Malvey Library, Villanova University, 40–41; Albert Castel, *General Sterling Price and the Civil War in the West*, 173.

16. *OR*, Vol. 34, Part 1, 516–517; and *B&L*, "The Defense of the Red River," by E. K. Smith, Vol. IV, 370.

17. *Ibid.*; and *OR*, Vol. 34, Part 1, 526.

18. *Ibid.*, 514.

19. *B&L*, "The Defense of the Red River," by E. K. Smith, 372; Taylor, *Destruction and Reconstruction*, 207.

20. *B&L*, "The Defense of the Red River," by E. K. Smith, 372–372; J. E. Sliger, "How General Taylor Fought the Battle of Mansfield, La.," *Confederate Veteran* (December 1923), 458; Taylor, *Destruction and Reconstruction*, 207–208.

21. *OR*, Vol. 34, Part 1, 571–572; and Johnson, *Red River Campaign*, 182.

22. Taylor, *Destruction and Reconstruction*, 224; and *OR*, Vol. 34, Part 1, 570.

23. Andrew F. Sperry, *History of the 33rd Iowa Infantry Volunteer Regiment*, 71.

24. Ira D. Richards, "Camden Expedition," University of Arkansas M.A. thesis, 11–12.

25. Christopher R. Gabel, *Railroad Generalship: Foundations of Civil War Strategy*, 1–5.

26. Anne J. Bailey and Daniel Sutherland eds., *Civil War Arkansas*, 64, 102, 119, 140, 196, & 214; Michael Dougan, "Life in Confederate Arkansas," *AHQ*, Vol. 34 (Spring 1972), 16–18; and Henry Cathey, "Extracts from the Memoirs of William Franklin Avera," *AHQ*, Vol. 22 (Winter 1963), 101–105.

27. *OR*, Vol. 34, Part 1, 661, 675–676; and Johnson, *Red River Campaign*, 178–179.

28. *OR*, Vol. 34, Part 1, 661–663; and Part 3, 162, 267–268.

29. *OR*, Vol. 34, Part 1, 541–543; and a post-war description in Taylor, *Destruction and Reconstruction*, 223–224.

30. Prushankin, "A Crisis in Command," M.A. thesis, 29, 96–102; Castel, *Sterling Price*, 173; *OR*, Vol. 34, Part 1, 476. In an April 16, 1864, letter to Jefferson Davis, Smith states, "of the three district commanders Major-Generals Magruder, Price, and Taylor, the latter is the junior and the only one of the three I consider suited to take charge of affairs of the department"; Taylor, *Destruction and Reconstruction*, 224–225; and Johnson, *Red River Campaign*, 177.

31. *OR*, Vol. 34, Part 1, 530–531.

32. U. S. Grant, *Memoirs*, 127; T. Harry Williams, ed., *Military Analysis of the Civil War*, "Military Strategy of the Civil War," U. S. Grant III, 9–10; and Foote, *The Civil War*, Vol. 3, 13–23.

33. Grant, *Memoirs*, 128–132; and T. Harry Williams, ed., *Military Analysis of the Civil War*, "Military Strategy of the Civil War," by U. S. Grant III, 13–14.

34. Johnson, *Red River Campaign*, 17, 36, 41–44 & 47–48; and Foote, *The Civil War*, 15–16.

35. Johnson, *Red River Campaign*, 6–11 & 45–48; *Report of the Joint Committee*, IV–V; and John G. Nicolay and John Hay, *Abraham Lincoln: A History*, 266–280 &285–286.

36. General Halleck had a habit of not issuing orders, but rather offering up courses of action he expected commanders to use. When they did not do as he suggested he would berate them as if he had issued actual orders.

37. *Report of the Joint Committee*, XXXI–XXXII [emphasis in original], 156–157.

38. Grant, *Memoirs*, Vol. II, 139.

39. *Report of the Joint Committee*, 338–339.

40. *OR*, Vol. 34, Part 1, 616.

41. *Report of the Joint Committee*, 159, 383–385; Grant, *Memoirs*, Vol. 2, 134–140; William T. Sherman, *Personal Memoirs*, Vol. 2, 26–17; and Johnson, *Red River Campaign*, 85, 105–106.

42. Michael Forsyth, *The Red River Campaign of 1864 and the Loss by the Confederacy of the Civil War*, 1–5.

43. Frank Vandiver, *Jubal's Raid*, 18–19, 25–26; Long, *The Jewel of Liberty*, 207–208; and Foote, *The Civil War*, Vol. 3, 446–461.

44. *Ibid.*; Long, *The Jewel of Liberty*, 210; and Jeffrey Wert, *From Winchester to Cedar Creek*, 230–233.

45. Sherman, *Memoirs*, 12–14; and Foote, *The Civil War*, Vol. 3, 357–358.

46. Sherman, *Memoirs*, 52; Castel, *Decision in the West*, 277; Long, *The Jewel of Liberty*, 206–207; and David G. Wills, *A Battle from the Start*, 216–217.

47. Chester G. Hearn, *Mobile Bay and the Mobile Campaign*, 125–137; *B&L*, "Land Operations Against Mobile," by Richard Irwin, Vol. IV, 400, 410–411 and "Farragut at Mobile Bay," by John C. Kinney, 391; and Long, *The Jewel of Liberty*, 209.

48. *Report of the Joint Committee*, 244–245; *Official Records of the Union and Confederate Navies in the War of the Rebellion*, Vol. 27, Part 1, 68–70 (hereafter cited as *ORN*); Porter, *Naval History of the Civil War*, 523–527; and Gideon Welles, *Diary of Gideon Welles*, Vol. II, 26.

49. Long, *The Jewel of Liberty*, 195 and 198–199.

50. Foote, *The Civil War*, Vol. 3, 102–103.

51. Williams, ed., *Military Analysis of the Civil War*, article by U. S. Grant III, "Military Strategy of the Civil War," 13.

2

The Rebel Commanders

To gain a full understanding of the decisions and events that occurred during the Camden Expedition requires a thorough examination of the character of the opposing command teams. The individual background and personality of each man reveals volumes about the outcome of both the Red River Campaign and the Camden Expedition. In addition, the manner by which these men interacted presents an intriguing study of the dynamics of combat command. The Rebel commanders came from diverse paths to fight on the fields of Arkansas and Louisiana. The contrasts and similarities make for an interesting story and enhance the historiography of the expedition.

General Edmund Kirby Smith held overall command of the Confederate Trans-Mississippi Department and had responsibility for defense of its vast territory. All decisions pertaining to her defense rested on his shoulders. Smith came from a distinguished yet modest family. The Kirbys and Smiths contributed sons who fought in the war for American independence and Smith's father Joseph served with some distinction in the War of 1812. Dissatisfaction over long separations from his family convinced Joseph to leave the army in 1821. Political connections enabled him to secure a federal judgeship in the newly formed Florida territory. Joseph soon moved with his family to the old city of St. Augustine.[1]

Early in his young life, Kirby Smith's parents recognized potential in him and made plans to provide him with an excellent education. In the 19th century a West Point education opened doors to further advancement, therefore Joseph and Frances Smith steered him in this direction. "Ned," as his parents affectionately called him, came under the tutelage of his older sister. Twelve years his senior, Frances[2] proved instrumental to the success in preparing Smith for an academy appointment. Through his early years in St. Augustine Frances assumed motherly responsibility for him, ensuring he attended to his studies. Smith had a somewhat mischievous streak exhibited by his tendency to play hooky. In spite of this Ned won admittance to the prestigious Hallowell school in Alexandria, Virginia. The school's rigid standards provided the discipline young Smith needed to pass the tough West Point entrance exams.[3]

At age 17 Smith easily met the requirements for admittance to the academy and accepted appointment in 1841. He got off to a fast start at West Point standing fifth in his class after his plebe year. Despite his high achievement in academic pursuits Smith chafed under the pettiness of the voluminous regulations. In a letter to his father he complained about the assessment of demerits "for a button off a coat, or because of his clothes, bed, windows, room, mantle, shelves, books, hands, or nails out of order." As a result of his disdain, Smith's class standing would drop to 25th in his class upon commissioning in 1845.[4]

Kirby Smith chose to accept an infantry commission and received orders assigning him to the 5th Infantry Regiment posted at Fort Jesup, Louisiana. Ironically, this area would someday fall under his responsibility as Rebel commander of the Trans-Mississippi and sit directly in the path of the opposing armies in 1864. In a further twist of irony, Smith's commanding officer in the 5th Infantry was Colonel Zachary Taylor, future president of the United States and father of one of his two primary subordinates during Camden and the Red River Campaign.[5]

Smith had little time to settle into his new assignment, for war with Mexico loomed on the horizon. Within weeks of his arrival Taylor, under orders from the War Department, deployed the regiment to the border with Mexico. Soon Taylor and his small army would see combat against the Mexican forces. Smith earned recognition from his commander for his courage in the battles of Resaca de la Palma and Cerro Gordo. Smith's company captured an enemy cannon and his performance under fire would bring him advancement in rank by brevet to first lieutenant.[6]

After the war Smith served as a professor of mathematics at West Point. This represented a turning point in his life as he decided to make military service his career. "I have chosen the army," he wrote to his mother, "or rather the army has been selected for me as a profession, and I see no prospect of its ever being changed … I am proud of it."[7] Smith therefore dedicated his life to the service, a characteristic that would manifest itself throughout the Civil War. He would unswervingly serve the cause and made decisions based on what he believed was the correct course of action.

After three years at West Point Smith joined the 7th Infantry Regiment guarding the western frontier against Indian incursions. He continued to perform in a competent manner over the next few years earning a promotion to captain and assignment to the new and elite 2nd Cavalry Regiment. Only officers considered a notch above the rest served in the regiment. The unit included such future Civil War leaders as Robert E. Lee, Albert S. Johnston, George Thomas, John Bell Hood, and Earl Van Dorn.[8] It was about 1855 when the question of secession began to generate discourse among the officer corps.

Smith, like many Southerners, was wary of such talk of dissolution of the Union. He believed the best interests of the South lay with remaining in the Union and finding a way to compromise over the explosive issues. Nevertheless, "right or wrong I go with the land of my birth," Smith told his mother. The test of his allegiance came soon after writing that letter as Florida seceded from the Union. With his native state joining the states of the lower south in secession, Smith painfully sent his resignation to the War Department and offered his sword to the South in March 1861. The new Confederate government was eager to have the services of officers of reputation and offered Smith a commission as colonel. Upon acceptance in April Smith received orders to proceed to Virginia to begin organizing recruits then arriving in droves at camps in Lynchburg.[9]

Within a month Smith would assume command of a brigade in General Joseph E. Johnston's army in the Shenandoah Valley. Smith's brigade reported for duty guarding the approaches south into Virginia at Harper's Ferry. After two months of uneventful service, General P. G. T. Beauregard sent a desperate request for reinforcement to Johnston's Valley Army. A large Federal force had moved south from Washington threatening to turn the Confederate defenses along Bull Run Creek near Manassas Junction. Johnston responded by placing his small army on rail cars en route to Manassas, including the brigade of newly promoted Brigadier General E. Kirby Smith's. Smith became one of the South's early heroes as a result of his actions at the Battle of First Bull Run. At a point in the battle when the Confederates appeared defeated Smith's brigade arrived just in time to swing the tide in favor of the Rebels. Upon arrival at Manassas Junction, Smith quickly disembarked his men and marched them at the double-quick to the sounds of a desperate battle. The hard-pressed Rebel left held and then counterattacked sending the raw Union recruits in a headlong retreat back toward Washington. While winning the sobriquet "Blucher of Manassas," Smith fell with a Minié ball through his thigh. Smith's actions won him accolades across the South and further promotion to major general and division command.[10]

Smith would spend most of the remainder of 1861 recovering from his painful wound finally returning to duty in November. He had just settled into his new command when the War Department summoned him to take command of the volatile Department of East Tennessee. This new assignment did not please him because his command was an area teeming with Unionist sentiment. Nevertheless, Smith accepted the challenge and took up his duties determined to make a positive impression on the citizens of the region while instilling discipline in the military units. Service in east Tennessee would prove an excellent training ground for future command of the Trans-Mississippi Department. Frustration became status quo for Smith as he struggled to stifle Unionist activities. In spite of the headaches, he systematically instituted a plan to gain control for Confederate authorities while building his meager troops into a force capable of offensive operations. Part of his program called for initiating martial law and exchanging troops of questionable loyalty with soldiers from other areas of the Confederacy.[11] This established a foundation that enabled Smith to turn his attention to other fields.

In mid-summer of 1862, Smith cast his gaze toward Kentucky and the "liberation" of that state from Federal control. In July he developed a plan to drive north into Kentucky in order to clear Tennessee of Federal forces and allow the state to recover from the destruction wrought by the war. Smith opened up a dialogue with

General Braxton Bragg in Mississippi to propose that they cooperate in the movement north. Bragg was amenable to Smith's suggestions as he had been considering similar operations himself. Both believed that transferring the seat of war to the Ohio Valley would relieve the ailing Confederate heartland of pressure, recover middle Tennessee, and possibly contribute to winning foreign recognition for the Confederacy. After a July 31 conference in Chattanooga, Bragg made arrangements to transfer his army from Mississippi to Chattanooga for the invasion.[12]

Smith led the foray, jumping off on August 14, 1862. At first the effort appeared destined for success as Smith moved rapidly over vast distances gobbling up Federal garrisons and pushing Union forces before him. At Richmond, Kentucky, his 18,000 men fought and won a tough battle bagging over 4,000 prisoners and nine pieces of artillery. Shortly, Smith had his army back on the road and soon occupied Lexington and the state capital at Frankfort. As Bragg's newly designated Army of Tennessee moved into central Kentucky, Smith sent him an enthusiastic letter recommending combination of their forces in the vicinity of Lexington. Unfortunately, the cordial cooperation between the two Rebel commanders would soon fade.[13]

The Confederacy formed commands based on territorial regions rather than enemy-oriented organizations. Time and again during the war Rebel armies failed to achieve decisive results, or worse, they met with defeat because of this flawed organizational structure.[14] This factor is behind the failed Bragg-Smith Kentucky Campaign. Because the Confederate War Department did not establish a unified command between Smith's Department of East Tennessee and Bragg's Department of Tennessee cracks in their cooperation formed soon after Bragg entered central Kentucky. Smith and Bragg moved into Kentucky with diverging objectives, lack of unity, and with ambition driving each man. When Bragg fought the indecisive Battle of Perryville squandering its opportunities, the invasion ended in ignominious failure. Smith bitterly criticized Bragg for his role in the campaign while exonerating himself and the decisions he made. The Kentucky Campaign was a precursor of events that would occur in the Trans-Mississippi later in the war.[15]

Following the debacle, Secretary of War George Randolph informed Kirby Smith that he had been promoted to lieutenant general. However, with promotion would come a new challenge. President Jefferson Davis summoned him to Richmond in January 1863 to discuss whether Smith might accept command of the Trans-Mississippi Department. Davis needed an energetic commander for a region that suffered under the uninspired leadership of Theophilus Holmes, poor transportation, few troops, and apathy. Though East Tennessee had supplied Smith with daily headaches, problems west of the Mississippi would dwarf anything yet seen. Smith did not necessarily want a command so far from the center of the war, but accepted out of patriotism and gratitude for the confidence shown him. Votes of approval for Davis' choice to command the department came from many quarters, but none were more important then Robert E. Lee's endorsement stating that he "consider[ed] him one of our best officers."[16]

Conditions in the region appalled Smith. During a tour of his new command he found "no soldiers, no arms or ammunition, and no money within the limits of the district." Further, Confederate national policy dictated that the department must become self-sufficient. With no help expected from the government, Smith set about improving conditions with his meager resources.[17] Any contributions to a Confederate victory would be of his own efforts and required effecting a solid command relationship with his headstrong and difficult subordinates. One of these men was a bear of a man named Sterling Price.

Major General Sterling Price commanded the Trans-Mississippi Department's District of Arkansas. He descended from a long line of Virginians who arrived at Jamestown in 1622. The Price family story is one of Welsh immigrants struggling to rise above the obscurity of itinerate farmers into the gentile and closed planter's society. The legacy of Sterling's forefathers' struggle to attain respectability would weigh heavily upon him and play a prominent role in defining his character. Sterling Price was born in 1809 in Prince Edward County, Virginia. Sterling's parents were of modest means holding a small farm with a comfortable home overlooking the Buffalo River. His father, Pugh, was a small slaveholder and first sergeant of the local militia company. He was a regular at all social functions in the area and everything he did was calculated to elevate him to the social position he craved.[18]

In 1812 Sterling's father and older brother left home to fight in the war against England. Young Sterling would have little recollection of this, but would fondly remember his youth growing up in tidewater Virginia. Frolicking on his father's tobacco farm would occupy his early childhood. Tobacco proved a boon to the Prices as the price of the leaf shot up to record levels in the years prior to 1820. This provided the opportunity to acquire more land to grow the family spread, an essential element to attaining gentleman planter status.[19] However, by the 1820s tobacco bottomed out and the opportunity to purchase more land in Virginia dried up as well. Since land acquisition was key to social advancement, the land depression guaranteed that Pugh Price could not rise above his status as a modest freeholder. Sterling absorbed all the lessons of operating the plantation as well as noting what it took to move up the social ladder from his father.

While tobacco figured prominently in Price's early education, his father intended for Sterling to have an education befitting a gentleman. After completing his primary schooling he passed the entrance exams to Hampden-Sidney College and started school in 1826. The independent-minded Price frequently disregarded the strict codes of the school as well as neglecting his studies. After one year Sterling dropped out of college instead choosing to take a law apprenticeship under a prominent lawyer. During this time Price began to form political opinions that would guide his judgment the rest of his life. The combination of his upbringing and education influenced him to become a Jacksonian Democrat.[20]

Virginia's competitive edge in tobacco waned in the 1820s, as did opportunities to expand plantations. Planters of the early 19th century needed to constantly find new land to maintain fertile holdings to grow tobacco. As the available land in Virginia gave out, many planters began to look further west to prime growing areas of

Major General Sterling Price, commander of the Confederate District of Arkansas, defended southwest Arkansas with a hodge-podge of cavalry in hopes of soon reentering his home state, Missouri. Courtesy the United States Army Military History Institute.

Kentucky and Missouri. Pugh Price knew that he had no chance to elevate his status in the closed Old Dominion society. With this in mind in 1830 he determined to pack up everything and make a westward trek to find a new life in Missouri. Although a young man of 21, Sterling decided to accompany his parents on the arduous journey west. He too sought the chance to better himself and felt that the ample land of Missouri made the best offer.[21]

The Price family settled in Chariton County, Missouri, in 1831 after purchasing a large 4,886 acre tract of land. The farm they bought lay along the fertile Missouri River Valley. The locality was perfect for establishing a tobacco plantation capable of producing high quality leaf. The county was just beginning to reap the benefits of a flourishing tobacco economy. As one of its early settlers with a gentleman's background, Sterling found it easy to achieve the social status his forebears had long sought to attain. The first step to climbing the social ladder came through winning election as captain of the militia company. At over six feet tall and 200 pounds, Price presented an imposing and martial appearance and enjoyed military airs.[22]

A rising citizen in the county, Sterling was able to parlay his position into business acquaintances and within a few years won recognition as a leader in the community. His success only whetted his appetite as he turned to politics to solidify his position. As a slaveholder Price fit naturally as an old line Democrat. He believed in limited government, the right to hold slaves, and opposed establishment of a national bank. The society he moved in reflected these core beliefs and his fellow citizens sent him to the state legislature in 1835.[23] With every success Price's self-importance, ambition, and vanity grew and associates in the Civil War would find these traits insufferable. In a mere two years his popularity propelled him to the speaker's chair of the state house.

Exemplifying his drive to maintain his status was the role he played in expelling the Mormons from Missouri. The Mormons arrived in Missouri after their expulsion from Illinois and had managed to put their lives back together. They built prospering communities on the Missouri upstream from Chariton County. However, their differing beliefs made many uncomfortable and some Missourians thought them subversive of tradition. As a result, citizens along the river valley began clamoring for the Mormon "threat" to clear out of the region. By 1839 unrest reached its zenith as the governor called out the militia to punish the "menace."[24]

Sterling Price as the leader of the militia enthusiastically answered the call to arms and assembled his unit. Brigaded with other county militia units, the whole marched upstream to quell the "uprising." In an ugly episode the Missouri militia went on a rampage of murder and plunder as they meted out what they called punishment. The remainder of the Mormon community in Missouri would join the great migration west following the events that destroyed their homes.[25] This was Price's first taste of military service. The success boosted his prestige and helped vault him to election to the U. S. Congress. Price enjoyed the popularity and came to believe in his own questionable abilities as a military commander. The laurels of the Mormon Expedition would pale in comparison to future campaigns in Mexico and the glory it would win him.

Price entered the House in 1846 and although he was known as a poor orator, he exuded charisma that enabled him to work behind the scenes to get what he wanted with an "unobtrusive but relentless pressure." This presence made him a highly successful legislator and helped him to make lifelong, beneficial alliances as well as jealous enemies.[26] During the Civil War such influence and powers of persuasion allowed him to gain what he wanted with Kirby Smith and created turbulent controversy with Jefferson Davis.

In 1846 the Texas question took front and center in American foreign policy. Sterling Price was a great supporter of immediate annexation of the fledgling republic and his support of the Polk Administration on the issue won him a controversial commission as colonel of volunteers.[27] Always seeking personal advancement, Price viewed the opportunity to command a regiment in combat as a ticket to even higher office in politics. He returned to Missouri in late 1846 to recruit and prepare for a long march to New Mexico.

Price exhibited an independent streak bordering on insubordination throughout his career as an officer. His commission authorized him to raise a regiment of infantry, yet Price ignored this directive instead opting to raise a mounted unit. His superiors did nothing to prevent his initiative and accordingly Price saw it as vindication of his military judgment.[28] His overestimation of his military prowess would cause him significant problems over the course of his military career.

Upon arrival at Santa Fe for duty in the New Mexico Territory, the 2nd Missouri Volunteers quickly gained a reputation as an undisciplined mob. His commanders—first Stephen Kearney and later Alexander Doniphan—criticized Price's inattention to discipline. His failure to control his men contributed to unrest in the territory as his men committed daily outrages against the local populous. Unrest soon boiled over into outright rebellion as the Mexicans and Indians rose up against the occupation forces. After the rebels assassinated the territorial governor, the Missourians brutally retaliated. After a sharp battle at the village of Puebla de Taos, Price's men wreaked havoc in the town. But they did restore order and Price had exercised sound military tactics in deploying his troops.[29] His lack of control over his men would carry over to the Civil War and many of his associates would question his competence because of this trait.

After long garrison duty it appeared that the Mexican War would end with no further action for Price and his men. Late 1847 changed the outlook as rumors of a Mexican thrust on El Paso began to surface in the Mexican province of Chihuahua. Promoted to brigadier general and independent command at Santa Fe, Price sought an opportunity to solidify his military reputation by proposing a campaign into Chihuahua to spoil the expedition before it started. The War Department denied Price's request. Yet, Price instead decided to disobey in a blatant display of insubordination, giving orders to his men to prepare to march in early 1848. Placing credence in his judgment over that of the War Department, he moved on February 23.[30] His disregard of orders would also crop up time and again in his career.

Lightly provisioned, Price moved with swiftness so that he could cover ground quickly undetected. However, he nearly defeated his own offensive by discounting the reality of needing logistical support in hostile territory. With provisions running low he arrived at the town of Chihuahua, the provincial capital, where 800 Mexicans barricaded themselves. He decided that he must attack the town immediately or run the risk of having to retreat. After arranging his assault force with admirable skill, Price stormed the city taking it with minimal casualties.[31] It was nothing short of stupendous and Price's reputation skyrocketed. In spite of his disregard for orders and failure to see to his own logistics, Price secured the U. S. border with Mexico. Instead of reprimand he received accolades and a promotion to major general of volunteers[32] and his confidence in his military ability reached new heights. The habits displayed in Mexico—lax discipline, arrogance, and flouting superiors—would carry over through to the 1860s making him a difficult and unreliable subordinate.

Price made a triumphal return to Missouri after the Mexican War receiving a hero's welcome. Having spent several years away from home Price attempted to spend time with his large family and tend to plantation business. But, as a popular figure in the state many sought his opinion on the pending sectional crisis. Lacking the gift of oration and mindful of public opinion, Price hesitated to take a stance until he gathered his thoughts and consulted close friends.[33]

At issue was whether or not to admit slavery into new states as the country expanded westward. Missouri stood at the center of the controversy and found itself torn by the competing interests. Democrats leaned toward allowing slavery in the territories while Free-Soil Whigs pushed to prevent extension of the institution. As a slaveholder and Democrat Price naturally opposed prohibition of slavery in the territories. Price attempted to remain neutral because he believed that the whole issue with the passions it spawned could explode into a civil war. As a politician he felt this was the best course to follow in order to maintain his public standing. His moderate stance, seen by some as fence-sitting, became a calming influence in state politics and won him an unexpected election to the governorship in 1852. Inaugurated in 1853, the Price Administration represented the calm before the storm of the 1860s in Missouri. As he was a supporter of the Compromise of 1850 and a fiscal conservative, Missouri experienced a rather tranquil and prosperous four years due to his quietly competent leadership.[34] Soon the secession question would thrust itself in full force upon the citizens of Missouri tearing the state apart.

Price, in spite of his slaveholding background, vehemently opposed secession. He believed that secession would only lead to a destructive war for both Missouri and the country. He aligned himself with Senator Stephen A. Douglas of Illinois and that faction of the Democratic Party that advocated sectional compromise. His support of the Union, however, was conditional. Should the North engage in an effort to suppress the South by force of arms, Price would then draw his sword in favor of the South.[35]

On April 12, 1861, Confederate forces at Charleston, South Carolina, fired on the 80-odd Federals holed up in the masonry post at Fort Sumter. Three days later President Lincoln issued a call of volunteers from the states remaining in the Union to put down the rebellion. This pushed the states of the Upper South into the rebel camp while the border states vigorously debated seceding as well. Lincoln's proclamation included a requirement for Missouri to supply a share of the volunteers. Claiborne F. Jackson, newly inaugurated governor of Missouri, responded with a terse note refusing to comply on grounds that it was "illegal, unconstitutional ... diabolical."[36] This did not mean Missouri desired secession; on the contrary, most Missourians remained loyal to the Union but believed it morally wrong to subdue the South by use of force. In effect, Missouri sought neutrality, but this would prove elusive as proponents of secession and Unionists prepared for a fight for the state.

Price officially maintained his loyalty; however, in private he stated that should Lincoln carry out his plan to coerce the South he as "a military man ... can't fight against the South." While Price guarded his counsel, Governor Jackson began a covert campaign to deliver Missouri to the Confederacy. Simultaneously, Missouri politician Francis P. Blair and Union brigadier general Nathaniel Lyon moved to hold the state in the Federal fold. Blair and Lyon gained the upper hand when they forcibly drove off pro-Southern militia at Camp Jackson outside St. Louis. Infuriated, Price now offered his service to the state. This offer was conditional as he intended only to fight for Missouri and not the Confederacy. Lyon consolidated his gains by moving Federal troops into the heart of the state. Price attempted one final effort to maintain Missouri's neutrality by meeting with Lyon on June 12, 1861, in St. Louis. The stormy meeting ended when Lyon boldly stated that he would see "every man, woman, and child in the state dead" before he would give up the Federal government's right to rule.[37] This event convinced Price of his course and he immediately declared his support for the Southern cause.

Price, commander of the State Guard, issued orders to mobilize the militia in readiness to meet the expected Federal move into the heart of the state. While Price scrambled to formulate a scheme for defending the state Lyon vigorously moved into central Missouri. In a matter of days he sent Price's rabble State Guard reeling into the southwest corner of the state as he occupied the capital at Jefferson City. Price now assembled his men at a place called the Cowskin Prairie.[38] Here began an irritating pattern of Price tactlessly calling for the liberation of Missouri with Confederate help.

Price's army more closely resembled a mob then a military formation. The State

Guard was devoid of organization, equipment, weapons, ordnance, and most disturbing, discipline. Price issued a series of general orders aimed at bringing order out of chaos. Some of these actually specified the number of tents allocated to the troops and authorized officers to procure them by any means possible.[39] Meanwhile, General Ben McCulloch, who had brought a Confederate force to the Cowskin Prairie, wondered if he had made a mistake coming when he saw the condition of Price's army. McCulloch considered going back to Arkansas, but impassioned objections by Price convinced him to remain.[40]

Price now began to plea for offensive action in spite of his lack of almost all military necessities reminiscent of his Mexican War campaign in Chihuahua. Lyon was now working his way into southwest Missouri in an effort to sweep the entire state clean of the State Guard. McCulloch once again reluctantly agreed to Price's entreaties and they began to move forward from the prairie on July 25. Lyon, now himself running short of supplies and suffering a loss of most of his army by expired enlistments, decided to strike Price first. He divided his forces into two striking columns and attempted to crush Price and McCulloch's combined army at Wilson's Creek on August 10. In a situation representative of the lax discipline in the State Guard, Price's cavalry had failed to post pickets and Lyon initially took the Confederates completely by surprise. Only fast thinking and courageous action by both Price and McCulloch saved the day for them. Recovering quickly they formed a line on Oak Hill and by the creek, first blunting Lyon's attack and then turning the tables. In the melee Lyon was killed and the Federals retreated back toward Springfield and hence to Rolla.[41]

The victory at Wilson's Creek passed the initiative from the Federals to the Rebels in Missouri and Price sought to follow it up with a triumphal sweep of the state. McCulloch once again balked and this time did return to Arkansas leaving Price to his own devices in Missouri. In spite of a continued deficit of resources, Price decided upon a drive to the Missouri River Valley with his objective Lexington. To assist his efforts he sought to rally public opinion by issuing grandiose proclamations to assure the citizens and attract additional levies to his army.[42]

In early September Price started his march northward. By September 13 his army was approaching Lexington garrisoned by 3,500 Federal troops under Colonel James Mulligan. The Union post was a formidable fortification encompassing extensive traverses, rifle pits, seven cannon, and obstacles in the form of sharpened stakes. Price, realizing the difficulty of taking the place by storm, invested the works in a siege. The threat of a Federal relief column convinced Price that he did not have time to wait out Mulligan; rather, he would have to storm the place. After an initial failed assault on September 18 his army attempted taking it again a couple of days later using a new tactic. Improvising, Price's men gathered hemp bales from the Missouri River wharves and placed them in a line for use as a rolling barricade. The Union troops were short of water and ammunition and quickly became demoralized by the sight of the slowly advancing line of hemp bales. When the Confederates moved to within 125 yards of the fort, Mulligan surrendered.[43] Lexington represents the zenith of Price's military career. It brought him accolades from fellow Missourians and the entire South. It also confirmed his inflated opinion of his abilities and reinforced his disdain for consideration of logistics in military operations.

Following Lexington Union forces mobilized to expel Price from the state. Price found himself in a slowly closing trap and decided that he must retreat or face destruction. Frustrated, he retreated from Lexington all the way to northwest Arkansas as the Federals launched a winter offensive. Yet, Price still searched for some way to move back into Missouri. He would not have to wait long to make an attempt. The Confederate government recently appointed an aggressive general, Earl Van Dorn, to take charge of all forces west of the Mississippi. The purpose behind appointing Van Dorn was to bring unity of effort to a chaotic situation. Van Dorn made a quick assessment of the status of his command and determined to make a counter-offensive much to the delight of Price. He had to temper his satisfaction as Van Dorn ordered him and McCulloch to unite their forces for the offensive, reestablishing a frustrating partnership for both men.[44]

The short-lived effort to recover Missouri culminated at an unknown corner of northwest Arkansas known as Pea Ridge. Van Dorn, much like Price, tended to ignore realities when planning the campaign and entered into the movement without considering logistics or the capabilities of his army. Van Dorn's plan initially appeared to work as the newly christened Army of the West stole a march on Brigadier General Samuel R. Curtis' Union Army of the Southwest. However, the inability to adequately supply the troops with subsistence and simply asking too much from mortals doomed the offensive. This allowed Curtis to recover from his own miscalculations and enabled him to meet Van Dorn's larger force at an advantage. After a hard-fought two day battle that saw Price wounded leading his troops with characteristic courage, the Confederates were forced to retreat.[45] Price bitterly criticized Van Dorn for his conduct of the campaign and the treatment of the soldiers. He could not dwell on this for long as his Missourians received a request to aid hard pressed Confederate armies east of the Mississippi.

The transfer of the Missouri troops to the east bank of the river represented a major change of Confederate national policy. The Confederate government had relegated the Trans-Mississippi theater to a backwater of the war—a fact that Price found hard to accept. Nevertheless, Price arrived in Memphis ready to beat back the blue tide and seek opportunity to advance his own agenda—Missouri. The Confederates in Tennessee and Mississippi were reeling after a series of setbacks in the spring of 1862. After a heartbreaking defeat at Shiloh in April, General P. G. T. Beauregard pulled out of the strategic rail center at Corinth lest the huge Union army under Major General Henry Halleck[46] encircle and capture his smaller Army of the Mississippi. Beauregard's retreat and the prospect of little action held no appeal for Price and his desire to assist fellow Confederates in the east waned. He now sought to turn attention back to the Trans-Mississippi and Missouri. He made a personal journey to Richmond to call on Jefferson Davis to discuss the early return of his troops to Arkansas. In addition, he sought overall command of Confederate troops west of the Mississippi.[47]

The trip to the capital brought many accolades as the entire South viewed Price as a hero. Unfortunately for Price, Davis did not share the same opinion of him as his countrymen. Davis believed that Price was the "vainest man" he had ever met and further was nothing more than a glorified military amateur. This set the tone for a stormy meeting between the two men on June 16. Colonel Thomas Snead, Price's chief of staff, recorded the results of the conference and described it as "contemptuous." Price presented his views of the situation in writing and expressed his desire to return to Missouri with his troops at the earliest date. Davis succinctly stated that he could not order Price west of the river. To this Price replied, "you cannot prevent me from doing that. I will send you my resignation and go back to Missouri ... and win new victories for the South in spite of the [G]overnment." This response angered Davis and he informed Price that his "resignation will be promptly accepted" and that should he win victories for the South no one would be "more pleased or, more surprised."[48]

"Indignant and furious" Price left Richmond intent on resigning and returning west to recruit a new army. Davis, however, had a change of heart sending word to Price that he would send him and his troops back to the west as soon as the situation permitted. Davis knew that Price's ability to attract recruits and his folk hero status in the South were too valuable to lose. This mollified Price and he agreed to stay on with the Confederacy.[49] His pattern of agitating superiors based on his own high opinion of his military skills would continue unabated throughout the war, but his strategy would change as he tried a different approach.

For now the situation in Mississippi had changed radically. General Braxton Bragg had taken over command of Beauregard's army and transferred it to Chattanooga in preparation for a drive into Kentucky. The seemingly invincible Federals were reeling in the face of the renewed Rebel vigor. The Union army had pulled back significant numbers from northwest Mississippi and west Tennessee in an attempt to stop Bragg. This left the important railhead at Corinth ripe for an attack and an offensive into west Tennessee in support of Bragg. Price, now in command of the Army of the West, prepared for offensive operations at the behest of Bragg. Further, he authorized Van Dorn to join forces with Price to ensure Grant did not shift more forces northward to Kentucky.[50] Van Dorn failed to reinforce Price in a timely manner causing more friction in an already strained relationship.

Bragg, concerned for his army's security in Kentucky, wrote to Price on September 6 urging him take action to prevent reinforcement of the Federal army facing him. Already impatient, Price could wait no longer for Van Dorn and decided to move immediately for west Tennessee. Price moved from Tupelo thence to Iuka in northeast Mississippi intending to push on from there to Nashville. The presence of a large Union force under Grant around Iuka forced a change of plan. Grant set a trap for Price, nearly snaring him on September 19 between the converging divisions of Major General William S. Rosecrans and E. O. C. Ord. Only an acoustic "shadow" saved Price from destruction as Ord's force never attacked because he could not hear Rosecrans in action to the south. Breaking off the action at Iuka on September 19, Price sought refuge at Baldwyn, Mississippi.[51]

Within a few days Van Dorn belatedly joined Price and characteristically called for offensive action in an attack on Corinth. Although Price held great disdain for Van Dorn he subordinated his lack of respect for him for the good of the cause. Despite his vanity Price had the good sense to ensure command harmony over self-interest. Price argued against making an attack on Corinth in light of the heavy fortifications surrounding the town. Van Dorn, as impudent as ever, refused to listen and laid out plans to attack Corinth. Against his better judgment Price agreed to the scheme, much to his chagrin.[52]

Corinth was a disaster for the Confederacy, Price, and his Missourians. On October 3–4 Van Dorn impetuously rushed the defenses in an uncoordinated manner and although in some sectors the Confederates enjoyed success, on the whole the Rebels met with bloody repulse. The Missourians suffered especially high casualties in the assault and Price determined that he would never serve with Van Dorn again and would cross back to the Trans-Mississippi.[53]

In order to ensure his and the Missouri troops' prompt return west, Price decided to make another trip to Richmond to plead his cause. He arrived in late January 1863 and held meetings with the new Missouri Governor Thomas C. Reynolds and Secretary of War James Seddon. On this second journey Price had greater success in achieving his purpose, but it was only a partial victory. While a command awaited Price west of the river, the secretary informed him that his troops were needed in Mississippi to defend Vicksburg. While leaving his men was distasteful Price's drive to get back to Missouri overrode his desire to remain with his division. Therefore, on March 18, 1863, Price finally returned west on orders from the War Department to assume command of a new division of Arkansas and Missouri troops.[54]

1863 would prove a disheartening year for Price as the Trans-Mississippi Department suffered setback after setback. First, Price participated in a disastrous assault on Helena, Arkansas, in an attempt to relieve pressure on Vicksburg. Then, Vicksburg itself fell cutting off the department from the rest of the Confederacy. Finally, in September Little Rock, the capital of Arkansas, surrendered to Federal forces under Brigadier General Frederick Steele as Price's small army took refuge in the southern part of the state. Much of the blame for the disasters fell to the aged and decrepit Lieutenant General Theophilus Holmes. Further, the Missouri congressional delegation lobbied for Holmes' removal since they believed he would do nothing to aid in the liberation of their state. In February 1864 Holmes resigned his post as commander of the District of Arkansas due to the "loss of confidence" in his abilities. Kirby Smith felt Price unequal to the command but the want of competent leaders in the Trans-Mississippi forced him into giving the appointment to Price.[55] On March 16, 1864, Price assumed his new command and would serve in this capacity throughout the Camden Expedition. During his tenure he continued to press for a move into Missouri, but his tone underwent a noticeable change. It seemed that the past few years had taught him a lesson in tact and he exercised it now to achieve his ends. His commander, Kirby Smith, was quite amenable to his proposals because of the irritating manner by which Smith's commander in Louisiana, Richard Taylor, pushed for his agenda.

Major General Richard Taylor, commander of the Confederate District of West Louisiana, vociferously disagreed with Kirby Smith's policy for defending the Trans-Mississippi and his home state, Louisiana. Courtesy Jack McCormack Irish Collection at the United States Army Military History Institute.

Major General Richard Taylor did not have a direct combat role in Arkansas since his command encompassed the District of West Louisiana. However, he exerted enormous influence over the decisions made regarding the expedition, and its outcome. He had a background paralleling that of Price while contrasting sharply with Kirby Smith. Therefore, an understanding of this complicated man in the context of his peers is necessary for a fuller appreciation of the expedition's results.

Taylor was the son of a president—Zachary Taylor—an army brat, and of aristocratic upbringing. His background contributed significantly to his social attitudes, political persuasion, and military command style. Though Taylor lived in a great many places as the son of a ranking military officer, he would claim Louisiana as his home state. Richard Taylor had a pronounced independent streak that his father attributed to the lengthy separations from his family required of him as a commander on the frontier. Zachary attempted to compensate for his absence by sending him to private schools with reputations for discipline. Nevertheless, Richard would develop an irascible personality noted for its combined sarcasm and childishness.[56] This would prove a source of irritation for Kirby Smith in 1864 while at the same time providing Sterling Price with an opportunity to fulfill his wish to liberate Missouri.

Taylor entered Yale after his time in private school and here he became stricken with a lifelong ailment, rheumatoid arthritis. It flared up throughout his life, and associates found his disposition unbearable when he was suffering bouts of the malady. As a result, Taylor's health impaired his judgment and soured his working relationship with subordinates and superiors alike.[57] A serious spell during the Red River Campaign would influence his tact and the decisions he made affecting all military operations in the Trans-Mississippi in the spring of 1864.

Like Price, Taylor was a full-time planter and a sometime politician in Louisiana. He would settle there after receiving his college education from Yale to live the life of a privileged planter. As a major land and slaveholder he was predictably a conservative and Democrat. He believed in maintenance of a classed society of planters, peasant farmers, and humble servants. Since this was the natural order he believed all should remain in their respective places for the good of the larger society. He viewed the secession crisis as disastrous for the country and felt that Louisiana's best interest lay with remaining in the Union. As a delegate at the Louisiana secession convention he opposed secession. When Louisiana left the Union he initially vowed to stay out of the war remaining at his plantation, Fashion. It took little time to change his mind when he received an invitation from General Braxton Bragg to serve on his staff. Bragg's exhortations convinced him to reluctantly join the Confederacy.[58]

Taylor had no formal military training like Price, once again diverging from Kirby Smith's background. Yet, as one contemporary noted, "probably no civilian of his time was more deeply versed in the annals of war." While having a great respect for the military profession, he held great disdain for the professional officer. He once stated that the frontier officer of the U. S. Army "furnish[ed] the most complete illustration of suppressed mental development."[59] When the war began Taylor quickly developed into an outstanding combat leader with sound grasp of tactics and operational art. Part of the reason for his rapid progress is his service under Stonewall Jackson. Taylor would adopt Jackson's philosophy of using lightning maneuver to gain advantage and then strike hard to finish the enemy.[60] After serving his apprenticeship with the aggressive Jackson, Taylor would find his service under the cautious Smith intolerable.

After missing the Peninsula Campaign in 1862 because of his arthritic condition, Taylor received a new assignment. The Trans-Mississippi held the distinction of being a junkyard for incompetent commanders in the Confederacy. Jefferson Davis—a former brother-in-law of Taylor's—realized the shortfall of leadership in the department and how it plagued efficiency. Additionally, state governors west of the Mississippi began demanding competent commanders for the army in that region. In response, Davis asked Taylor to accept command of the District of West Louisiana. Taylor accepted the challenge and assumed command in his home state on August 20, 1862. The situation he found defied description as he noted shortages of everything from men to ammunition. Through herculean efforts he brought a semblance of order out of the chaos.[61] His incentive was a driving ambition to succeed as a commander and the attachment he felt to the home state he was defending.

Soon after taking charge Taylor began to clash with the department commander over matters of resource distribution, priorities of defense, and where the decisive point of the region lay. Taylor tactlessly pummeled Smith with his thoughts on how best to defend the department with the primary focus in Louisiana. Every barb grated on Smith in spite of the deference he paid Taylor and eventually Smith would have enough. Price also proffered his opinions to superiors on the best course of action for the Confederacy west of the Mississippi. In his opinion the liberation of Missouri should be the top priority of the department. However, having been unsuccessful for so long in his hard-nosed efforts, Price would change tactics in 1864. He became more agreeable while suggesting what he believed Smith should do. By April 1864 Smith was receptive to Price while conversely agitated by Taylor, directly leading to his decision to move into Arkansas.

The Smith-Price-Taylor triumvirate would decide the fate of the Confederate Trans-Mississippi Department and in a larger sense affect the outcome of the war. The interaction of these men influenced decision-making and set the tone for the Red River Campaign and the Camden Expedition. The inability of Taylor to get along with Smith would have an overall detrimental effect on events. Price's moderation of his tone enabled him to win over Smith and set the military priorities of the department. His deference to Smith would also allow him to realize his fondest wish, reentering Missouri.

Notes

1. Joseph H. Parks, *General Edmund Kirby Smith, C. S. A.*, 1–6.

2. Namesake of her mother, also Frances Smith.

3. Parks, *General E. K. Smith*, 9–12.

4. *Ibid.*, 15–19, 36–39; Edmund Kirby Smith "Papers," in a letter to his father Joseph Smith dated February 1842.

5. Parks, *General E. K. Smith*, 39–41.

6. *Ibid.*, 61–62.

7. Smith "Papers," in a letter to his mother dated September 28, 1852.

8. Parks, *General E. K. Smith*, 87–88.

9. Smith "Papers," in letters to his mother dated November 23, 1860, and December 24, 1860; Parks, *General E. K. Smith*, 121.

10. *Ibid.*, 130–137; and Nina Buck Smith, "Blucher of the Day at Manassas," *Confederate Veteran*, VII (March 1889), 108.

11. *OR*, Vol. 5, 1072–73 and 1078; Parks, *General E. K. Smith*, 154–158, 165–167, and 174–175.

12. *Ibid.*, 197–199.

13. Frank T. Ryan. "The Kentucky Campaign and the Battle of Richmond," *Confederate Veteran* XXVI (April 1918), 158–160; *OR*, Vol. 16, Part 2, 833–834.

14. U. S. Grant, III, "Military Strategy of the Civil War," article from *Military Analysis of the Civil War*, 11–13; Archer Jones, *Civil War Command and Strategy*, 78–79 and 110–127.

15. Parks, *General E. K. Smith*, 220–239.

16. *Ibid.*, 251; *OR*, Vol. 19, Part 2, 643.

17. Parks, *General E. K. Smith*, 252–256.

18. Robert E. Shalhope, *Sterling Price: Portrait of a Southerner*, 1–4.

19. *Ibid.*, 5, 10–11.

20. *Ibid.*, 6–8.

21. *Ibid.*, 12–13.

22. *Ibid.*, 15–16.

23. Albert Castel, *General Sterling Price and the Civil War in the West*, 3.

24. Shalhope, *Sterling Price*, 27–29.

25. *Ibid.*; and B. H. Roberts, *History of the Church of Latter Day Saints*, Vol. III, 205–206.

26. Shalhope, *Sterling Price*, 39–40 and 46–47.

27. James K. Polk, *Diary*, Vol. I, Quaife, ed., 440.

28. Shalhope, *Sterling Price*, 58–59.

29. William E. Connelley, *Doniphan's Expedition*, 515–516; Joseph D. Gill III, "American Civil-Military Government: The Service of Colonel Alexander Doniphan in the Mexican War," *Armed Forces and Society* (Summer 1996), 558–559; J. S. D. Eisenhower, *So Far From God*, 236–240.

30. Shalhope, *Sterling Price*, 70–71; Quaife, ed., *Polk Diary*, Vol. III, 450–451.

31. Cadmus Wilcox, *History of the War with Mexico*, 538–541; Shalhope, *Sterling Price*, 72.

32. Quaife, ed., *Polk Diary*, Vol. IV, 8–9.

33. Shalhope, *Sterling Price*, 78–82.

34. *Ibid.*, 98–99, 102–103, and 130.

35. Castel, *General Sterling Price*, 7–11.

36. Thomas L. Snead, "The First Year of the War in Missouri," *B & L*, Vol. I, 264.

37. Shalhope, Sterling Price, 157–158; Anthony Monachello, "Missouri in the Balance: Struggle for St. Louis," *America's Civil War* (March 1998), 44, 47–52.

38. Shalhope, *Sterling Price*, 164–167; Castel, *General Sterling Price*, 25.

39. Castel, *General Sterling Price*, 28; Price "Papers," Western Historical Manuscript Collection, University of Missouri Columbia, G. O. #8.

40. Castel, *General Sterling Price*, 35.

41. *OR*, Vol. III, 53–129; N. B. Pearce, "Arkansas Troops in the Battle of Wilson's Creek," *B & L*, Vol. I, 299–303.

42. Price "Papers," Western Historical Manuscript Collection, August 12, 1861, proclamation to the people of Missouri and Price "Papers," Special Collection Library, Rice University, August 13, 1861, G. O. to the Missouri State Guard.

43. James A. Mulligan, "The Siege of Lexington," *B & L*, Vol. I, 307–312.

44. Earl J. Hess and William Shea, *Thunder in the Ozarks: The Pea Ridge Campaign*, 22 and 56–57.

45. *Ibid.*, 311–313.

46. Halleck had taken personal command of the army recently commanded by U. S. Grant after the latter's near-defeat at Shiloh.

47. Castel, *General Sterling Price*, 87; Thomas L. Snead, "With Price East of the Mississippi," *B & L*, Vol. II, 723.

48. Thomas L. Snead, "With Price East of the Mississippi," *B&L*, Vol. II, 724.

49. *Ibid.*, 725.

50. Snead, "With Price East of the Mississippi," *B & L*, Vol. II, 725–726; *OR*, Vol. 17, Part 2, 656. Price also had command of what was known as the District of Tennessee.

51. *OR*, Vol. 17, Part 2, 694, 705–706; C. S. Hamilton, "The Battle of Iuka," *B & L*, Vol. II, 734–736; and Castel, *General Sterling Price*, 97–104.

52. Castel, *General Sterling Price*, 106; Peter Cozzens, *The Darkest Days of the War: The Battles of Iuka and Corinth*, 139–140.

53. Peter Cozzens, *The Darkest Days of the War: The Battles of Iuka and Corinth*, 270–273; Castel, *General Sterling Price*, 126–128.

54. Castel, *General Sterling Price*, 134–139.

55. *Ibid.*, 165–171.

56. Michael T. Parrish, *Richard Taylor: Soldier Prince of Dixie*, 3, 10–15.

57. Jack Welsh, M.D., *Medical Histories of Confederate Generals*, 210–211.

58. Parrish, *Richard Taylor*, 69, 105–107; Richard Taylor, *Destruction and Reconstruction*, 10. Containing an extract of the letter from Braxton Bragg.

59. Parrish, *Richard Taylor*, 125.

60. Taylor, *Destruction and Reconstruction*, 91.

61. Parrish, *Richard Taylor*, 241; Taylor, *Destruction and Reconstruction*, 119–120.

3

The Yankee Commanders

The commanders in blue were a mixture of hard-bitten regulars, frontier volunteers, and German immigrants. By 1864 all had a long record of service that included combat in all the major battles west of the Appalachians such as Fort Donelson, Shiloh, Pea Ridge, Prairie Grove, and Vicksburg to name a few. While their Rebel antagonists suffered from uncooperative relationships, the Union leaders maintained a more professional discourse. The Federals did have moments of disagreement; however, the manner of their official conduct demonstrated discipline and focus on the objective. The men in charge of the Camden Expedition included Major General Frederick Steele, and Brigadier Generals John M. Thayer, Eugene A. Carr, and Frederick Salomon. The character and conduct of these men enabled them to save their army — and in the larger scheme General Bank's army on the Red — when they had their backs to the wall, in order to fight another day.

Frederick Steele commanded the Federal Department of Arkansas and the 7th Army Corps. He would reluctantly lead the thrust from Arkansas toward Shreveport in March–May 1864. Steele came from humble beginnings as the eldest son of Nathaniel and Dameras Johnson Steele. He was born in the small New York village Delhi on January 14, 1819. His forbears emigrated from Britain in 1715 and co-founded modern-day Hartford, Connecticut. Eventually the Steeles migrated west to settle as farmers in the wilderness of upstate New York.[1]

Little is known of Steele's childhood prior to his entry into West Point in 1839. What is known is that Frederick had a large and extended family. His mother's first husband died leaving Dameras with four young children. She would soon remarry to Nathaniel and this marriage produced five more children. Among Frederick's siblings and half-brothers and sisters, he was closest to his half-brother John. John maintained a close relationship with his younger brother until Frederick's early death in 1868. He was a sounding board for Fred as well as mentor and confidant.[2]

Steele became interested in a military career later than most of his peers at West Point. Most cadets entered the Point as teenagers of sixteen to eighteen years of age. Fred Steele began his military training in July 1839 at the ancient age of twenty years, five months and as a result became something of a mentor to the younger men. Steele would find satisfying camaraderie and make lifelong friendships during his time at the academy. Among his closest friends were future Civil War generals Nathaniel Lyon, William Tecumseh Sherman, and perhaps his most intimate associate, Ulysses S. Grant.[3]

Fred Steele had a respectable first year at the academy finishing in the upper fifth of the class at 17th out of 73 cadets after examinations in January 1839. His standing would fall steadily in the succeeding years to 27th of 54 in 1841 and by his 1843 graduation to 30th of 39 graduates. His slide is probably attributable to the reputation he earned as a prankster. One observer notes that Steele was "marked for humor and mischief ... quick repartee, a wiry, shrill-voiced wag whose friends could tell by an odd snapping of his eyelids when he was preparing to tell a joke." His penchant for levity earned him 108 demerits, a low class rank, and an infantry officer's commission.[4]

At the time of his commissioning in 1843 the regular army had no vacancies for officers. Therefore, Steele received a brevet second lieutenant's commission in lieu of full rank until positions opened to accommodate all the graduates. Steele finally received his second lieutenancy three years later in 1846. In the meantime, he reported for duty with the 2nd Infantry Regiment in his home state of New York. Although his army service was uneventful he did lead an unusual expedition in 1845 through his home county. At this time, his brother Osman served as sheriff of Delaware County and was murdered by local agitators. Frederick requested and received a furlough intent upon chasing down the perpetrators and bringing them to justice.[5] While there is no record of the result of this expedition, it reveals much of Frederick Steele's character. Though he had a happy-go-lucky reputation at West Point, beneath the surface lurked a serious, driven man. Further, Steele demonstrated an uncompromising loyalty to his older half-brother, a characteristic he would exhibit toward many throughout his military career.

Steele's service proved uneventful until the outbreak of the Mexican War in 1846. He was still a second lieutenant, but the war provided the opportunity for advancement and excitement in contrast to the stagnation and mundane activities of the peacetime army. The war also tested the U. S. Army's young officer corps and the mettle of the West Point educated officers. Fred Steele, like the majority of his peers, validated the confidence the nation placed in him by serving with distinction in several of the war's fiercest battles, particularly Contreras and Chapultepec.[6]

Steele's performance at Chapultepec earned him the recognition of the commanding general, Winfield Scott. The battle for the Mexican palace at Chapultepec was the culminating event of the war. Everything hinged on the battle's outcome, as a victory would win the war for the U. S. while a defeat quite possibly could dash hopes for success by destroying the army. To enable the main force to successfully assault Chapultepec's precipitous walls, 265 select officers and men were picked to breach the obstacle with scaling ladders. Among the group was Lieutenant Frederick Steele from the 2nd Regiment. Called a "forlorn hope" by some of the participants, the storming party suffered heavy casualties in its approach to the walls of the palace.

Several of the commanders fell dead or severely wounded as a result of the galling fire. Lieutenant Steele, seeing his own superiors down, assumed command and pushed the soldiers across the killing ground to secure the breach.[7]

In his report Winfield Scott noted that Steele, "after the fall of Lieutenant Gantt," took charge of the storming party and led it in a "most distinguished" manner.[8] For his service, Steele earned two brevets to the rank of captain, but more important he had invaluable combat experience. Of the many lessons learned, he would remember how the American army suffered under the hardship of a tenuous line of communication deep in enemy territory. Undoubtedly, with this in mind he attempted to avoid launching the Camden Expedition in the Civil War due to similar conditions in Arkansas.

Steele spent the inter-war years on the frontier serving in a variety of positions at far-flung locations. He saw little combat against Indian bands since slow-moving infantry was inadequate for chasing such a wily enemy. He maintained his warm friendship with fellow officer U. S. Grant. Even after Grant left the army in 1854 he would inquire of his old friend Steele to all mutual acquaintances.[9] This comradeship proved a boon for Steele, as Grant would confidently place him in important commands in the Civil War.

Promotions in the old army came at a snail's pace and only when a vacancy opened due to the resignation or death of another officer. In spite of his gallantry in the Mexican War Steele reverted to the rank of first lieutenant after the war. He did not regain a captaincy until 1855. Nevertheless, he continued in his duties serving for six years as adjutant of the 2nd Infantry Regiment, on court-martial boards, and patrolling the upper Great Plains.[10]

The tragedy of his mother's death broke up the monotony of frontier service and reveals another glimpse of the strength and determination of Frederick Steele. While he grieved tremendously, he exhorted his brother that "there is no use in … making ourselves miserable." Instead, he stated, "we should make use of all reasonable means to stifle immoderate sorrow."[11] He believed his mother would want the family to move forward rather than looking back and he encouraged his siblings to remember her by living full lives. Such determination carried him and his army through trying times at Camden.

In the late '50s the secession question began to enter conversations among the officer corps of the army. As a northern man there is little doubt of Steele's loyalty to the country. While the record contains scanty evidence of his stance on the issues of the day, one can surmise from his associates and his efforts in organizing and raising troops in 1861 that he was a staunch Union man. As the southern states seceded in early 1861 Steele and other officers looked on with bewilderment. The regular army numbered slightly more than 16,000 men in 1861 and found itself scattered across the frontier. With Lincoln's call for volunteers the army attempted to assemble into regiments and brigades. The start of the war found Steele at Fort Leavenworth and in May the army promoted him to major in command of a battalion in the 11th Infantry Regiment.[12]

In June, newly appointed Brigadier General Nathaniel Lyon, Steele's old academy friend, began consolidating all available Federal forces in and around Missouri to mount an offensive against hastily assembling Missouri State Guardsmen. Lyon knew he had to move quickly in order to secure strategically located Missouri for the Union. Among the forces called upon to form Lyon's army was Steele's battalion of regulars and volunteers. Frederick Steele's performance during the upcoming campaign would solidify his reputation as a cool, fighting commander.

General Lyon occupied Springfield, Missouri, on July 13, 1861, having forced Sterling Price and his Missouri State Guard into the extreme southwest corner of the state. This gave Federal authorities complete control of the state, but Lyon remained unsatisfied with his bloodless occupation of the state. He knew that he had to inflict a crushing blow on the rebels in order to consolidate the Federal hold on Missouri. Additionally, Lyon's command had several three-month regiments whose enlistment would expire within thirty days. Loss of these men would reduce Lyon's 7,000-man army to around 4,000 soldiers, barely enough to hold St. Louis not to speak of the entire state.[13] In light of these circumstances Lyon decided to mount a drive against Price to eliminate him as a threat to Missouri.

Lyon assigned Steele's battalion as the spearhead of the army's advance and the regulars quickly drew first blood at Dug Springs. On a sweltering August morning Steele's skirmishers ran into a Rebel cavalry patrol. Steele assessed the situation and deployed his battalion to drive away the mounted Confederates. After a sharp engagement the battalion routed the Rebels, in the process appropriating a wagon loaded with rations.[14] In his first fight Steele had discharged his duties in battalion command in commendable fashion, but the true test of his mettle could come at a little known corner of Missouri called Wilson's Creek.

On August 12, 1861, the little Union army under Lyon attacked the combined Confederate force under Price and Ben McCulloch near Wilson's Creek. Catching the larger Rebel force by surprise in their camps, Lyon nearly annihilated them as they struggled to form a coherent line. The quick reaction of Price and McCulloch prevented disaster and soon they directed a counterattack up what today is known as Bloody Hill. Anchoring the defense on Bloody Hill was Steele's battalion. After repulsing the initial assaults, the much larger Confederate army overwhelmed Lyon's army killing him in the process. Command of the Union army fell on Major Samuel D. Sturgis who assigned Steele responsibility for covering the army's retreat. Steele conducted a stubborn defense that arrested the Confederate pursuit and allowed the Federals to retreat in good order, bringing along their wounded. In his report of the battle Sturgis commended Steele for "gallantry ... from the beginning to the close of the battle."[15] Steele took great pride in his battalion's performance in this first battle. He stated "with some exultation of feeling" that his "gallant little battalion" had held its ground against every assault, and indeed it had.[16]

Steele would not long remain a major. Competent commanders were hard to come by for the Union early in the war. Steele's performance at Wilson's Creek came to the attention of none other than the President. Learning of Steele's exploits, Lin-

Major General Frederick Steele, commander of the Federal Department of Arkansas and the VII Corps, reluctantly embarked on the Camden Expedition to aid Nathaniel P. Banks' Army of the Gulf in the Red River Campaign. Courtesy Massachusetts Commandery Military Order of the Loyal Legion and the United States Army Military History Institute.

coln penned a note to the Secretary of War on December 31, 1861, requesting that he "[L]et Frederick Steele of the Regular Army ... be appointed Brigadier General of Volunteers." "Let it be done," stated Simon Cameron in his endorsement, and on January 29, 1862, Steele assumed duties as a newly minted brigadier general.[17]

Frederick Steele would distinguish himself again in operations against Vicksburg. The Vicksburg Campaign extended over several frustrating months before culminating in the Confederate surrender in July 1863. The campaign found Steele reunited with under the command of his old friend U. S. Grant and leading a division in Sherman's 13th Army Corps. In every phase Steele played a prominent role while always finding himself where the action was hottest. During the attack on Chickasaw Bluffs in December 1862 Steele found himself "dodging bullets" as he aligned his division for the assault. He was among the lucky ones that day as his division suffered 856 casualties in what Grant later termed a "very unfortunate attack."[18]

While Steele continued to demonstrate courage and competence as a commander, he also demonstrated the qualities of versatility and cooperativeness. For the attack at Chickasaw Bluffs Sherman placed Steele "in support" of his 3rd Division commander Brigadier General George W. Morgan and responsible to his orders. Rather than quibble over matters of rank, Steele graciously rendered full assistance and support to him as Morgan confirmed in a post-war account.[19] This aspect of Steele's character would prove critical to his ability to command effectively in Arkansas. Commanders expect subordinates to act in a loyal and responsive manner. However, these same commanders sometimes find it difficult to willingly subordinate themselves to the wishes of others. The result in many cases is infighting among men with big egos that leads to military failure. An example of this is the command climate that existed between Edmund Kirby Smith and Richard Taylor on the Confederate side in the Trans-Mississippi. Steele's ability to provide unqualified support combined with his recognized talent for command enabled him to foster a cooperative command environment during the Camden Expedition.

Following Vicksburg, Grant appointed Steele commander of the "Army of Arkansas." Grant formed this new force for the purpose of "break[ing] up Price and occupy[ing] Little Rock." This represented Steele's first independent command and led to his initial tangle with the Confederate commander of the District of Arkansas, Sterling Price. Upon arrival at Helena in July 1863 to take up his duties, Steele pronounced his troops "the poorest command I have ever seen." Nevertheless, he quickly organized his men for a thrust in the direction of Little Rock.[20]

Steele commenced his march on August 5, 1863, with about 12,000 men against light resistance from Price's cavalry outposts. Steele had closed on the outskirts of Little Rock by the first of September. Price hoped that Steele would throw himself against the fortifications protecting the city. Steele, although outnumbering his foe, would not be so obliging of Price's wishes. Instead, he developed a clever plan to turn Price out of his prepared defenses. If Price failed to react to the movement Steele even had a chance to bag Price and the city, laying the rest of Arkansas open to occupation. Steele sent his cavalry south of the Arkansas River to threaten Price's rear while he took the infantry up the north bank to attack Price in front of the city. Realizing his plight, Price prepared to evacuate the Arkansas capital. Steele had won an outstanding victory at a cost of only 136 casualties. In addition, Steele had captured the state arsenal thus depriving the Trans-Mississippi rebels of a primary source of arms manufacturing.[21] He did fail to "break up" Price though and would have to deal with him again in 1864.

Steele spent the rest of 1863 in Little Rock dealing with a host of command, civil administration, and logistical problems. So far in the war he had earned a reputation for solid command in subordinate and independent positions. His judgment had proved sound in every campaign. In 1864 his military opinions would again be shown as prescient. However, he would find himself trumped and forced to launch an expedition he did not believe his army could carry through to success. It would take all of his determination and ability of command to prevent a disaster from befalling his army and the Union war effort.

Steele's most important subordinate in the Camden Expedition was a driven frontier lawyer-turned-general, John M. Thayer. Thayer epitomized the Union soldier from the Midwest and it was appropriate that he commanded the Frontier Division. Thayer, like Steele, came from the humblest of beginnings. Thayer was born in Bellingham, Massachusetts, on January 24, 1820, to Elias and Ruth Thayer. His father held a captain's commission in the army and had fought in the War of 1812. John was the eighth generation of the Thayer family in America. The family arrived in the colonies in 1635 and family members took great pride in the fact that the males had all served in the colonial militia or American army.[22]

John Thayer was the youngest of nine children and grew up on the family farm. Little is known of his early life, but one could surmise that his father put him to work at an early age on farm chores. In addition, as the youngest Thayer he likely took part in his share of mischief directed at his older siblings. His childhood would be cut short though, as his father died suddenly when John was twelve. With only two other siblings remaining at home "much care and responsibility ... fell upon his shoulders" for the care of his mother. The family attempted to maintain the farm, but it proved too difficult and Ruth Thayer sold the land in favor of moving to a smaller home.[23]

In spite of the family hardships, Thayer's mother did not neglect young John's education. She sent him to prepare for college under the tutelage of Reverend Calvin Newton. Although not noted for his intellectual attainment, Thayer performed well enough to earn admission to Brown in 1837. He developed a keen interest in history and classical literature at Brown. Between class terms Thayer taught primary school to earn tuition. He graduated in 1841 with honors and entered into a law apprenticeship under Isaac Davis of Worcester.[24]

Thayer spent the next thirteen years practicing law in Massachusetts working various legal matters ranging from land claims to pensions. He had a keen interest in moving west to join the rush to open the continent. He felt the push westward offered him the best opportunity "to make a name for himself." Yet, his devotion to his widowed mother would not allow him to make the journey.[25] Loyalty is a key trait of Thayer's character as a man. Though he had great ambition to achieve a high position in society, he was unwilling to sacrifice his relationship with his mother for personal advancement. Throughout trying days during the Camden Expedition Thayer provided solid support to his commander, Fred Steele, demonstrating his loyalty.

Thayer's mother died in the early 1850s and within a year John made the trek west settling in Nebraska. Nebraska in the 1850s was a howling wilderness fraught with many dangers including hostile Indians. Nevertheless, Thayer became one of the founding fathers of present-day Omaha and a leading citizen of the fledgling territory. He believed Omaha's position on the Missouri River made the location the perfect site to act as the gateway to the west.[26] He would gain his initial military experience protecting the portal.

Indian uprisings among the Pawnee nation forced the territorial legislature to raise a militia force to quell the unrest. Thayer commanded great respect within the body and as a result the legislature commissioned him as a brigadier general in charge of the territorial militia. The Pawnees were upset over white encroachment on their hunting grounds and began raiding in wide swaths across the countryside. It was during their raid of the Elkhorn Valley that Thayer soundly defeated the Pawnees and gained invaluable combat experience. The victory over the tribe demonstrated Thayer's force of will and audacity. Though his territorial militia stood outnumbered 1,500 braves to 200 soldiers, he decisively defeated the foe. In addition, he placed the governor, who had accompanied the march, under arrest for issuing orders directly to his subordinates while intoxicated.[27] Throughout the Civil War Thayer would exhibit cool leadership under tough circumstances combined with bold determination.

The Pawnees never again rose up against white settlement in Nebraska, but Thayer's talent for combat leadership was not to end. By 1860 the sectional crisis placed Nebraska at center stage of the controversy and Thayer would play a major role in the state's contribution to the preservation of the Union.

Upon the outbreak of the war the various states answered Lincoln's call for volunteers by providing levies of the young men. Nebraska, although still a territory, contributed more than its share as Thayer raised the 1st Regiment of Nebraska Volunteers. Raising the thousand-man contingent from the territory represents a remarkable feat considering the total population of the territory did not exceed 28,000. Commissioned colonel of the regiment, Thayer marched them to St. Louis to join Union forces gathering in the city. The 1st Nebraska would become part of the nucleus of the army commanded by U. S. Grant in the first Federal drive south.[28]

Thayer became something of a minor hero within the Army of the Tennessee in short order. In January 1862 Grant began assembling his forces for a drive into the Tennessee Valley. His initial target was the twin forts guarding the Tennessee and Cumberland rivers. The fall of Forts Henry and Donelson would open up the Confederate heartland to invasion and expose critical industrial and agricultural regions to destruction. Grant launched the offensive in the first week of February and achieved satisfying success at a time when Union morale was at low ebb. Fort Henry easily fell almost exclusively by naval bombardment, but Fort Donelson proved a tougher nut to crack. Garrisoned by 17,000 troops and situated on a hill overlooking the Cumberland, Donelson first battered the Union navy and then repulsed an assault by Grant's army from its land face.

On the second day of the battle the Confederates attempted to break out of the slowly tightening noose Grant was applying to the Fort. The foray threatened to unhinge the siege as the Rebels pushed Federal forces off a key escape route. Acting quickly, Grant ordered the gap plugged. Into the breach Brigadier General Lew Wallace sent elements of his division including a newly formed brigade commanded by John M. Thayer.[29]

Wallace noted a "stampede" streaming from the front as he pushed his division through stragglers and walking wounded. As the division approached the battlefront, Wallace placed Thayer at a critical location on the Wynn's Ferry Road. Thayer coolly deployed his brigade squarely along the axis of the Rebel attack. As he supervised the placement the Federals could clearly see the Rebels "coming up the road." Thayer's men waited until the Confederates moved to within a few paces and then opened fire. The gray infantry tumbled before the fire but reformed to attack again. Thayer's men held against three separate assaults enabling Grant to seal off the break in his lines. Thayer's stalwart defense at Fort Donelson singled him out for praise from Grant in his official report.[30] Thayer at Fort Donelson proved himself as he had against the Plains Indians—a reliable, unflappable leader in combat. He would retain and build on this reputation throughout the war.

Grant's army followed up the victory at Fort Donelson pushing deep into Rebel territory to sweep the Tennessee Valley clean. In the first week of April the army camped at Pittsburg Landing where they would soon engage in an epic struggle. Thayer would again distinguish himself in battle winning the recognition of his superiors. Thayer's 2nd Brigade of Lew Wallace's Division spent the first day of the battle of Shiloh floundering about as conflicting march orders kept them out of the fight. Disaster nearly befell Grant's army on April 6 as General Albert S. Johnston's Confederate army surprised Grant's unsuspecting bivouac. Grant's skill and determination allowed the army to hold as darkness came on that evening.

Wallace's Division arrived on the field after dark on the 6th and immediately filed into line of battle to help stiffen the right flank of the Union defenses. At 5 A.M., April 7th, Wallace gave the order to move forward in accordance with Grant's counterattack along the whole front. Thayer's brigade hit the left flank of the Confederate line. Advancing through deep ravines and heavy timber, Thayer wheeled the brigade maintaining alignment "as unbroken as upon the parade ground." Wallace's Division broke through Confederate resistance in the early afternoon and continued to pursue until 5 P.M. While Grant doled out criticism of Lew Wallace's ineffectual performance at Shiloh, Thayer once again found favor as he received a promotion to brigadier general for his service.[31]

Thayer's next major engagement came at Vicksburg. It was during the long effort to take the citadel that Thayer first served under the command of Frederick Steele. Thayer became a stalwart, dependable leader within the division leading key assaults at Chickasaw Bluffs in 1862 and on the Vicksburg fortifications in May 1863. At Chickasaw Bluffs his brigade gained an advanced position, but was forced to retire as supporting units failed to render timely assistance. Thayer's brigade suffered severe losses in the assault and Thayer's son claimed later that the general wept at receiving the order to retreat. Throughout the arduous campaign to take Vicksburg Thayer performed in an exemplary manner. He worked well with Steele as well as his peers earning the recognition of corps commander William T. Sherman. When Steele left to assume his new command in Arkansas, Sherman chose Thayer to succeed him.[32]

Thayer would remain in command of Steele's old division and participated in Sherman's Meridian Campaign. Competent commanders were in short supply for the Union west of the Mississippi just as in the Confederacy. In order to shore up the rickety command situation the War Department transferred him to Steele's Department of Arkansas. Thayer assumed command of the District of the Frontier on February 22, 1864, reuniting him with his former division commander. The troops in the district became known as the Frontier Division and would assume a major role in the upcoming Camden Expedition.[33] The solid working relationship established between Steele and Thayer at Vicksburg would receive a severe test during the expedition, but Thayer's loyalty and determination would bear up well against the strain.

Eugene A. Carr commanded Steele's cavalry division in the Camden Expedition. Carr also descended from several generations of Americans. His family arrived in Rhode Island in 1631 among the earliest of the colonists. Carr's forebears worked in various occupations — they ranged from ministers to legislators to colonial militia officers. The family — as in the case of the Steeles and Thayers — typified the early American experience. Eugene Asa was born to Clark and Delia Carr on March 10, 1830, in Erie County, New York. All that is known of his adolescence is anecdotes related by the general in his later years. However, by his own account, Carr led a happy childhood.[34]

Tragedy beset Carr at age nine when his mother died unexpectedly. Carr's aunt — his father's sister — assisted the young family in their time of need and as a result Eugene developed a close relationship with her. As the oldest sibling additional responsibility fell to Eugene in maintaining the household.[35] A deep sense of duty was a hallmark of Carr's character and career and it probably germinated from the loss of his mother.

Having rarely ventured out of Erie County he received an appointment to West Point at the young age of sixteen. His nomination to the academy would begin a long military career characterized by much travel and numerous battles. He entered the "Point" on September 1, 1846, at the start of the Mexican War. While Carr demonstrated excellent academic skill his conduct left much to be desired. He maintained a class standing in course study consistently in the upper third of the class. However, his penchant for horseplay kept him near the bottom in demerits. Nevertheless, he graduated high enough to earn a much-desired commission in the cavalry.[36]

One of the subjects Carr excelled in at West Point was ethics. A prominent point of emphasis in the course was the concept of devotion to duty. One biographer suggests that Carr's dedication as an officer resulted in large part from this course. The program of study stated that "the officer has no right to question the *goodness or wisdom*" of an order, "his only duty is to execute it."[37] The influence on his character evidenced itself in the Camden Expedition. While Carr would staunchly fight for the welfare of his men, he would always give loyal service to Steele in the spring of 1864.

Carr graduated from West Point on July 1, 1850, with an appointment as brevet second lieutenant. His orders assigned him to the 3rd Cavalry Regiment (at that time known as the Regiment of Mounted Rifles) at Jefferson Barracks, Missouri. The 3rd Cavalry contained a large proportion of southern officers who would offer their services to the Confederacy. Ironically, Carr's company commander, John G. Walker, would oppose him on the battlefield during the Camden Expedition. Over the course of the next ten years Carr bounced around from frontier post to post engaged in mostly uneventful, mundane duties of an old army officer. He did receive his baptism of fire while posted in Kansas and Texas.[38]

Carr's first engagement was almost his last. In pursuit of Comanches in west Texas, Carr impetuously led a charge on a group gathering ponies and galloped far ahead of the troops. Warriors surrounded the young lieutenant and shot him "full of arrows." The wounds were not serious, but Carr's exploits found favor with the department commander. In his official report General Persifor Smith expressed admiration for "his [Carr's] coolness" and recommended him for promotion.[39] With the congressional authorization for two new cavalry regiments, Carr received his promotion to first lieutenant in 1855 and transfer to the 1st Cavalry Regiment.

Action would find Carr again in Kansas as the 1st Cavalry became reluctantly involved in restoring order amidst civil unrest. The sectional crisis erupted into outright civil war in the territory as slave and free-state factions fought over control of the legislature. In the summer of 1856 pro-slave state fanatics ransacked Lawrence killing many free-state advocates and by-standers. In retaliation John Brown hacked several pro-slavery leaders to death with a broadsword at Pottawatomie Creek. President Franklin Pierce called in the 1st Cavalry to restore the pro-slave legislature. Pierce deemed the free-state legislature illegitimate and ordered it disbanded. While

Carr personally disagreed with this "mistaken policy" he nevertheless felt compelled to "be on the side of the established government." [40] Carr's statement symbolized his dedication to duty, an inseparable aspect of his character.

The regular army managed to avoid a physical engagement between either faction, but did witness some tense moments. Carr became personally involved as General Winfield Scott assigned him as aide-de-camp to the new territorial governor. As a first-hand spectator of the struggle for Kansas, Carr became irreversibly connected with the sectional issues and the war that erupted from it in 1861.[41] He formed his ardent opinions in favor of the Union and governance of the Constitution as a result of his experience and the influence of his father. Clark Carr held exceptionally strong views in favor of the Union cause. On the eve of the Civil War he penned a particularly scathing letter to his son denouncing the nonchalance by which some of the southern states chose to leave the Union.[42] Carr's opinions of the sectional crisis are reflective of his father's strong assertions against slavery and the right of secession. There is good reason to believe the elder Carr held great sway in the formulation of Eugene's thoughts on the issue.

Eugene A. Carr received another promotion on the eve of the Civil War to captain and command of Fort Washita in the Indian Territory. War came to the country as Carr's garrison patrolled the Southern Plains. In March 1861 orders came from department headquarters to consolidate several posts including Fort Washita in preparation for putting down the expected rebellion. Carr trudged north to Fort Leavenworth with his command — a 500-mile trek — in accordance with the order to bring the frontier army together for the war.[43]

Carr made an excellent reputation as a troop commander in several battles during the conflict, particularly at Wilson's Creek and Pea Ridge. His rise in the army started at Wilson's Creek while commanding a company of cavalry in Nathaniel Lyon's small army. Carr led the vanguard of the army, screening its advance. At 6 A.M., July 10 Carr identified the Rebel encampment near the creek and notified his commander Franz Sigel, an officer of German descent appointed for his political connections. Sigel immediately deployed his flanking column for an assault on the unsuspecting Confederates. After enjoying initial success the Rebels rallied and turned the tables on the bluecoats. Some of the raw levies under Sigel misidentified approaching Confederates wearing blue jackets as friendly and did not fire on their advance. Moving to within ten paces, the blue-clad Rebels decimated Sigel's lead ranks precipitating a rout. In a letter to his father, Carr related his disgust at Sigel's amateurish performance. He added that "the Ad'm [Lincoln Administration] makes a terrible mistake in appointing such generals."[44] Major Samuel Sturgis — now in command of the army after Lyon's fall — called upon Carr to cover the stampede with his regulars. Carr's 56 cavalrymen successfully fought a running rear guard action allowing the remnants of the army to retreat safely from the field.[45] Although Wilson's Creek was a clear defeat for the North, Carr earned plaudits for his ability to command under fire. In recognition, Lincoln himself released Carr from duties with the 1st Cavalry so that he could accept a commission as colonel of the 3rd Illinois Cavalry proffered by the governor of the state.[46]

Brigadier General Eugene A. Carr, commander of the Federal VII Corps cavalry division, competently led Steele's horsemen providing reliable service throughout a trying expedition in southwest Arkansas. Courtesy Massachusetts Commandery Military Order of the Loyal Legion and the United States Army Military History Institute.

If Carr's performance at Wilson's Creek is described as outstanding, his exploits at Pea Ridge could be characterized as nothing short of brilliant. Pea Ridge would forever mark Carr as one of the best combat commanders in the army as he earned the Congressional Medal of Honor. Samuel R. Curtis assumed command of the remnants of Lyon's army after Wilson's Creek and dubbed it the Army of the Southwest. In conjunction with his ascension to command he reorganized the subordinate units and appointed Carr to command of the 4th Division of the army. Curtis boldly launched a winter offensive in February 1862 to clear Missouri of armed Confederates as Lyon had attempted in 1861. By March the Army of the Southwest had nearly bloodlessly forced Sterling Price out of Missouri and "penetrat[ed] ... far into the region of secessiondom [sic]." Curtis did not believe the Confederates would "make a stand short of Fort Smith, Ark. beyond the Boston Mountains."[47] However, the Rebels had a new commander in the West that superseded Price and McCulloch. Major General Earl Van Dorn came to Arkansas intent on reversing fortunes and launching an immediate counteroffensive to take back Missouri for the Confederacy. Within three days of taking the reins, Van Dorn turned Price and McCulloch around to strike back at Curtis.

Van Dorn's plan was bold bordering on rash. In the midst of a blinding winter storm and a tenuous supply situation, Van Dorn attacked a surprised Curtis near Elkhorn Tavern. Although Curtis had constructed prepared defensive works to meet the Confederates, the Rebels did not oblige him by attacking frontally. After a grueling all night march Van Dorn appeared behind Curtis' fortifications on March 7, 1862. Curtis immediately turned the army about to meet the unexpected threat. Curtis' scouts discovered that Van Dorn's army had marched on two separate avenues with two miles of heavy timber and the Pea Ridge intervening between the columns. Armed with this information, he dispatched three divisions to the small hamlet of Leetown to defeat the column commanded by Ben McCulloch. He sent his 4th Division under Carr to Elkhorn Tavern to delay Price's column rounding the ridge in order to prevent the wings of the Confederate army from linking up.[48]

Carr force marched his division at breakneck speed to the tavern and quickly deployed his men into line. Price's column outnumbered Carr's division over three to one and had a four to one advantage in artillery. Shortly after 11 A.M., Carr had his line set and within minutes his division was heavily engaged. Price launched head-on assaults against Carr's line several times from first contact until late afternoon. Having little success, Price began moving to the left to flank Carr's defense. Price had pummeled the lone Federal division for hours wounding Carr three times in the process. For several weeks after the battle Carr had to dictate all correspondence to an aide due to a severe wound to his wrist and one to his spine that left him temporarily paralyzed. In spite of the pain Carr remained on the field throughout the engagement inspiring his division to greater exertions through his example.[49] Carr now realized that it would be difficult to hold without reinforcements if Price found and hit his exposed right. In a precarious situation, Carr sent a hasty dispatch to Curtis requesting additional troops to bolster the line. Curtis responded that he had nothing to spare and that Carr must "persevere"[50] and hold the line with his own resources. Price forced him to fall back several hundred yards, but darkness set in granting Carr a reprieve. As a result of Carr's action, he bought precious time for Curtis' column near Leetown to defeat McCulloch's force. On a wintry March 7 night Curtis consolidated his army at Elkhorn Tavern with a view toward finishing off Price in the morning. The next morning Curtis struck hard thoroughly defeating Van Dorn and company.[51]

Curtis recognized the importance of what Carr had done at Pea Ridge and complimented Carr's gallantry in his official report.[52] Carr would soon receive a brigadier's star and later the Medal of Honor for service beyond the call of duty. In addition, Carr would receive a transfer to Grant's Army of the Tennessee and begin his association with Frederick Steele as a fellow division commander in the effort to take Vicksburg. Carr continued to build on his reputation during the campaign, shining at the Battle of the Big Black. Leading the pursuit by the Union army by Grant's personal orders, Carr caught up with the Confederate rear-guard near the railroad bridge spanning the river on May 17, 1863. The Rebels had suffered several setbacks since Grant had crossed to the east side of the Mississippi, especially following their recent defeat at Champion's Hill. Assessing the Confederate lines to be in utter confusion, Carr decided to launch an immediate assault. Carr maneuvered his 2nd Brigade into a position to turn the Confederate position. Upon leading the attack "the enemy were completely routed, and fled in confusion across the Big Black River."[53] The Confederates retreated to the safety of the Vicksburg fortifications sealing the fate of the city and army.

Carr's actions had been near flawless throughout the campaign to take the city; however, controversy tainted his performance. Major General John A. McClernand — Carr's corps commander and a "political" general — filed a skewed report attributing the laurels of the campaign to his leadership. Simultaneously, the report denigrated the performance of Carr and his troops. Incensed, Carr wrote to Grant pointing out the inconsistencies of McClernand's statements and that "he always tried to show him [McClernand] the respect due to my commanding officer." Grant, no fan of McClernand either, felt that the democratic politician was more interested in self-promotion than the welfare of his troops or the cause. Accordingly, he would relieve McClernand of command within weeks of the incident.[54] The McClernand-Carr confrontation does provide more evidence of Carr's character as a leader. While he might disagree with a senior, he always paid proper deference to the rank that commander held. Regardless of his loyalty to the commander, he would never hesitate to stand up in defense of his troops revealing his first loyalty. This is an admirable characteristic for the professional officer and Carr displayed it consistently throughout his career.

Following the victory at Vicksburg Carr took leave for a time before returning to his division. With campaign plans crystallizing for 1864, Grant realized that Steele needed a competent cavalry commander for the Camden Expedition. Steele's cavalry commander, Brigadier General John W. Davidson, had publicly criticized his civil-military program known as the "conciliatory policy." Davidson had even sent an open letter to the *Missouri Democrat* newspaper denouncing Steele's efforts in Arkansas. Irritated by this lack of loyalty from a senior subordinate leader, Steele sought to relieve Davidson and replace him with a more palatable man. He did not hesitate to appoint Carr to the post in light of his mounted background and aggressive leadership.[55] This would prove an excellent selection, as Carr would serve Steele with loyal, solid leadership. The Federal leadership in the Trans-Mississippi improved with each transfer and Carr only added to a noticeable upturn in the efficiency of Union endeavors.

Brigadier General Friedrich (Frederick) Salomon commanded Steele's Third Division during the Camden Expedition and is the wild card among the leaders of the army. His background differs radically from that of his peers within the army. Yet, while he maintained opinions diverging from that of the commander, Salomon invariably demonstrated proper deference and loyalty to Steele. This factor prevented dissension in the ranks from lessening the effectiveness of the commander in conducting operations and is a credit to Salomon's professionalism.

Frederick Salomon was born on April 7, 1826, in the province of Saxony, Prussia. While not of noble birth his parents managed to obtain a solid education for their son. His education included military instruction and Salomon would earn a commission as a lieutenant in the Prussian army. Following a short term of service Salomon went to Berlin to study architecture. Germany during the 1840s was undergoing a long period of upheaval as various factions struggled for control of the individual states. Salomon became swept up in the furor, but participated on the wrong side in the revolution of 1848. With retribution sure to follow, Salomon and three of his brothers immigrated to the United States.[56]

Salomon settled in the midwest, as would many thousand German immigrants. He made Manitowoc, Wisconsin, his home and his talents as a surveyor and engineer enabled him to rise to prominence among the German community. Salomon prospered as the sectional crisis began to tear his adopted country apart. Most German immigrants gave full allegiance to the Union because they identified closely with its principles. Most had fought for these same principles during the 1848 revolutions and Salomon was no exception. Young Germans turned out by the thousands to enlist when the Civil War broke out to show their commitment to the nation. Prominent Germans like Frederick Salomon were actively sought out by the government for commissions in the army because they believed this would solidify German support for the war. Salomon volunteered to serve and received a commission as a captain of volunteers.[57]

Salomon's training in the Prussian army and experience in the 1848 revolution would serve him and his adopted country well. His first engagement came at Wilson's Creek as a company commander in the 5th Missouri Infantry — his brother Charles' regiment. He performed competently under fire in the battle and within a couple of months had command of his own regiment, the 9th Wisconsin.[58] He would continue to serve quietly and solidly in all the major engagements in the Trans-Mississippi, including the battles of Prairie Grove and Helena.

The defense of the river town Helena would shine as the jewel of Salomon's service during the Civil War. He had risen to brigadier general and command of a division by July of 1863 and had the task of defending the town under the supervision of district commander Major General Benjamin Prentiss. Vicksburg was on the verge of capitulation in late June and Confederate leaders sought for a way to relieve pressure on the citadel. Theophilus Holmes, commander of the Confederate District of Arkansas, hatched a plan to capture Helena to cut Federal river traffic southward and draw off Union troops from Vicksburg. Salomon had prepared the defenses of Helena and when the Rebels attacked the fortifications they received a hot reception. In the early morning hours of July 4, 1863, Holmes launched a series of desperate assaults against the fortifications. Sterling Price managed to make a temporary lodgment, but lack of support forced him to retreat. The Confederates suffered over 1,000 casualties to Salomon's 239. Salomon had performed excellent service in holding the town.[59] Following Helena, Salomon's division would be rolled into the newly created Federal Department of Arkansas headed by Frederick Steele. In this capacity Salomon would command during the Camden Expedition.

Somewhere along the way, Salomon developed a great disdain for West Point educated officers. Captain H. A. Heinemann, a staff officer on Salomon's staff, captured some of his commander's thoughts on academy graduates during the Camden Expedition. "They [regular officers] map out battles on paper, draw their salaries, and smoke cigars," recorded Heinemann in his diary after a conversation with Salomon.[60] There is significant evidence to demonstrate that Salomon's brigade commanders shared this prejudice concerning West Pointers. However, as an officer trained in the culture of the Prussian army, Salomon did not allow this attitude to enter into his official discourse.[61] This element of loyalty helped to prevent any dissension that might have arisen as it did in the Confederate army in the Trans-Mississippi.

The Rebel commanders west of the Mississippi were a mix of contentious egos bent on satisfying personal interests. The Rebels would engage in vociferous infighting over the course of events in 1864. Thus, they lost the chance to inflict an irrevocable loss on the Union army invading Louisiana. By contrast, the Federals under Steele's direction maintained an atmosphere of professional cooperation in spite of their individual attitudes and aspirations. Each man placed a premium on duty and loyalty that would pay off when the expedition turned sour. These attributes not only preserved their own force, but forced the Confederates to divided their armies at a time when they had the opportunity to destroy a large army and fleet in the Red River Valley. In sum, the Union commanders performed admirable service for their country rather than seeking self-gratification.

Notes

1. Patricia Palmer, *Frederick Steele: Forgotten General*, 6 and 14.

2. Ezra J. Warner, *Generals in Blue*, 474.

3. John F. Lacey, "Major General Frederick Steele," *Annals of Iowa*, 424–425; Frederick Steele "Papers," Stanford University, Special Collections Library, Collection #M0191. In a November 21, 1861, letter Steele speaks of his sorrow after the death of Lyon at Wilson's Creek an associate of "over twenty years" and "intimate friend"; Lloyd Lewis, *Captain Sam Grant*, 72.

4. *Ibid*; and Lacey, "Major General Frederick Steele," *Annals of Iowa*, 427.

5. Frederick Steele "Papers," from a September 9, 1845, letter from Frederick and Nathaniel Steele to Erin Steele of Amherst, Ohio.

6. Lacey, "Major General Frederick Steele," *Annals of Iowa*, 427–428.

7. Winfield Scott, *Memoirs*, Vol. II, 517–518; J. S. D. Eisenhower, *So Far From God*, 340–342; Cadmus Wilcox, *History of the Mexican War*, 460–461.

8. Scott, *Memoirs*, 516–517. Extract from his report to the Secretary of War.

9. Lewis, *Captain Sam Grant*, 218–219; and Lacey, "Major General Frederick Steele," *Annals of Iowa*, 428.

10. Steele "Papers," containing a copy of his promotion orders from the War Department dated March 14, 1855, and other documents, including courts-martial appointment orders dated November 15, 1855, detailing his activities.

11. *Ibid.*, from a February 23, 1860, letter from Frederick Steele to Edgar W. Steele.

12. Palmer, *Frederick Steele: Forgotten General*, 6 and 16.

13. Edwin Bearss, *The Battle of Wilson's Creek*, 1–2.

14. *Ibid.*; 15–16 and Steele "Papers," containing an excerpt of Steele's official report of the affair in an undated *St. Louis Republican* newspaper article.

15. Bearss, *The Battle of Wilson's Creek*, 81, 106, 124, 131, and 135; Steele "Papers," from Sturgis' official report.

16. Steele "Papers," from a letter dated November 21, 1861, recounting the events of Wilson's Creek.

17. Steele "Papers," from a December 31, 1861, note from Lincoln to Simon Cameron; A. A. Stuart, *Iowa Colonels and Regiments*, 179.

18. Foote, *The Civil War*, II, 76; *B&L*, III, order of battle and casualties, 471; and Grant, *Memoirs*, I, 438.

19. Sherman, *Memoirs*, I, 290–291; George W. Morgan, "The Assault on Chickasaw Bluffs," *B&L*, III, 467.

20. Stuart, *Iowa Colonels and Regiments*, 180–181; Thomas L. Snead, "The Conquest of Arkansas," *B&L*, III, 456–457; and *OR*, Vol. 22, Part 1, 472 and Vol. 24, part 3, 553.

21. Castel, *General Sterling Price*, 154–158.

22. John M. Thayer "Papers," from a biographical sketch of General Thayer by his son, John, 2.

23. *Ibid.*

24. John M. Thayer "Papers," "John M. Thayer, '41, Soldier and Civilian," reprint from *Brown Alumni Monthly*, 2. Found in the Thayer collection.

25. John M. Thayer "Papers," from biographical sketch by his son, 3–4.

26. *Ibid.*, 4–5.

27. John M. Thayer "Papers," *Brown Alumni Monthly*, 2.

28. *Ibid.*, 3.

29. Benjamin F. Cooling, *Forts Henry and Donelson: The Key to the Confederate Heartland*, 148–149.

30. *Ibid.*, 178–179, 183, & 251.

31. *OR*, Vol. 10, part 1, 173, 193–195.

32. George W. Morgan, "The Assault on Chickasaw Bluffs," *B&L*, Vol. 3, 466–470; Thayer "Papers," biographical sketch by his son, 6; Edwin C. Bearss, *The Vicksburg Campaign*, Vol. 1, 202–211; and *OR*, Vol. 24, Part 3, 554.

33. *OR*, Vol. 34, Part 2, 394.

34. James T. King, *War Eagle: A Life of General Eugene A. Carr*, 8–9.

35. *Ibid.*, 10.

36. *Ibid.*, 11–13.

37. *Ibid.*, 13. Emphasis added.

38. *Ibid.*, 13–14.

39. *Ibid.*, 15–16.

40. *Ibid.*, 20–21.

41. *Ibid.*, 22–26.

42. Eugene A. Carr "Papers," United States Army Military History Institute from a letter written by Clark Carr to Eugene Carr dated March 20, 1861.

43. King, *War Eagle*, 35–36.

44. Carr "Papers," in a letter from Eugene to his father dated August 16, 1861, describing the Battle of Wilson's Creek.

45. Bearss, *Wilson's Creek*, 54, 70–71, and 95.

46. King, *War Eagle*, 40–41.

47. Carr "Papers," in a February 23, 1862, letter to his father days before the Battle of Pea Ridge.

48. Shea and Hess, *Pea Ridge*, 93.

49. Carr "Papers," from a March 15, 1862, letter to his father that Carr dictated to an aide. The letter is in the handwriting of this unidentified officer.

50. Shea and Hess, *Pea Ridge*, 184; and *OR*, Vol. 8, 258–262.

51. *Ibid.*, 191, 201–203.

52. *OR*, Vol. 8, 192.

53. Grant, *Memoirs*, I, 518; and *OR*, Vol. 24, part 1, 617.

54. King, *War Eagle*, 66–67.

55. King, *War Eagle*, 68; *OR*, Vol. 22, part 1, 709 and Vol. 34, Part 2, 105, 175, 187, 403, 427–428, and 433.

56. Ezra J. Warner, *Generals in Blue: Lives of Union Commanders*, 417–418.

57. *Ibid.*

58. *Ibid.*

59. Foote, *The Civil War*, II, 604–606.

60. M. A. Elliot, ed., *The Garden of Memory*, "Diary of Captain Heinemann, U. S. A.," 76.

61. *OR*, Vol. 34, Part 1, 671.

4

Toward a Common Center?

Times had become desperate for the Confederacy in 1864, particularly in the Trans-Mississippi region. The capture of Vicksburg in 1863 had severed communications with the eastern Confederacy leaving the territory west of the river to fend for itself. Confederate national policy dictated that the region would have to conduct the war without help from the east using its own meager resources. Kirby Smith knew this was problematic at best and near impossible at worst, but as commander of the department he would defend the region to the utmost extent of his power. The Union forces were in a better position to exploit Confederate weaknesses, but a question arose as to whether the Federal armies really needed to conduct significant operations in the Trans-Mississippi in 1864. Competing demands in the east would require the preponderance of northern resources; however, some in the Federal high command desired to "clean up" the rear areas before conducting further offensives in the east. 1864 was a year of decision in the Civil War and events in the Trans-Mississippi had the potential to have a major impact.

The Confederates designated all the territory west of the Mississippi River the Trans-Mississippi Department. The department encompassed some 600,000 square miles of territory that included the states of Texas, Arkansas, and Louisiana, except for the parishes east of the Mississippi. The Confederacy also claimed Missouri, still a Union state, Indian Territory (modern-day Oklahoma) and Arizona Territory. Arkansas, Louisiana, and Texas were the focus of Rebel and Federal actions in the Civil War with the far western territories playing a minor role. The region produced large amounts of cotton and sugar cane, and had the potential for producing foodstuffs to sustain Rebel armies. While the department had substantial natural resources, these would remain largely untapped due to the undeveloped infrastructure. Rail transportation west of the Mississippi lagged far behind the east with no coherent system connecting key points. Water transportation proved more robust due to the existence of several navigable rivers, including the Red, Arkansas, Ouachita, and Saline. The area also had hundreds of miles of coastline, the number one port in the south, New Orleans, and an uninterrupted trade outlet by land with Mexico. Trade with Mexico represented the one source of foreign trade that the Federal blockade proved unable to shut down throughout the war. By 1864, though, Union naval power had seriously constricted southern sea lines of communication. The Federal authorities had control of New Orleans and the entire length of the Mississippi. The terrain varied widely, from rugged hills in Arkansas and forested lowlands in Louisiana, to open plains in Texas.[1] While deficient in many aspects the department did have some significant advantages.

On the surface it appears that the Trans-Mississippi Department was completely unimportant, but a closer look reveals that it was an area of vast strategic importance — at least early in the war. Both the Confederacy and the Union dismissed the area as a backwater in their policy making. Each combatant tended to focus its war effort on the east bank of the Mississippi as a result. Jefferson Davis' Administration wrote off the Trans-Mississippi by mid-1862 deciding on an eastern strategy centered on Richmond and the Confederate heartland — the area between the Appalachians and the Mississippi River. In addition to these, Davis dispersed forces around the nation to protect vital points. This territorial strategy would prove the undoing of the Confederacy. Federal policy early in the war aimed at capturing the Confederate capital and isolating the Trans-Mississippi by wresting control of the river from the Rebels. However, by disregarding the Trans-Mississippi, the Confederacy unwittingly failed to leverage a vast pool of resources that included manpower and previously mentioned agriculture and raw materials.[2]

The Confederate Trans-Mississippi Department encompassed a vast landmass and a substantial population. Of a total white population of 6.51 million, approximately 2.16 million lived in the Trans-Mississippi or 33 percent of the total.[3] The Confederate government recognized that here was an excellent source of military age men to fill the armies. Indeed, in 1862 Richmond virtually stripped the department of soldiers to stem the Federal tide after the defeat at Shiloh. Throughout Lieutenant General Theophilus Holmes' tenure as departmental commander, the Rebel War Department badgered him for transfers to serve in Confederate armies east of the Mississippi River. The manpower drain served to diminish the strength and morale of the people for a couple of reasons. First, since the Rebel government considered the main theater of war to be the area east of the Mississippi, it made sense that the bulk of Confederate soldiers should serve in the east. Believing that there was only a minimal military threat to the region, the Confederacy continually demanded that the Trans-Mississippi supply troops to the main armies across the great river. Second, the Trans-Mississippi became the junkyard of incompetent officers for the Confederacy. As the war intensified in 1862 failed officers were sent packing to this "quiet" area where they could do little harm. Men the likes of Holmes and John Magruder filled the upper echelons of leadership in the department. The combination of these factors caused a serious problem among the citizens and a resulting recruiting challenge.[4]

The citizenry believed that the Richmond government had abandoned them and taken all of their soldiers, and they were reluctant to serve in the army. Why, many asked, in the face of a very real Federal threat should the male population join the

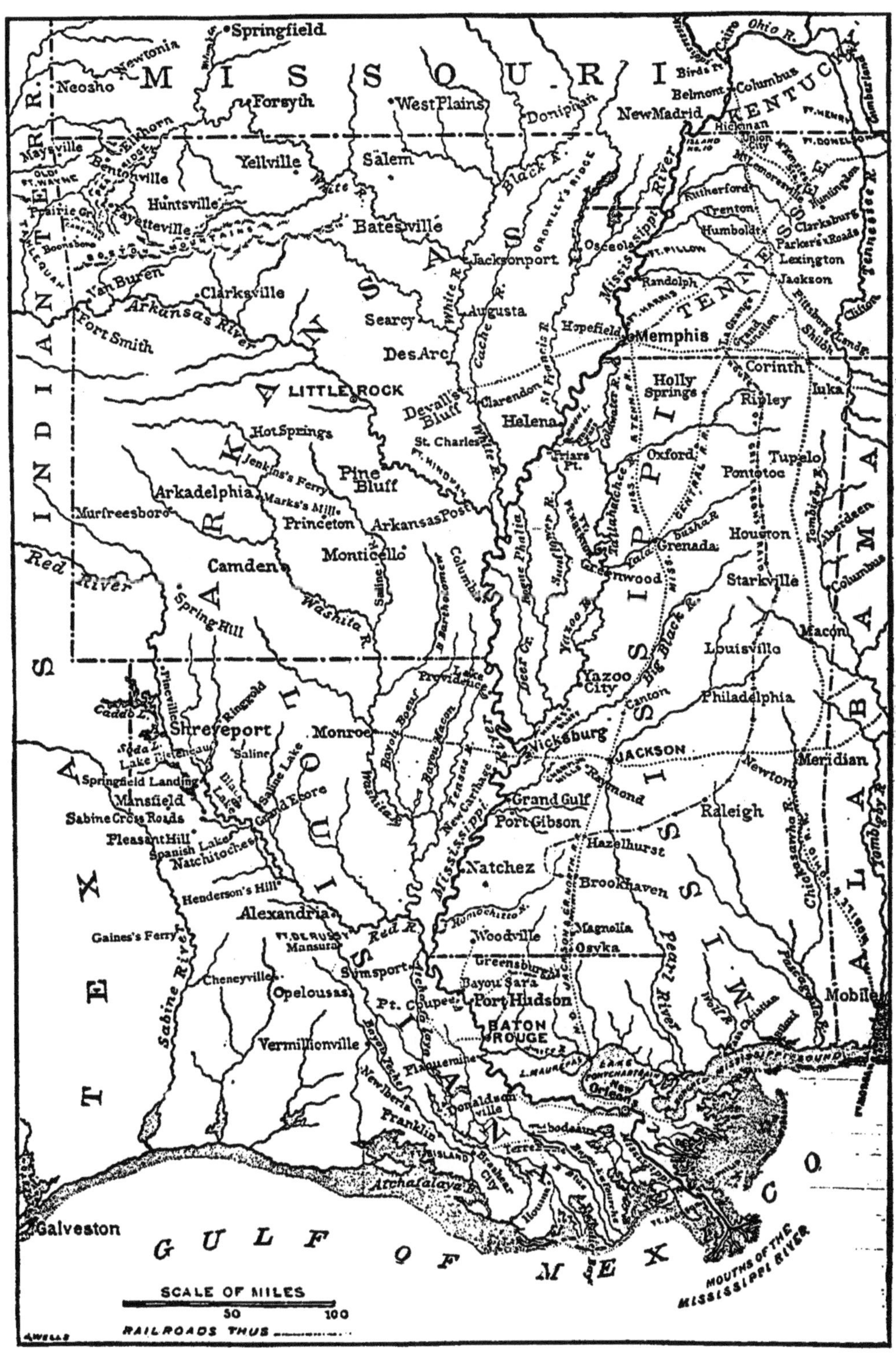

Theater of Operations, Trans-Mississippi Department. Source: *Battles and Leaders of the Civil War: Retreat with Honor,* Vol. 4, p. 348.

Confederate army only to be sent east to fight? This would lay their homes open to pillage, and the resultant resentment led to anti-government sentiment. The out-of-touch Rebel government did not realize the true extent of the Federal military threat even as the bluecoats steadily gobbled up territory. The demand for soldiers, constant Union incursions, and weak leadership produced an air of pessimism that strangled the potential positive contribution the department could have made to the war effort. To make matters worse Richmond did little to remedy the problems.[5]

Rather than forming a coherent strategy for the defense of the Trans-Mississippi, the administration simply made a change in the top man. By doing so, the Davis administration demonstrated its belief that the problem in the west lay in the realm of leadership rather than policy and it did little to allay the fears of the people. While a change in command was warranted, it proved only a half measure in the face of the challenges west of the Mississippi. President Davis replaced the decrepit and aged Holmes with the more energetic and youthful Kirby Smith in order to rejuvenate the stagnating theater and lift sagging morale. In doing so, Davis also informed Smith not to expect much in the way of material help from the Confederate government. Thus, he formally stated the previously implied policy that the Trans-Mississippi region would have to make do with its own resources. Upon arrival in the west, Smith conducted an inspection tour and what he found appalled him. "The male population," Smith reported, "are old men, or have furnished substitutes, are lukewarm, or wrapped up in speculations and money making."[6] In sum, no simple change of command would restore the confidence of the people of the Trans-Mississippi in their government. The administration would have to demonstrate true concern by changing the damaging policy that made the citizens west of the Mississippi feel abandoned.

Kirby Smith had approximately 30,000 men in his department — of whom many were not combat troops — available for defense. While this sounds like a substantial number, a closer look reveals some inherent flaws in organization. Smith's department was sub-divided into four separate districts, each with its own distribution of the total manpower. These districts were the Districts of Arkansas, West Louisiana, Texas, and the Indian Territory. The field returns from January 1, 1864, show Arkansas with about 11,000 troops, West Louisiana with another 11,000, Texas at 9,800 and the Indian Territory with 1,800. Therefore, Smith's troops were actually dispersed across several hundred miles. While the Confederates had the advantage of operating on interior lines, the poor transportation infrastructure would minimize this strength somewhat.[7]

The disposition of Rebel forces stemmed directly from the prevailing military strategy of the Confederacy. In essence, Jefferson Davis' policy was one devoted to maintaining the territorial integrity of the fledgling nation. Political considerations were largely to blame for the decision to implement such a strategy, as state governors demanded that Davis provide troops to protect the interests of their individual states. This meant that the already small Rebel armies had to disperse themselves across many points to repulse any Federal incursion. The obvious problem with such a strategy is that a much larger Union army could puncture this cordon at any time while simultaneously gobbling up the very territory the Confederates were supposed to defend. Additionally, a real danger existed in that as the concentrated Federals pushed forward they would capture or destroy the scattered, diminutive Confederate armies as at Fort Donelson and Vicksburg, steadily eroding precious strength.[8]

Kirby Smith's strategy mirrored the overarching Confederate policy on paper and in practice. Smith coined his strategy a Fabian policy. Based on his limited resources, Smith planned to make maximum use of interior lines to quickly concentrate against Federal thrusts. Once he detected a threat the confronting district would slowly fall back before the enemy advance. Meanwhile, he would order the other district commanders to reinforce the threatened district. When Smith had the force he needed to repulse the enemy, he could then pounce and defeat it. The policy traded space in order to gain time while placing scattered Confederate forces at minimal risk.[9] In light of the disposition of his forces, Smith's policy was probably the wise choice, but the policy caused tremendous friction within the department. The various district commanders, particularly Richard Taylor, did not like the policy. The dissension caused by the disagreement would spark fireworks in the Rebel command and doom hopes for a decisive victory in the Trans-Mississippi in 1864.

Arkansas had witnessed the hard hand of war for three years by 1864 and it had been thoroughly ravaged. Early 1862 saw the first large engagement as Brigadier General Samuel R. Curtis' Federal army defeated Major General Earl Van Dorn's Rebels at Pea Ridge. While this campaign locked in Missouri as a Union state, it also lay Arkansas open to further encroachment. It began a cycle of depredations and hardships that would demoralize the state's citizens. "Hit shore was mighty hard for us gals o' th' war [*sic*]," one northwest Arkansas woman recalled after the war. She continued, "[T]h' boys had all tuck t' th' hills, an' th' horses was all gone, an' nothin' for we-uns t'eat, nohow." Indeed, food became a scarce commodity for those left behind when the men left for the war, and times were especially tough for the women. Yet, the depredations were not the work of Yankee soldiers exclusively. The same Ozark woman recalled, "when ol' Sterlin' Price was a-raidin', th' Choctaw Injuns was with him, an' they et up ever' last stalk o' sugarcorn even — jest all set down an' peeled it an' chawed it for th'sweet. We did make a leetle crop o' corn thet year, but th' dang Yankees come an' tuck most of it."[10]

Such constant danger and struggle for survival sent morale sinking in Arkansas making it ripe for re-incorporation into the Union. In September 1863 Frederick Steele took Little Rock, the state capital. The taking of the seat of government was a serious blow to the Confederate cause in the state. Everything north of the Arkansas River was now under Federal control and much of the eastern part of the state close to the Mississippi River. This left the Confederates a small enclave in the southwest corner of the state. Losing the entire state in 1864 would represent a failure of Confederate arms and policy and likely deliver the state up to Federal authority. Many in the Lincoln administration had just such a scenario in mind in 1864 and Henry Halleck had a military plan in the works to bring these aspirations to fruition.

Henry Halleck was the general-in-chief of all Union armies in late 1863 through early 1864. Halleck, known by the nickname "Old Brains," was a cerebral commander in every sense. He had authored *Elements of Military Art and Science* before the war and the text served as unofficial army doctrine. While Halleck knew much of the theory of war he continually demonstrated a lack of understanding of the art of war in practice. His cautious nature and tendency to insist on tidying up his rear area as a pre-requisite to a forward advance always robbed the Federal armies of momentum. This aspect of his character exhibited itself in the formulation of plans for 1864.

Halleck proposed a movement up the Red as early as August 1863 after the fall of Vicksburg "to restore the flag" to Texas. The reason for Halleck's suggestion was the recent French intervention in Mexico. In mid–1863 Napoleon III, Emperor of the French, had installed Austrian archduke Maximillian I on the throne in Mexico City as head of a puppet regime. This was a clear violation of the Monroe Doctrine, but there was little that the Lincoln administration could do about it while engaged in a civil war. However, Napoleon dangled the possibility of a rapprochement to Confederate diplomats in Paris. Foreign recognition had long haunted the Confederacy and now it seemed achievable. This, of course, would be unacceptable to Lincoln and he solicited potential solutions to the problem. Lincoln's personal secretary recalled that the president was "very anxious that Texas should be occupied and firmly held in view of French possibilities."[11] Halleck's proposal for a campaign in the Trans-Mississippi in 1864 appeared to be a viable solution to Lincoln's dilemma.

Major General Nathaniel P. Banks rebuffed Halleck's suggestions at that time, counter-proposing that incursions up the Sabine River or landings on the Texas coast might suffice to discourage the French in establishing ties with the Confederacy. Neither of Banks' courses of action came to much as both were attempted in late 1863. Major General William B. Franklin attempted to establish a foothold in Texas by running through the Sabine Pass and occupying Galveston. This small-scale expedition failed miserably as a scratch force of Rebel artillerymen turned back the Federal gunboats and troop transports before Franklin could effect a landing. Additional attempts to "restore the flag" did little more than occupy worthless strips of bare beach on the Texas coast and proved equally abortive. Halleck expressed his displeasure with Banks in a series of dispatches between December and January.[12] While the French situation troubled the administration, other factors closed in on the President and pressed Halleck to push Banks to more concrete action.

The most compelling reason for action in the Trans-Mississippi was political in nature. 1864 was an election year in the United States. Under normal circumstances elections produce excitement, but this election would prove particularly interesting. This is because the United States was the first representative government to undergo a national election in time of a civil war. While 1864 dawned bright for Lincoln's prospects for reelection due to the military successes in 1863, his retention in office was by no means a foregone conclusion. This was the third year of a bloody war. Scarcely anyone north or south remained unaffected by the fighting. With few exceptions all families either had a loved one or a friend that had died or been maimed in the war. The protracted nature of the conflict tended to drive morale down in the North the longer it continued.[13]

In 1864 there were significant anti-Lincoln factions operating in the North, the most prominent among them was the Copperheads. Not only did they have the potential to sway the election; they also exhibited subversive tendencies. In light of this threat to his reelection, and consequently pursuit of his war aims, Lincoln and his handlers devised what became known as the Ten Percent plan. Under the plan rebellious states could gain readmittance to the Union when ten percent of its citizens reaffirmed loyalty to the Union and it adopted a new state constitution recognizing the Union. The state would then form a new government and its citizens — those who had taken the oath of allegiance — could participate in the national election in November.[14] The key to this policy was that the Federal government, through the army, would have to exert control over the state before Lincoln could carry the scheme out. Many supporters of the Republican Party wholeheartedly agreed with this policy believing it would deliver an electoral boon for their cause.[15] Thus, here was a major motivation for conducting an otherwise unnecessary campaign in what both sides considered a minor theater.

Frederick Steele's occupation of northern Arkansas and Little Rock figured prominently in the Ten Percent plan. With Federal forces in control of over half the state, Lincoln could institute his policy. Steele carried out Lincoln's wishes as instructed in the winter of 1863 through spring 1864. Steele's "conciliatory policy" drew both raves from the loyal citizens of Arkansas while simultaneously drawing the ire of Radical Republicans in Congress. Many of the Radicals felt that Steele's focus on conciliation and restoration of loyal civil government came at the expense of his military duties and there is an element of truth to this. Less than one week from the start of the Camden Expedition, Steele could be found engrossed in the details of supervising the civil election rather than campaign preparations. Nevertheless, as a soldier he conducted himself as a professional in executing his instructions from the President.[16]

In addition to the election, economics had a role in initiating the Red River Campaign and Camden Expedition. Northern textile interests had suffered under a severe shortage of cotton since 1862 with mills operating at one quarter of capacity. Textile magnates began to exert pressure on New England lawmakers to do something to prop up their ailing industry. The textile interests asserted that a military offensive in the Trans-Mississippi would give them access to an unlimited source of the crop. In addition to extracting cotton, prominent German-American citizens were calling for the "liberation" of their kinsmen in Texas. A significant population of Free-Soil German farmers lived in Texas and utilized no slave labor in their production of cotton. These people felt no particular loyalty to the South and this resulted in Confederate repression of the Germans. A campaign to Texas up Red River then would produce several benefits. First, it would provide a source of cheap cotton to jump start New England's textile economy. Second, liberation of the Germans in

Texas would appease the influential pro-German lobby thus solidifying the loyalty of German soldiers then serving in the Union armies. Also, the German farmers would help wrest control of Texas from Rebel authorities and provide a source of additional voters for Lincoln in the upcoming election. Finally, cotton produced by free labor would prove a propaganda boon for the abolitionists because it would demonstrate to the South that a profitable cotton crop did not require the use of slave labor. While showing the Confederate states that their economic system was defunct, Lincoln would also reap the side benefit of quieting the abolitionists who constantly criticized his policy toward the South as being too soft on slaveholders.[17] On the surface an 1864 campaign in the Trans-Mississippi appeared to have many benefits and a potentially high payoff for Lincoln, the war effort, and his reelection prospects.

A more in depth look however, reveals that the reasons for launching such a campaign were not as compelling as they originally appeared. U. S. Grant received appointment to the rank of lieutenant general and command of the Union armies on March 12, 1864, based on his long series of successful campaigns in the west. Lincoln believed that Grant had the necessary qualities to finally provide the Union the strategic direction it had lacked the three previous years. Lincoln had at last made a wise choice in appointing a general-in-chief after a long period of trial and error. Grant indeed had an excellent plan in mind to bring the South to its knees.

Throughout the early years of the war the Union conducted operations with no centralized direction in spite of the presence of a series of generals holding the top command. "For the first two years the Civil War on the Union side was largely an experiment; we were learning how to fight, ..." one observer noted.[18] The Union had pursued a territorial strategy somewhat similar to the southern strategy. Grant pointed out in his memoirs that the "Union armies were now divided into nineteen departments." All had "acted separately and independently of each [other].... I determined to stop this," he stated emphatically.[19]

Grant's plan to end the war was simple yet brilliant in conception. It called for simultaneous offensives by all Federal armies directed at the principal Rebel armies. In his orders to George Meade, commander of the Army of the Potomac, he admonished that "Lee's army will be your objective point. Wherever Lee goes, there you will go also." In his order to Sherman he further stated that the armies will "work all parts ... together and somewhat toward a common center." In essence, he scrapped the territorial strategy in favor of a force-oriented framework. The Army of the Potomac would attack Robert E. Lee's Army of Northern Virginia in the east. At nearly the same moment, Sherman would advance against Joseph E. Johnston's Army of Tennessee in the west. Additionally, Major General Benjamin Butler's Army of the James would make a lunge at a nearly defenseless Richmond and Grant wanted Banks to mount a campaign to take the port of Mobile, Alabama. By attacking the Confederacy's main armies with overwhelming force simultaneously, Grant meant to prevent the Rebels from using their interior lines to shift forces as they had so many times in the past. The plan would strangle the Confederacy and finally bring the war to an end.[20]

Henry Halleck devised the plan for the Red River Campaign and Camden while he was still the Union general-in-chief, months before Grant rose to the command. Red River is vintage Halleck as it represents his habitual operating paradigm. On numerous occasions during the war, Halleck had dispersed Union armies ostensibly to tidy up the rear area. Now with the reduction of Vicksburg and the Franco-Confederate rapprochement it appeared that Halleck would follow the same pattern. In January 1864 he had written Banks badgering him to "restore the flag" to Texas suggesting "that the Red river [*sic*] is the shortest and best line ... of operations against Texas." Additionally, he enlisted the support of Generals Sherman and Schofield to convince Banks of the correctness of his proposal. Banks, faced with a wall of support from prominent officers, relented and agreed to conduct a campaign up the Red in March. Halleck now wrote to Steele expressing his "[hope] that you might cooperate with General Banks ... and thus secure Arkansas."[21] This set the wheels in motion for a mid-March jump off for a combined army-navy operation up the Red River and overland from Little Rock to Shreveport.

The problem with Halleck's plan, in contrast to Grant's comprehensive plan for 1864 is that Halleck did not aim "toward a common center." In modern military parlance this common center is known as the enemy center of gravity, the hub of all power.[22] Grant identified the Rebel center of gravity as her principal armies. Halleck's plan diverted precious assets away from the common center. Even Kirby Smith realized the error of Halleck's scheme while recognizing the strategic significance of what his own forces would do to frustrate the plan. He recorded, "I still think that the enemy cannot be so infatuated as to occupy a large force in this department when every man should be employed east of the river, where the result of the campaign this summer must be decisive of our future...."[23] Though Grant disagreed with Halleck's plan, he did not call it off. There were two reasons for this. First, Grant did not want to embarrass Halleck, his former superior, and further the Red River Campaign was already well under way when he assumed command.[24] This provided the Confederacy with an opportunity to upset the Federal program for 1864 with a workable counter-strategy.

For the Confederates, 1863 had been a serious blow to their cause. For all intents and purposes the Confederacy had little hope of winning the war in 1864 on the battlefield in the face of an ever-stronger Union. As already alluded to, the Rebel government had heretofore conducted a "territorial" strategy for defense of the young nation. Thus far the strategy had failed ignominiously and even Jefferson Davis stated in his *Papers*, "I acknowledge the error of my attempt to defend all the frontier."[25] By spring of '64 there was no longer a need to defend all Rebel territory for a good portion of it now came under Federal control. As a result, Jefferson Davis revised Confederate strategy to meet the changing situation.

The foundation of the strategy for winning the war centered around influencing the presidential election in the North. By adopting a coherent strategy for 1864 it was still possible that events on the battlefield could convince war weary northern voters to cast ballots for a peace candidate. Davis reasoned that in order to win the war at the polls the Rebel armies could not lose on the battlefield. With the Trans-Mississippi cut off from the rest of the South, only the Rebel heartland remained. The heartland consisted of the area between Richmond, Savannah, and Mobile. The principal Confederate armies—the Armies of Northern Virginia and Tennessee—would focus on defending this axis in active operations. These armies would attempt to avoid decisive engagements, yet at the same time inflict maximum losses on the Union armies. Where opportunity offered, Confederate forces would launch limited counteroffensives to demonstrate their still potent capability. The design would maintain the heartland and present the image that the Federal armies could not beat the Confederates. The northern public's confidence in Lincoln would finally shatter and they would reveal their disapproval by electing the peace candidate. In other words, the South could win by not losing.[26]

In addition to military operations, Davis approved of efforts to elect an alternate candidate in the North itself. This would consist of secretly contributing cash to the Democratic Party and fomenting unrest in the north through subversive organizations. Covert agents operating out of Canada would funnel money into the Democratic coffers and peace movements operating in the Midwest. Other agents would help the Copperheads organize civil disturbances, as election day approached in hopes that the public would realize the Lincoln Administration could not even maintain peace at home.[27] Altogether, military and covert operations were calculated to give the South a victory through the ballot box vice one on the battlefield.

The Union decision to launch the Red River Campaign fit neatly into Confederate strategy for 1864. Here the Federals obliged the strapped Rebels by diverting a major force away from the main theaters of the war. This force consisted of several army corps from Banks' and Sherman's armies and a host of gunboats from Admiral Porter's Mississippi Squadron. Rather than assaulting Mobile as Grant wished, Banks would move up the Red with his Army of the Gulf to Shreveport and thence to Texas. By not attacking Mobile, Polk's Confederate army corps in Mississippi was now free to join Johnston around Atlanta providing a material increase in his manpower. Halleck added more weight to Banks' force by coordinating with Sherman to detach two of his army corps—the XVI and XVII—to make the movement up the Red. This detachment from Sherman reduced his forces needed for the Atlanta campaign at a time when Johnston's strength was increasing. Additionally, the ubiquitous Halleck wrote to Gideon Welles to enlist the "cooperation" of the navy to provide transport, logistics, and fire support. Finally, Halleck corresponded with Steele expressing his "hope that you [Steele] might cooperate with General Banks."[28] It is interesting to note that Halleck never gave any of the generals an order. He merely suggested or cajoled subordinates to do his bidding so that if an operation went sour he could sidestep responsibility.

Nevertheless, Halleck's plan and method of carrying out the Red River Campaign and Camden Expedition had several gaping holes. First, as previously noted, the whole operation diverted precious Union manpower away from Rebel centers of gravity at a critical juncture of the war. Second, while Halleck sought to create cooperation between the services in this joint venture, he failed to ensure that one of the principals in the operation had overall command. Third, he did not define how Banks and Steele would establish command and control to coordinate their simultaneous movements. Steele and Banks would have to move separately from Little Rock and New Orleans to affect a link up in the middle at Shreveport at a pre-appointed time. With the primitive communications of the day, this would prove a fantasy. On the whole, Halleck's planning and preparations for the campaign looked amateurish rather than the scheme of a leading military professional.

While Halleck's plan left much to be desired, it did have one positive attribute. By designating two major assault columns—Steele in Arkansas and Banks in Louisiana—he confused the Confederate high command as to which force represented the primary threat. Had Halleck not pushed for Steele's inclusion in the scheme for the Red River Campaign, the Confederates could have focused their entire efforts on Banks' hapless army, very likely with disastrous results for the Union. The column from Arkansas in the end would have the major role in deciding the campaign.

Edmund Kirby Smith found himself confronted by two armies converging from different directions and a large fleet all aimed at Shreveport. Shreveport by 1864 was the capital of the Trans-Mississippi and a substantial military-industrial complex. Loss of the city would deal the Confederate cause west of the Mississippi a serious, if not fatal blow. However, Smith had devised his Fabian strategy as a framework to deal with just such a crisis and had about 30,000 troops in his department to oppose the threat. When Union forces jumped off in mid-March, Smith immediately implemented his strategy ordering Taylor and Price to give ground. Simultaneously, he ordered forces scattered across Texas to begin assembling at Shreveport. Smith reasoned that as he drew his forces closer together he would have time to determine which threat constituted the main effort. "Our role must be a defensive policy," he stated in a dispatch to Richard Taylor. Further, "where the enemy is largely our superior, and where our columns come within a practicable distance of each other, [we will] concentrate rapidly upon and crushing one or the other of the enemy's column."[29] Once he identified the main effort, Smith would mass the preponderance of Trans-Mississippi forces against the supporting effort, defeat it, and then turn to dispose of the main.[30] The plan made maximum use of the interior lines the Rebels enjoyed and took advantage of the inability of Banks and Steele to cooperate because of the nature of the geography. The plan was not only an admirable conception; it was also within the capability of the Trans-Mississippi Department's limited manpower and material resources. Smith's true challenge lay not in defeating the enemy, but within the army itself.

Neither Richard Taylor nor Sterling Price liked the Fabian policy. Each believed that his own domain was the most important in the department and each had a history of openly expressing his views on the subject. Taylor's distaste for Smith's strategy began in 1863 during the Teche Campaign. In mid–1863 Banks had launched a limited effort along the Bayou Teche to clear away Rebel forces threatening New Orleans. To deal with Banks' advance, Taylor employed his own paltry force and obtained a pledge from Kirby Smith to provide another division — Walker's— of reinforcements. Smith reneged on his word shortly after consulting with Missouri Governor Thomas C. Reynolds and Sterling Price. Reynolds and Price convinced Smith that he should retain Walker's Division in Arkansas in preparation for a move into Missouri. They jointly persuaded Smith that a failure to demonstrate an affinity for the citizens of Missouri would result in a corresponding loss of face by Confederate authorities in the state. Walker's Division eventually became paralyzed in an abortive attempt to relieve Vicksburg from the Louisiana side of the Mississippi. Taylor became incensed by the decision and this marked the beginning of the Smith-Taylor feud that continued until Taylor's relief following the Red River Campaign.[31]

Price held a long track record of badgering military superiors and also the Confederate government with propositions for the liberation of Missouri. His latest offering to Smith had done much the same as his previous attempts to influence military policy. It had embarrassed Kirby Smith while angering President Davis. Keenly aware that his past efforts had been largely ineffective in winning support for a Missouri expedition, Price unnoticeably changed his tactics. Rather than boldly and arrogantly pressing his position with Smith he would engage in a "fly and honey" strategy. He would drop light hints of his aspiration for an advance into Missouri, but at the same time he would mix in a compliment of the commanding general's efforts. Price even went further by providing unquestioning, cheerful support for the very strategy that he vehemently disagreed with.[32] From the Confederate perspective the stage was set for a drama in a forgotten corner of Arkansas that would have far reaching effects on the outcome of the Civil War.

Halleck planned to throw a total of 50,000 troops into the Red River Campaign. Banks with reinforcements from Sherman and Porter's Mississippi Squadron in cooperation had about 35,000 troops to make the advance. Frederick Steele's Department of Arkansas would bring approximately 15,000 soldiers in support of the campaign through the Camden Expedition.[33] Initially, Steele expressed enthusiastic support for the campaign as he offered to launch a supporting effort in cooperation with Banks. However, his enthusiasm for carrying out the Camden part of the campaign gradually waned. His correspondence between January and March 1864 bears out his misgivings as he chronicles a host of challenges.[34]

In February Steele penned a dispatch to Banks describing his intent "to advance with 10,000 well-appointed troops" in cooperation with his move up the Red. However, he also begins to exhibit his reasons for not moving. "The roads," he states, "are now in such condition that an army could not move from here to the Ouachita with artillery or trains, and I am told that they will be impracticable for several months to come." There is also evidence that Banks was becoming frustrated with an inability to communicate with Steele due to the long distance between the commanders. At one point Banks sarcastically asked Steele to "have the goodness ... to inform me fully of your intentions."[35] Here is the initial inkling of the difficulty of coordinating the campaign and the possible outcome as a result.

Three weeks later Steele informed Banks of his "apprehension" about the ability to move south. He once again identified the "severity of the weather" as a tormentor, but he now also states his deficiencies in logistics. Specifically, the "want of long forage [and] our loss in animals has been very heavy, but we shall make every effort to overcome these deficiencies." Logistics would prove the Achilles' heel of the Camden Expedition. Admiral Porter reinforced Steele's assertions with an endorsement stating his belief that "I do not think General Steele will be able to move unless his quartermasters show more energy. At present half his supplies are blocked up in [the] Arkansas River."[36] As the evidence of Steele's desperate supply situation mounted, so did his determination to avoid jumping off in mid-March to support Banks.

Another reason for not moving also entered the equation as March drew near. In a February 28, 1864, letter to Banks, Steele declared that he could not "move at so early a day as that named in your dispatch" (March 5th). Among the reasons enumerated by Steele was President Lincoln's desire to have the Ten Percent Plan implemented in Arkansas. "The President," he stated, "is very anxious" to conduct the election. In order to carry out Lincoln's wishes Steele had to use troops at the various polling stations to maintain order and ensure the credibility of the process. The date set for the plebiscite was March 14 — nine days after Banks proposed to initiate operations. The Rebels, he believed, would attempt to "break up the election" which required security. Due to the dispersion of his men protecting the election sites, Steele concluded that he "could not now concentrate anything like the force named in my former letter." He did offer to "make a demonstration" in order to confuse the Rebels about which column represented the Federal main effort.[37]

Steele routed his letter through General Sherman, newly appointed commander west of the Appalachians replacing the freshly promoted Grant. Sherman failed to appreciate the difficulties facing Steele in Arkansas in spite of Steele and Porter's efforts to articulate the true nature of the situation in the state. In a dispatch to Banks three weeks earlier, Sherman discounted Steele's assertions assuring Banks that Steele would make the expedition with 15,000 troops. Now, Sherman wrote an endorsement to Steele's letter stating his misgivings about carrying out the Ten Percent Plan. "The civil election is as nothing compared with the fruits of military success," he wrote to Banks. Further, "I will advise Steele to send you work ... of his movement."[38] Sherman realized that Steele had to undertake a full-fledged operation in conjunction with Banks' Red River movement to give it a reasonable prospect of success.

Steele, however, did not intend to accept Sherman's advice and conduct a full-scale advance without a direct order from the highest authority. Instead, Steele made plans for the demonstration he spoke of in his letter to Banks. Steele described in a letter to Sherman his belief that Banks' force was more than sufficient to defeat Richard Taylor and that the Confederates would "run without giving battle." Additionally, he made the grandiose assertion that "Price and some members of his staff have gone to Europe — deserted."[39] All this seems calculated to excuse Steele from making any effort, much less a demonstration. In fact, he wrote to Halleck and his old friend Grant to convince them of his views and request permission to back out of the campaign. In his letters Steele outlines his belief that "Smith will run" from the forces that Banks could bring to bear in the Red River Valley. In light of this opinion, Steele proposed to "move to threaten the enemy's flank and rear with all my cavalry." This would provide Banks with the cooperation he wanted and allow Steele to secure his own lines of communication from the wide-ranging Confederate cavalry.[40]

Steele's letter troubled Halleck immensely. Halleck, like Sherman, realized that a failure by Steele to conduct a full-scale operation in Arkansas would jeopardize Banks' thrust in Louisiana. The Confederate cavalry under Price would quickly identify Steele's demonstration for what it actually was, a ruse. If this happened Kirby Smith would certainly mass all Trans-Mississippi forces against Banks. This made the prospect of restoring the flag to Texas much more difficult to attain. Upon receipt of Steele's dispatch he immediately responded stating that "I advise that you proceed to co-operate in the movement of Banks and Sherman on Shreveport, unless General Grant orders otherwise." Halleck, now Grant's chief of staff in Washington, could not order Steele to carry out the original plan. Halleck then appealed to Grant in a telegram that the new general-in-chief give Steele "positive orders ... to move in conjunction with them for Red River." He also added that "Sherman and Banks are of the opinion that Steele can do much more."[41] In effect, Halleck also discounted Steele's objections in favor of the opinion of two generals unfamiliar with the situation in Arkansas.

Halleck's logic was not lost on General Grant. While he had not supported the Red River Campaign, Grant realized that if the campaign had any chance to succeed Steele would have to conduct a full-scale offensive to link up with Banks near Shreveport. Grant's motivation to see Banks succeed had nothing to do with an interest in the events west of the Mississippi. He wanted Banks to take Shreveport and then turn over responsibility for "defence [*sic*] of the Red River to General Steele and the navy." This is because he wanted Banks' army ready to conduct operations against Mobile in consonance with his offensives in Virginia and Georgia. Grant was so adamant that Banks wrap up the Red River Campaign quickly that he instructed him to abandon the "main object" if he could not take Shreveport in ten to fifteen days." In twin letters written on the 15th of March Grant reassured Banks that "I have directed General Steele to make a real move, as suggested by you, instead of a demonstration."[42] To Steele he sent a curt note stating:

> Move your force in full cooperation with General N. P. Banks' attack on Shreveport. A mere demonstration will not be sufficient. Now that a large force has gone up Red River it is necessary that Shreveport and the Red River should come into our possession.[43]

The stage was now set for a clash of armies far from the primary seat of the war. More than 50,000 Union soldiers now moved from widely scattered locations toward a rendezvous in the vicinity of Shreveport. Meanwhile, General Edmund Kirby Smith was working frantically to concentrate the 30,000-odd available Rebel forces and attempt to determine which Federal army constituted the greatest threat to his department. The Federal move represented an unfavorable diversion of forces away from the Confederate vitals. Kirby Smith understood the nature of what the Federals had done by sending such a large force into the Trans-Mississippi region. However, his Fabian policy — a reflection of the Davis administration's territorial defense — diminished the eventual outcome of the campaign. Confederate squabbling among Smith, Taylor, and Price created a paralysis in the high command in the Trans-Mississippi Department. But, this paralysis of leadership would not have materialized if Steele had been successful in lobbying Halleck and Grant to call off the Camden Expedition. Indeed, Smith's task would have been much simpler had he only to deal with Banks. Banks might have met destruction in the Red River Valley, altering the outcome of the war. This did not happen as Steele reluctantly launched his forlorn expedition. While the tactical outcome would appear a disaster, Camden redeemed Banks' army to fight on other fields.

Notes

1. E. B. Long with Barbara Long, *The Civil War: Day by Day*, 700–702.

2. Anne J. Bailey, "The Abandoned Western Theater: Confederate National Policy Toward the Trans-Mississippi Region," *Journal of Confederate History*, 35–37.

3. *Ibid.*, 36; and E. B. Long with Barbara Long, *The Civil War: Day By Day*, 700–702.

4. Bailey, "The Abandoned Western Theater: Confederate National Policy Toward the Trans-Mississippi Region," *Journal of Confederate History*, 47–49; and Lynda L. Crist, Mary S. Dix, and Kenneth Williams, eds., *The Papers of Jefferson Davis*, vol. 9, 279.

5. Bailey, "The Abandoned Western Theater," *Journal of Confederate History*, 48–49.

6. *Ibid.*, 49–51 and 54; and Parks, *General Edmund Kirby Smith*, 257.

7. *OR*, Vol. 34, part 2, 814.

8. Gabor S. Borbitt, *Jefferson Davis's Generals*, essay by James M. McPherson, "Jefferson Davis and Confederate Strategies," 164.

9. Robert L. Kerby, *Kirby Smith's Confederacy: The Trans-Mississippi South, 1863–1865*, 245.

10. As quoted in Michael B. Dougan, *Confederate Arkansas: The People and Policies of a Frontier State in Wartime*, 105–106.

11. Crist, Dix, and Williams, eds., *The Jefferson Davis Papers*, Vol. 9, 372; Robert Garlick Hill Kean, *Inside the Confederate Government*, 131; John G. Nicolay and John Hay, *Abraham Lincoln: A History*, Vol. 8, 266–280; and John Hay, *Lincoln and the Civil War in the Diaries and Letters of John Hay*, 77.

12. *Report of the Joint Committee*, XVIII-XXII; Foote, *The Civil War*, vol. 3, 26.

13. Donald D. Jackson, *Twenty Million Yankees*, 149–150; Foote, *The Civil War*, vol. 3, 103; and John C. Waugh, *Reelecting Lincoln*, 149.

14. Ludwell Johnson, *Red River Campaign*, 10–11 and 45–48.

15. Carr "Papers." From a March 20, 1864, letter from Clark Carr to Eugene Carr expressing the importance of the Ten Percent Plan to the Administration.

16. Palmer, *Frederick Steele: Forgotten General*, 8; and Steele "Papers," from letters dated December 10, 1863, and January 24, 1864, written by Mr. G. S. Miller and provisional Union Governor Isaac Miller complimenting Steele's "conciliatory" policy.

17. Johnson, *Red River Campaign*, 9–17 and 47–48.

18. Williams, ed., *Military Analysis of the Civil War*, essay by U. S. Grant, III, "Military Strategy of the Civil War," 10.

19. U. S. Grant, *Personal Memoirs*, II, 127.

20. *OR*, Vol. 32, Part 3, 245–246 and Vol. 33, 827.

21. *Report of the Joint Committee*, XXIV-XXV.

22. U. S. Army Field Manual 3-0, *Operations*, 5-7.

23. *OR*, Vol. 34, Part 1, 494.

24. U. S. Grant, *Personal Memoirs*, II, 139; and Williams, ed., *Military Analysis of the Civil War*, essay by U. S. Grant, III, "Military Strategy of the Civil War," 9-10.

25. Crist, Dix, and Williams, eds., *The Papers of Jefferson Davis*, Vol. 8, 100.

26. Foote, *The Civil War*, Vol. 3, 101-103.

27. Larry H. Nelson, *Bullets, Ballots, and Rhetoric: Confederate Policy for the U. S. Presidential Contest of 1864*, 25-26; David E. Long, *The Jewel of Liberty*, 96-101; Oscar A. Kinchen, *Confederate Operations in Canada*, 219; and Crist, Dix, and Williams, eds. *The Papers of Jefferson Davis*, Vol. 10, 368-369.

28. *Report of the Joint Committee*, XXIV-XXXI.

29. *OR*, Vol. 34, Part 2, 1027-1030, and Part 1, 516; and *B&L*, E. Kirby Smith, "The Defense of the Red River Valley," IV, 369-370.

30. *OR.*, Vol. 34, Part 1, 494.

31. Jeffery S. Prushankin, "A Crisis in Command," M.A. thesis, Villanova University, 26-27; Castel, *General Sterling Price*, 137-138 and 142; Richard Taylor, *Destruction and Reconstruction*, 145 and 157, 159-160; and Robert L. Kerby, *Kirby Smith's Confederacy*, 247-248.

32. Castel, *General Sterling Price*, 172-173; Ira D. Richards, "The Camden Expedition," M.A. thesis, University of Arkansas, 20-22; Mike Fisher, "The Camden Expedition," M.A. thesis, Pittsburg State College, 26-27; *OR*, Vol. 34, Part II, 1028-1029.

33. *OR*, Vol. 34, Part 1, 167-168 and 657.

34. *Ibid.*, Part 2, 15-16 and 55-56.

35. *Ibid.*, 144-145, 246-247, 305, 415, and 491.

36. *Ibid.*, 422-424.

37. *Ibid.*, 372, 448-449 and 483-484; and Steele "Papers," from a dispatch dated February 28, 1864, from Steele to Banks.

38. *OR*, Vol. 34, Part 2, 267 and 449.

39. *Ibid.*, 517-518 and 522-523.

40. *Ibid.*, 546-547; and *Report of the Joint Committee*, XXXI-XXXII.

41. *Report of the Joint Committee*, XXXII.

42. *Ibid.*, 383-384.

43. *OR*, Vol. 34, Part 2, 616.

5

Starting "in style"

Frederick Steele belatedly began making preparations to conduct operations upon receiving Grant's message. General Banks' force including Porter's naval flotilla was already well under way by the 15th of March. A day earlier troops from Sherman's army under Brigadier General Andrew Jackson Smith had captured the formidable earthwork on the Red known as Fort DeRussy. Within two more days lead elements would reach Alexandria, only 90 miles from Shreveport. Meanwhile, Steele was still in Little Rock, over 150 miles from the capital of the Trans Mississippi having made little effort to begin any advance. In addition to Steele's lack of preparedness, some major obstacles stood in the way of success. These included a poor rail transportation network, an obstructed river, lack of accumulated supplies, the election, dispersion of his forces, and the vigilant forces under Sterling Price. Grant's peremptory order afforded Steele little time to make careful arrangements for offensive operations. Nevertheless, the longer Steele waited, the more vulnerable to destruction he made Banks' move up the Red. Therefore, Steele hastily issued orders to his quartermaster and subordinate commanders to prepare to move south within a week. Herein, lay the seeds of tactical failure, yet the expedition salvaged Banks from strategic disaster.

On March 17, 1864, a frustrated Steele issued his initial orders to concentrate his small army for the expedition. He instructed General Thayer commanding the Frontier Division at Fort Smith "to cooperate in a movement toward the Red River." Thayer was to leave sufficient forces behind to secure his district yet mass as much of his division as possible to make the march. Thayer and Steele would move nearly simultaneously, converging on Arkadelphia. Under optimal conditions it should have taken about a week for the separate columns to reach the link-up point.[1]

Thayer immediately began making arrangements to carry out his orders, but issues conspired to slow his efforts. First, there was an on-going tug-of-war in the Union command west of the Mississippi over which department had authority to give Thayer orders. The Frontier Division had previously operated under the command of the Department of Kansas, but in February the War Department had detached the Frontier Division and placed it under Steele's Department of Arkansas. After a series of dispatches between all parties the War Department settled the dispute with orders positively placing Fort Smith and Thayer's division under command of Steele's department.[2] Second, Thayer's Frontier District suffered under a constrained logistic situation similar to Steele's at Little Rock. There was no rail service to Fort Smith from supply depots in eastern Arkansas. Additionally, the Arkansas River proved unable to support Thayer's needs and he had inadequate stockpiles to begin the movement. Steele had instructed Thayer to "depend upon the country for meat and corn meal." But, as Thayer pointed out, "the resources of the country [are] exhausted by the rebel troops." Therefore, Thayer concluded that his move south would prove difficult, but the resolute general stated, "I mean to be at Arkadelphia before the 1st of April."[3]

Steele struggled to make hasty plans to push his scattered command forward. Steele's supply situation at Little Rock proved intractable in the winter of 1863–64. The reasons for this were twofold and the repercussions of it would have far-reaching negative effects on the Camden Expedition. Little Rock seemingly had many advantages with reference to transportation. The Little Rock & Memphis Railroad had been started in the 1850s to connect the city to Memphis, Tennessee and the Arkansas River provided water transport linking the VII Army Corps to the Mississippi. The railroad had not been completed by the start of the war resulting in a fifty-mile gap between Madison and De Vall's Bluff. Additionally, the Little Rock & Memphis had different gauges further complicating the movement of supplies because of the requirement to transload rolling stock.[4] The line between Duvall's Bluff and Little Rock proved unreliable in delivering as well because it frequently required repairs from normal wear and as a result of Rebel raids. This caused a want of supplies for man and animal alike in simply subsisting the army in camp. One soldier recorded in a post-war account that "for several days about the last of January ... the troops at Little Rock, had actually no rations on hand for several meals."[5] Before the army could execute a major offensive, it had to stockpile sufficient supplies to move. Steele complained in a report of "a want of long forage [and] our loss in animals has been very heavy" producing a lack of haul capacity of the draft animals when the expedition kicked off.[6] It would be difficult for Steele to move artillery and quartermaster stores with gaunt horses and mules in the days to come.

The river also proved unreliable, as events would have it. Early spring is the rainy season in Arkansas which, under normal conditions, should have resulted in a rise in the level of the water. This had not yet occurred making movement of food, forage and ammunition prohibitive. Admiral Porter filed a report confirming the status of the river. "At present," he wrote, "half his [Steele's] supplies are blocked up in Arkansas River, with low water, and some of his transports sunk on snags."[7] The commander of Porter's 6th Division, Mississippi Squadron, confirmed Porter's assertion and added that the very nature of the Arkansas "afforded great facilities" for setting ambushes to interdict transports.[8] Price's aggressive cavalry commanders would surely take advantage of the geography to further exacerbate Steele's situation.

Steele issued orders to alleviate the transportation and supply problems. His Field Order #1 emphasized that the army would need to live off the land to supplement the scanty rations available. Yet, even as Steele issued the order he understood that obtaining adequate sustenance on the march would be difficult since the Rebels had previously picked over the area. He wrote:

> The proposed expedition is through a country scant of supplies. The troops composing the Command [*sic*] will undoubtedly have hardships to encounter, which the General Commanding doubts not they will cheerfully endure for the expected results. The country must yield all it can of food and forage, without bringing starvation upon the people. This fact will not, however, justify plundering or indiscriminate seizure of anything. Commanders of Divisions will avail themselves of every opportunity to supply their commands, but always under lawful direction and accountability...."[9]

Steele also required strict accountability of ammunition. Austere transportation on the march would require that ordnance stores remain tightly controlled to prevent carelessness or indiscriminate expenditure.[10] Without such measures Steele knew he would never successfully reach Shreveport. Even with his regulations he would not achieve this goal.

Steele's next challenge was to determine the best route of march. The route had to facilitate ease of resupply while enabling the VII Corps to reach Shreveport at the proper time to link up with Banks. To this end there were three possibilities. Each had potential advantages and drawbacks that the commanding general had to consider. The routes included the old Military Road via Arkadelphia, or Pine Bluff, and finally by way of Camden. The route through Camden was the shortest route, but it led through lowlands that could make it difficult to pass an army. The onset of the spring rains would surely transform the dirt roads into quagmires. Pine Bluff-Monroe made sense in that Steele could use the Arkansas and Ouachita to supply the army as he moved. Steele, however, had "serious objections" to using this route because he believed Price's large mounted arm would slip in behind his line of march threatening Little Rock. This left the Military Road. While it was more roundabout, the road conditions would support the passage of the army while keeping Price to his front forcing him back on Shreveport. Banks exhorted Steele to move via Monroe in order to mass forces at Natchitoches. From there Banks could then move on the Trans-Mississippi capital with an irresistible army forcing Kirby Smith to defend Shreveport or abandon it for Texas. Steele rejected the advice concluding that moving via Arkadelphia was the most judicious choice. He therefore issued orders to commence movement by this route early on the morning of March 23.[11]

The total strength of Steele's Department of Arkansas in March came to approximately 16,000 men of all arms. This included about 5,000 in Thayer's Frontier Division, 5,100 in Frederick Salomon's 3rd Division, VII Army Corps, 3,400 in Eugene Carr's cavalry division, and 2,500 at the Pine Bluff garrison. From these Steele would assemble a striking column to conduct the expedition while leaving enough troops behind to garrison Fort Smith, Little Rock, and Pine Bluff. Steele had already issued orders to Thayer to effect a link up at Arkadelphia. In this force Steele would personally lead the 3rd Division and the cavalry division, for a total strength of around

12,000 once both columns had combined. The garrison at Pine Bluff commanded by Colonel Powell Clayton would launch a supporting effort with about 1,100 men to prevent Confederate forces in his front from reinforcing their main force to the west. Steele would leave about 4,000 behind to secure the rear areas with Colonel Nathan Kimball commanding at Little Rock. The large Confederate mounted forces worried Steele, as they would surely slip around his flanks to attempt to capture Little Rock or Pine Bluff or cut his tenuous supply lines. However, to move with less than this number was to risk a decisive defeat in enemy country. Accordingly, Steele issued the appropriate directives to assemble the army for movement on March 23. Steele also lodged pleas with the War Department to recall furloughed veteran regiments in order to beef up his meager forces along "the line of the Arkansas."[12]

John Thayer's Frontier Division, having a longer distance to march, started for the rendezvous at Arkadelphia on March 21. Thayer's line of march would prove extremely challenging. His route would cover 170 miles of the roughest terrain in Arkansas including the Ouachita Mountains, wetlands, and areas under mob control where guerrilla factions freely roamed. Added to these difficulties, the weather now intervened as torrential spring rains turned dirt roads into swamps slowing the movement to a crawl. This resulted in it taking two days for Thayer's troops to clear Fort Smith. Steele had set April 1st as the date for the columns to combine, but with seven days to march 170 miles it was doubtful that Thayer could move that quickly. Shortly after departure Thayer realized that his original route by way of Waldron would not support the movement for want of forage. Changing directions in midstream, he chose the more circuitous route through Booneville, Danville and then to Mount Ida and Caddo Gap as "it is the only route I [Thayer] can get corn."[13]

Meanwhile, Steele's hasty preparations concluded on March 23 as Salomon's division preceded by Carr's cavalry division moved out shortly after nine o'clock in the morning. "The march seemed hard[er] at first, from our having been in camp so long," observed Private Andrew Sperry of the 33rd Iowa. "But," he continued, "we made the nine miles marked out for the first day without difficulty." In contrast to the poor weather encountered by Thayer's men, Steele's column was blessed by a "clear and beautiful" day. Each man carried forty rounds, his knapsack, and two days' provisions moving in cadence to Yankee Doodle. By all accounts the Camden Expedition was starting out "in style," but things would not take long for the situation to deteriorate. After another day's hard march the men received the unwelcome news that the quartermaster would issue only half rations, except coffee, for the duration of the march. As could be expected this action immediately touched off a round of grumbling in the ranks as the soldiers speculated about the relative intelligence of the officers at headquarters. A half ration amounted to "two hardtacks, a little salt pork, a little salt, and some coffee." As Private Sperry pointed out in his post-war account, this meager sustenance would hardly keep up the strength of soldiers on a march through mud, hills, and broken terrain. Nevertheless, the men trudged on making good time, approaching the banks of the Saline River by the evening of the 24th.[14]

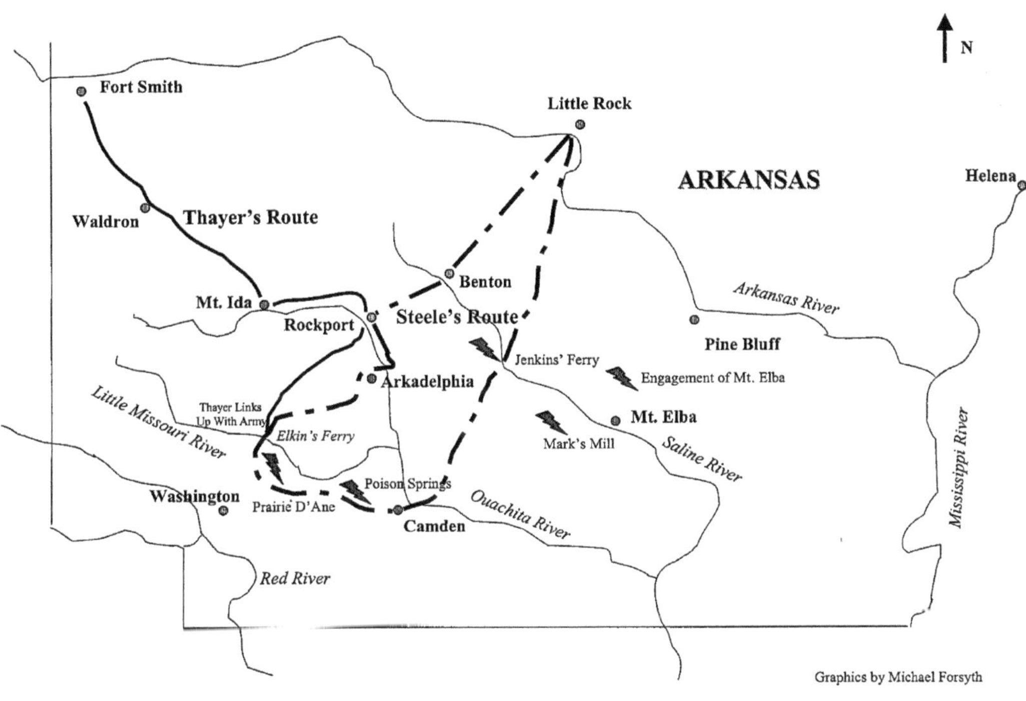

Camden Expedition Overview

The Confederates had not been idle over the winter months of 1863–64. Kirby Smith anticipated the Federal offensives in January and accordingly made preparations to defend the interior of the Trans-Mississippi. In Arkansas Smith's program included construction of a series of supply caches, the wholesale relocation of the civilian population along the expected avenue of the Union thrust, construction of fortifications at key locations, and reorganization of forces. The cache sites extended from Camden to Shreveport. The purpose of them was to provide a regular system that the Rebels could use to sustain their forces in country destitute of resources. The intent behind removal of the populace was to further denude southwest Arkansas, so the advancing Federals would find it difficult to forage as they moved further from their own supply base. Camden figured to be a major objective of the Federal thrust given its strategic location astride a prime avenue to Shreveport and as a potential logistic hub on the Ouachita. As such, Smith authorized construction of a series of fortifications to protect the city. Finally, Smith provided the impetus behind a reorganization of forces in the District of Arkansas when he relieved the aged Theophilus Holmes with Sterling Price.[15]

In addition to Price's usual scheming for a Missouri expedition, he had been busy reorganizing his new command and planning for the defense of Arkansas. Price's command consisted of his old infantry division and two divisions of cavalry commanded by Brigadier Generals John Sappington Marmaduke and James F. Fagan in five brigades. Upon Holmes' relief Kirby Smith in short order split Price's division into two small divisions now commanded by Brigadier Generals Thomas Churchill and Mosby Parsons for ease of management. Upon taking command Smith alerted Price of the impending advance and implored his new district commander "to exert all your energies in preparing to meet the storm." Additionally, Smith informed Price that he held Brigadier General Samuel Maxey's division from the Indian Territory in readiness to cooperate with his command should it become necessary. Finally, Smith needed intelligence from Price in order to make decisions regarding the defense of the department.[16]

Price's troops were disposed in a wide swath across southern Arkansas to watch all possible Federal approaches to Shreveport. Churchill's and Parsons' divisions concentrated their infantry forces around Camden as Price anticipated the main Federal advance would move through this city. Marmaduke's cavalry patrolled northwest of Camden to observe the routes leading to Washington while elements of Fagan's troopers spread out northeast toward Pine Bluff to contest an advance from that direction. The dust had barely settled from making these dispositions when orders came from Kirby Smith ordering Price's infantry to Shreveport on March 18. Banks' campaign along the Red was already a week old and at Alexandria, Louisiana, while Steele had not even started from Little Rock. Though Smith was not sure if Banks' force represented the greatest threat to the department, it was certainly closer to Shreveport and had to be dealt with immediately. Therefore, he wanted Price's infantry to augment Taylor's forces to turn Banks back. Perhaps sensing that Price would have strong objections to the taking of all his foot soldiers, Smith ordered Maxey from the Indian Territory to reinforce Price partially making up for the loss of the infantry. Uncharacteristically, Price cheerfully complied with the order and promptly sent the troops to Shreveport.[17] His support made Smith's job much easier as Price offered no argument and also, to Price's benefit, Smith became amenable to future designs in Missouri.

Price's strategy for opposing the Union advance was dictated by Kirby Smith in a final piece of guidance as operations commenced. Smith instructed Price to:

> Retard the enemy's advance. Operate on their communications with your cavalry if practicable. Time is everything with us. Do not risk a general action unless with advantage to yourself. You fall back toward reinforcements.[18]

This represents the implementation of Smith's Fabian defensive strategy and Price would prove adept at parrying with the Federals as they moved south.

The Federals under Steele had enjoyed fair weather and steady progress over the first 48 hours of the march from Little Rock. However, late on the night of March 24–25 the heavens opened up thoroughly drenching the army and turning the lowlands in the Saline River Valley into a sea of mud. As the Federals attempted to ford the river they quickly bogged down in the mire as the innumerable vehicles churned up what had been the road. In response, the Pioneer Corps began corduroying the road to provide a foundation and traction for the movement of vehicles and men. Andrew Sperry of the 33rd Iowa described the march "as a tiresome and disagreeable one … for it necessitated slow marching [and] sometimes a good deal of work in getting out of the mud." The struggles through the bottomlands exhausted the already weakened animals forcing the Federals to cut short their march on the 25th.[19]

On the 26th, now out of the bottom and moving through rolling terrain, the army closed in on Rockport on the east bank of the Ouachita. As they advanced, troopers from Carr's cavalry began coming into contact with elements of Marmaduke's gray squadrons probing for intelligence. Confederate resistance while light, stepped up significantly as the blue clad cavalry approached the nearly deserted river town of Rockport late in the afternoon. The Ouachita at Rockport was normally fordable at several locations around the village. Steele, now faced with unpredictable weather, ordered the army pontoon bridge erected to span the river should another downpour further swell the river. Such an event could endanger the army if it suddenly became separated in crossing a now unfordable stream in the face of the enemy. Chief of Engineers Junius Wheeler worked his pioneers all night to have the bridge in place by morning on the 27th enabling the army to continue its tramp to Arkadelphia. Wheeler's engineers completed the task and the army began crossing the span at daylight, only two days' march from Arkadelphia and the rendezvous with the Frontier Division.[20]

Price had anxiously observed Steele's movements since he had departed Little Rock. In order to execute Kirby Smith's order to "retard the advance of the enemy" Price first had to determine which avenue the Federals would use to advance on Shreveport. The Military Road to Washington had a couple of branches leading to Camden and other points suitable for use by the Federal army. However, once the army reached Rockport it had to commit to a single direction for the next several days. The moment the Federals began crossing the pontoon, Price knew they were headed toward Arkadelphia and Washington. Armed with this information Price now mobilized his minions to begin contesting the Federals' march in earnest. He ordered Brigadier General William Cabell and Colonel Colton Greene to challenge Steele in front while he directed Brigadier General Joseph Shelby — described by one author as a sort of Trans-Mississippi Nathan Bedford Forrest[21] — to "operate upon his rear." The march of Steele's men would now face ever-increasing resistance as Price would do his best to delay Steele so that Smith could land a blow on Banks in Louisiana.[22]

Thayer's Frontier Division was not having as easy a time of it trudging toward Arkadelphia. One trooper recounted that the men spent hours laying rails to firm up roads and "pushing wagons up mountains." Compounding the problem was the shortfall of rations causing the soldiers to exhaust their energies.[23] Thayer had chosen a somewhat roundabout route of march in order to maximize his ability to forage for the animals. The line of march led through the Arkansas River Valley greatly increasing the distance required for the movement. Before making the move Thayer made no intimation that he could not complete the march to Arkadelphia by April 1 and never informed Steele of the change of route. Within a few days Thayer realized that he could not make it by the appointed time. In an attempt to quicken the pace of his march he took to destroying superfluous equipment in an effort to lighten up his load. While knowing he could not make it in time, Thayer had no way of communicating this to Steele. With both Steele and Thayer on the move there was simply no way to send a message by telegraph. Attempts to send couriers would prove futile as well because the region of the Arkansas Valley literally teemed with guerrillas and partisans.[24] Steele could not even communicate with Little Rock once he reached Rockport. Guerrillas had turned back messengers with dispatches bound for Nathan Kimball in the rear area. Therefore, Steele continued to move resolutely forward oblivious to the fact that Thayer, with almost half the force required for the expedition, would be delayed for several days. This made Steele vulnerable to attack and worse, forced him to consume precious supplies while waiting for Thayer's arrival at Arkadelphia.

Steele's logistic posture, as already discussed, was strained before commencement of the march. By the 28th — only five days from Little Rock — Steele began to feel the squeeze caused by his rickety arrangements. He reported in a dispatch to Sherman:

> More than half of my cavalry are dismounted, and most of the rest very
> poorly mounted. Artillery horses and transportation in the same condition....
> We have had to haul most of our forage 30 and 40 miles.... Still I am
> confident of being able to do my share of the work before me.[25]

Steele's confidence was only a façade for he knew that he could not push on indefinitely with failing transportation and fast dwindling stocks of supply. Should the rendezvous with Thayer's wayward division cause a significant delay in forward movement, it would force a major change in the course Steele would follow if the expedition was to have any chance of success.

While Steele and Thayer struggled forward a splendid little action took place at a place called Mt. Elba that would have a positive effect on the expedition for the Federal VII Corps. Colonel Powell Clayton commanded the garrison at Pine Bluff. The post at Pine Bluff was a key supply depot and strategic location in Arkansas. Situated on the west bank of the Arkansas River, it controlled access to Little Rock by boat. Clayton's command consisted of a small brigade of three cavalry regiments, two infantry regiments and a battery of artillery, which secured Pine Bluff from Rebel incursions. Elements of two Confederate brigades under Brigadier General Thomas Dockery and Colonel William Crawford opposed Clayton's diminutive brigade. Steele worried that the Rebels would make a lunge at the base and capture it. Rebel possession of Pine Bluff would disrupt Steele's source of supply, as they would be able to interdict river traffic to Little Rock while simultaneously destroying the depot itself. To prevent such an eventuality, Steele wanted Clayton to employ aggressive tactics to deceive the Rebels. He instructed Clayton to move forward in cooperation with his own advance and "if our movement shall cause them to fall back" he continued, "press them with all force you can use, making the entire safety of your post the primary object."[26] Clayton dutifully complied and in the process the pugnacious cavalryman delivered a smart victory to Federal arms.

Clayton initially sent out two small probes of forty picked men under Lieutenants Grover Young and Frank M. Greathouse of the 5th Kansas Cavalry and 1st Indiana Cavalry respectively to determine enemy dispositions and intentions. Departing on the evening of March 24th they returned on the 26th with troubling intelligence. The lieutenants reported that they had observed the Confederate horsemen encamped around Monticello apparently making preparations to break camp for a march. Clayton surmised that Dockery and Crawford would move off to stiffen Price's effort to slow Steele's main column or worse, slip in behind Steele to cut his line of communication with Little Rock. Clayton resolved to prevent this by striking an immediate blow on the enemy. His plan combined boldness, deception, and decisive action to produce favorable results.[27]

First, Clayton again sent his trusty lieutenants out on a critical mission, this time with one hundred troopers to destroy the bridge over the Saline River at Long View to prevent a hasty retreat in that direction. Second, he planned to make a demonstration from Pine Bluff toward the Rebel camp at Monticello to make the Confederates believe he would attack from this direction. Finally, with the balance of the force, Clayton would personally lead them to Mt. Elba on the Saline. Here he would cross the river and make a feint toward Camden to further deceive the baffled Confederates. Then by quick marches he would retrace his steps back across the Saline to come down on the Rebel camp from the south — an unanticipated quarter.[28] If everything clicked according to the scheme, Clayton would potentially remove two brigades from Price's order of battle making Steele's advance infinitely easier.

Clayton's plan to first destroy the bridge at Long View provided an unexpected coup. As Lieutenants Young and Greathouse approached their objective they corralled several prisoners who informed them that a large wagon train with supplies intended for Dockery and Crawford had crossed the Saline headed for Monticello only a short time before. Taking some liberty with their orders, the lieutenants decided to follow the train with a view toward destroying it. The raiders tracked it for several hours before the train halted for the night. The party surrounded the camp and rushed it just after dark demanding surrender from the train guard. The Rebel pickets on outpost duty had mistaken the raiders for their own comrades and never fired a warning shot to alert the train guard. The frightened guards quickly submitted to the entreaties of Greathouse and Young. The evening's haul came to 250 enlisted men, eight officers, over 30 wagons, and 300 horses and mules.[29] The raiding party now turned to burn the bridge in accordance with their original instructions, now with over 200 prisoners in tow. The Federal troopers made short work of the Saline bridge destroying it and dumping some 200 small arms into the river from their prisoners. Their primary objective completed, the raiders, prisoners, animals, and dozens of runaway slaves made their way back to Pine Bluff arriving there a mere 24 hours after starting. The lieutenants' exploits electrified Clayton, who reported in his account of the action at Mt. Elba that their acts were "brilliant" and "almost without parallel." The small raiding party accomplished all expected and had succeeded in throwing the two Rebel brigades off balance.[30]

The demonstration at Monticello commanded by Lieutenant Colonel Samuel

Marks of the 18th Illinois Infantry and Lieutenant Colonel Wilton Jenkins of the 5th Kansas Cavalry also had its desired effect as the Rebel troopers seemed confounded about Federal intentions. Clayton now moved with his main body across the Saline toward Camden to further compound Confederate confusion. Dockery and Crawford moved out of their cantonments toward Marks and Jenkins to confront what they believed was Clayton's main column, but was actually the demonstration. After making a quick stab toward Camden, Clayton turned back to attack the Rebel rear. By the time the Union colonel reached the Confederate encampment on March 30, the Rebels had already moved to assault Marks and Jenkins.[31]

A courier from Jenkins now reached Clayton informing him that he was under attack by a large force of the enemy. Clayton, hearing the report of artillery in the distance, had his troopers in the saddle riding with "utmost dispatch" to assist the beleaguered lieutenant colonels near Mt. Elba. Upon arriving Clayton discovered his small demonstration force had "handsomely repulsed" the assault of the much larger force, but the Rebels were preparing another attack imperiling Marks and Jenkins. Clayton, squarely in the rear of the unsuspecting Confederates, deployed his force to deliver a surprise. Once his artillery was in position, Clayton ordered a charge through a peach orchard resulting in a rout. Clayton reported:

> The enemy broke in the wildest confusion, and from this out [sic] his retreat was a perfect rout. The road and timber were strewn with blankets, saddle-bags, hats and guns, and prisoners were being constantly brought in and sent to the rear. The pursuit was vigorously kept up until we arrived at a point about 5 miles from Mount Elba, where the road crosses Big Creek. Here the enemy succeeded in tearing up about 20 feet of the bridge, carrying off the plank. The creek could not be forded. We were consequently very suddenly and effectively checked.[32]

Sergeant August Bondi, an Austrian immigrant from the 1848 revolutions turned Union soldier, confirmed Clayton's report in his recollections while adding a few details from the perspective of the common soldier. He stated:

> As the 5th Kansas [Cavalry] came in from across the river the engagement began to wax warm. We dismounted and deployed. Company K ordered to support two howitzers of the 1st Indiana and a detail of the 28th Wisconsin Infantry already in position: went in, on double quick with the 28th Wisconsin detail, to an old log corn-crib for shelter, using the cracks for loop-holes. This being just opposite the enemy's center, greatly contributed to the repulse of his charges. During the action one of the 28th Wisconsin men by the cabin was hit in the forehead and fell back dying. While I tried to raise him up, both of the howitzers ... discharged ... and my left ear became deaf and has remained so since then. The enemy, without artillery, retreated, and Colonel Clayton ordered me to take a squad across the river and scout.... The cavalry was ordered to charge and harass the retreating enemy, which we did till we came to a very defective bridge, partially destroyed, where we halted.[33]

The engagement of Mt. Elba cost the Confederates about 260 men and scattered the remainder of Dockery's men in all directions. On top of the success Lieutenants Young and Greathouse had achieved, the expedition from Pine Bluff realized brilliant results effectively removing two brigades from the Confederate order of battle and eliminating a serious threat to Steele's line of communication. With the exception of the logistic problems, the Camden Expedition was meeting and exceeding expectations. Unknown to the Federal high command, the neat little Mt. Elba engagements would represent the only solid success of the entire expedition.

While Powell Clayton's Yankee cavalry had dazzled their opponents, Frederick Steele's column continued to press on to Arkadelphia. Amid the advance there were visible signs of increasing pressure from Price's horsemen, as clashes became more frequent. Nevertheless, the army had little trouble in reaching the town brushing aside Rebel resistance. Andrew Sperry took note that the area surrounding Arkadelphia "looked much fresher and greener than anywhere else. The change was great and noticeable.... It had almost the appearance of magic." The change of scenery from the dank bottomlands of the Saline to the rolling, forested hills surrounding Arkadelphia served to lift the spirits of the army.[34]

Arkadelphia rests on the west bank of the Ouachita River and this point represented roughly the halfway mark between Little Rock and Washington. From Washington it is another 90 miles to Shreveport where Steele hoped to link up with Banks to deliver the death blow to Kirby Smith's Trans-Mississippi Confederacy. Thus far, Steele's column had progressed with relative ease losing no men along the way. Even Rebel major John Edwards, aide to General Shelby, recounted that "Steele's movements were admirable and precise."[35] Now Steele would wait to link up with Thayer's column from Fort Smith. Once concentrated the unified VII Corps would continue the march to Washington and Shreveport. Steele expected Thayer by April 1, two days after arriving, but as we have already seen, the Frontier Division was behind schedule. For the time being Steele would have to wait at Arkadelphia for the rest of his forces.

The village, even in 1864, had a fine appearance and the soldiers looked forward to a restful couple of days waiting for their comrades. The men were disappointed as their stay became consumed in the never-ending quest for food. Private Sperry provided a glimpse of the Federal army's repose in Arkadelphia. The town reminded the Iowa infantryman of quaint northern villages in contrast to the "dilapidated huddles to which [we] had been more accustomed." Oddly, the inhabitants seemed to welcome the newcomers. Sperry recalled the women commenting that, "Yur [sic] men treat us better than our own do." As the soldiers supplemented their diet with what was available, they were confounded by the fact that the locals refused to accept payment. Upon further inquiry they discovered that the people worried that the Rebels might retaliate against those who accepted Yankee greenbacks as collaborators.[36] Arkadelphia, however, had little surplus food and within hours of arrival the stocks of available victuals dried up. With a tenuous supply line and little local forage the Federals could not long remain in town.

No one in Steele's army was more concerned about logistics than the quartermaster, Captain Charles A. Henry. Without any inkling of the length of their stay, Henry took the initiative to organize foraging parties to fan out around town and bring in provender. Surprisingly, the area provided much more than expected as the Confederates had failed to destroy granaries surrounding Arkadelphia. If Thayer could reach his destination by the April 1 deadline, the Federals would remain in good shape to continue the advance.[37] Steele had other considerations aside from uniting his forces and logistics. He had to achieve a concentration with Banks in Louisiana as soon as possible and could not afford to wait too long for Thayer. But, what was happening in Louisiana?

Steele's ability to communicate with Banks was poor when the army remained in Little Rock, but now with both columns on the move it became impossible. Neither general knew where the other was and since Halleck had not established an over-all commander to coordinate the far-flung elements, lack of information would plague Steele and Banks. Brigadier General Nathan Kimball commanding the rear echelon troops at Little Rock did have access to newspapers and from these he gleaned what intelligence he could. Kimball reported on March 30 that he "had no news from General Banks other than newspaper reports of the capture of Fort DeRussy."[38] But this information was already sixteen days old and on the 30th the bulk of the Army of the Gulf had already reached Grand Ecore upriver from Alexandria. What Kimball did not report, since he had no way of knowing, was that Grant had ordered Banks to wrap up the Red River Campaign by April 10 in order to return Sherman's troops to Mississippi and begin preparations for an assault on Mobile. Banks received this message on April 1 at Grand Ecore, the same day of Thayer's expected combination at Arkadelphia with the rest of the VII Corps.[39] April 10th was only nine days away and Banks still had over 60 miles to go and an army between him and his quarry. Banks made a hasty decision to save time that would lead to his demise at Mansfield. Steele, however, was still 100 miles away and not yet massed for the final leg of the march. Meanwhile, Kirby Smith had concentrated the bulk of Trans-Mississippi forces south of Shreveport under Richard Taylor, and his irascible subordinate meant to strike a blow. It seemed unlikely that Steele would be able to give full cooperation.

Steele had spent only three days in Arkadelphia by April 1, but with no word from Thayer and worried over his supply vulnerability, he resolved to continue the march without the Frontier Division. Thayer would have to catch up with Steele to unite their forces further south. Accordingly, Eugene Carr's cavalry swung out onto the Military Road in the direction of Washington that morning. The previously light Confederate resistance took a noticeable up-tick as Price's minions began to resist in earnest. The terrain favored hit and run tactics and the Rebels used them to perfection. The Military Road beyond Arkadelphia ran through a pine forest down to the Little Missouri River and then to Washington. The woodland forced the Federals to lengthen their line of march over many miles as the army snaked southward. The Rebel division commander in this sector was Brigadier General John S. Marmaduke and he had laid his plans out carefully. With two brigades in front, Greene's and Cabell's, Marmaduke would slow Steele's forward progress while Jo Shelby circled around to the rear to snap at the Federal's heels and if opportunity offered to attempt a foray at the supply train.[40]

Colonel Samuel J. Crawford, commander of the 2nd Kansas Infantry (Colored) of the Frontier Division, was quite critical of Steele's decision to push on from Arkadelphia without forming a junction with Thayer. He asserted that Steele had not considered the length of Thayer's march before setting the April 1 deadline and exposed the separate columns to destruction by moving forward before uniting. This criticism is unfounded since as a regimental commander Crawford was not privy to the fact that Thayer had not raised any objections to the deadline or informed his superior of the change of his route of march. Further, Crawford failed to consider Steele's logistic situation which fast became untenable every day that the army sat idle. When these factors are taken into account, Steele's decision to move on was probably his only available alternative.[41]

Incessant skirmishing with the pesky Rebels took its toll on the ability of the Yankees to make progress. Much time was spent deploying from march column into line of battle in the dense forest. One Union infantryman remembered "double-quicking a good deal of the time, first to the rear as reinforcements, and then back … again."[42] This necessarily slowed the advance to a crawl and exhausted the men. In an attempt to accelerate the movement Steele closed the column into a tight mass and elements of Carr's cavalry set dry leaves in the forest on fire foolishly believing this would help screen the march of the army from the searching eyes of the enemy. Rather than screening anything, they succeeded in choking the men struggling along in the rear in a pall of acrid smoke and stifling heat. The slowing rate of march in the pine woods continued to exacerbate the logistic situation.[43] Marching through wooded areas cannot provide forage for man or beast and the incessant deployment to skirmish with elusive Rebels increased the appetite of soldiers who already had little to eat. Rebel pressure from Marmaduke was beginning to pay dividends and Smith's Fabian strategy worked to perfection.

Brigadier General Samuel A. Rice led Steele's rear guard on the march from Arkadelphia. As such he would bear the brunt of fierce little attacks by Jo Shelby's troopers. Around noon of April 2 near Terre Noir Creek Shelby's men announced their presence as the blue mass slowly made their way south. Shelby's brigade mounted an all-out charge with about 1500 troops supported by three pieces of artillery. Rice, near the front of his column, became alarmed by the crash of fire near the rear of the column. He perceived by its sustained nature that this was not harassing fire, but an attempt to snatch the precious supply train and pontoon bridges. He therefore "proceeded at once to the field of action" and deployed his whole brigade including a battery of artillery to repel the assault. "This was a hard day all around," Private Sperry recalled as Rice's brigade engaged in a running six hour fight before the onset of darkness finally broke off the fight near Okolona. Shelby compared the fight to a posse on a manhunt with his men as "eager as bloodhounds" to get at the Yankees. The newly promoted Shelby nearly succeeded in his attempt to break through to the train, but the determination and agility of Rice saved the day for the Union army.[44]

The exhausted army arrived on the Little Missouri River on the 3rd of April amid continued pressure from Marmaduke's Division at Okolona in rear and at the river crossing sites in front. Steele's frustration began to mount as he still had no word from Thayer, and because of the fresh fighting and a deteriorating food supply. For some days he had been considering a modification in his route. The Military Road had served well as a line for rapid movement, but as discussed earlier it was a rather circuitous path to Shreveport. In addition, keeping his army supplied by road from Little Rock was infeasible. He now began to contemplate diverging from the Military Road in favor of a move to Camden. Camden had the advantage of position since it rested on a high bluff overlooking the Ouachita River — a sort of "Confederate Gibraltar on the Ouachita." If Steele could take Camden he could use the river — which the Union navy controlled — to resupply and refit his troops before pressing on to Shreveport.[45]

There were, however, three problems with adopting this modified course of action. First, the Confederates were in full possession of Camden, the most heavily fortified location in southern Arkansas. A perimeter of several redoubts and strongpoints ringed the town making it virtually impregnable to assault. Should Steele move east to Camden and fail to take the town, his army could starve in hostile country. Second, he could not move in this direction without having established positive communications with Thayer as the latter would have no idea where Steele had gone. Finally, sidestepping back to the east would further delay his movement south to make the junction with Banks on the Red. This would upset Banks' very tight timetable and jeopardize success of the enterprise.[46]

While Steele could immediately put this plan into execution, instead he determined to first set the conditions for its possibility later. To do this Steele decided to stay on course toward Washington on the Military Road. This would enable him to establish communication with Thayer as soon as he came in range. Also, continuing south to Washington would have a deceptive effect on Price. Since Washington now stood as the seat of Confederate authority in Arkansas, Steele reasoned that by threatening the place Price would have to draw in his own forces to defend the capital. This would result in a corresponding weakening of Rebel defenses at Camden. By throwing forward a cavalry screen to cover his movements, Steele could then turn quickly off the Military Road toward a thinly defended Camden. Then with a head start and hard marching the VII Corps could reach the relatively undefended town and refit for continuation of the expedition.[47]

The Confederates held the far side of the Little Missouri and planned to contest Steele's crossing on the Military Road. The wily Steele had no intention of butting his head against a wall in a foolish attempt to force a river crossing under fire. Instead, Steele sent out reconnaissance parties to find an alternative crossing location. These detachments found Elkins' Ford a few miles to the east only lightly guarded by graybacks from Marmaduke's division and Steele quickly sent out Colonel William E. McLean's 2nd Brigade of Salomon's 3rd Division to seize the ford. McLean assigned Lieutenant Colonel Francis Drake — after whom present-day Drake University is named — to lead the advance of three companies each from the 43rd Indiana and

36th Iowa Infantry regiments to establish the foothold. Upon arrival Drake found elements of the 1st Iowa Cavalry already skirmishing with Marmaduke's men on the far side. The small Rebel contingent put up an unusually stiff resistance and Drake reported that he could not take control of the ford with the force at hand. McLean reinforced Drake with a section of Lieutenant Charles Peetz' 2nd Missouri Light Artillery and orders to assume command of all forces at the ford. This action enabled Drake to push the Rebels back and assume a commanding position at the crossing site. Marmaduke was not yet ready to let the Federals have the ford without a fight and he heavily reinforced his men at Elkins to prevent the Federals from advancing. Launching a fierce counterattack, Marmaduke placed enormous pressure on Drake holding the ford, but his small contingent held long enough for the van of Steele's army to reach his position ensuring it would serve as the crossing place for the VII Corps. The skirmish at Elkins had been sharp indeed, but the Federals claimed a tactical victory that would allow them to make a smooth crossing, and further they took great delight in capturing Marmaduke's own aide-de-camp in the fight. The Federals began crossing that evening while a frustrated Marmaduke fell back from the river in the direction of the Prairie D'Ane.[48]

On the 4th Steele redoubled his effort to make contact with the tardy Thayer sending out patrols to find the erstwhile division. As these feelers fanned out the Federals continued to push across the Little Missouri when another spring deluge unleashed itself on the hapless Yankees. Once again the blueclad soldiers supervised by Junius Wheeler's pioneers had to corduroy the roads to enable the ponderous artillery and wagons to make their way out of the bottoms to higher ground. About this time the Confederates stepped up their own efforts to delay and harass the Union army. Rice's brigade, now on advanced guard, once again bore the preponderance of the action as Marmaduke pressed home an assault. While the army was never in any real danger the attack did fray nerves and sap more strength from the tired Union soldiers. Rice again demonstrated his fortitude as a leader, personally directing the defense, and in the process he received a painful wound that carried away "a piece of his scalp."[49] The Federals finally completed the crossing late on the 4th and moved forward to the Prairie D' Ane where a showdown awaited.

On April 5 Steele finally received the intelligence he had been anticipating hearing for over a week. A courier arrived that day informing him that Thayer had just passed through Rockport. It would take another three to four days for the Frontier Division to reach the Little Missouri. Rather than continue the advance Steele decided to call a halt in order to wait for Thayer. Steele ordered the army to a place known locally as the Widow Cornelius' plantation. This location would secure the crossing from further Confederate assaults. Further, it would allow Captain Wheeler, chief engineer, the breathing space he needed to improve the roads and build a pontoon at the ford. The rains had turned the bottoms into a swamp and caused a three-foot rise in the river at the crossing site.[50]

The Confederates were not idle as the Federals finally effected their concentration on the Little Missouri. Several events occurred that would set the stage for the rest of the expedition. First, Price, believing from his own sources and from a message penned by Kirby Smith, that Steele intended to continue down the Military Road to Washington, ordered all his available forces to mass at the Prairie D' Ane. This uncovered Camden as Price left only a token force in the earthworks and had all the public stores removed. The brigades already at the prairie began to throw up breastworks across the Federal line of march to contest the advance. Second, the van of Maxey's Division, Gano's Brigade, commanded by Colonel Charles DeMorse, arrived in southern Arkansas giving Price his first accession in strength since the infantry had left for Louisiana and the disaster at Mt. Elba. Third, Dockery and Crawford had reconstituted their cut up brigades in record time making good the embarrassing losses south of Pine Bluff. Price left Camden on the 5th to take personal command in the field. He arrived on April 7th with a plan to frustrate the Federals in his front and make his contribution to Kirby Smith's overall campaign to defeat Steele's VII Corps.[51]

Thus far, Price had slowly drawn back within the space of southern Arkansas extending Steele's lines of communication to the breaking point. The guerrillas and partisans had assisted his efforts by harassing couriers and making it extremely dangerous to pass wagon trains down the difficult roads from Little Rock. Every mile that Price moved backward drew the spring more taut on a trap. He now intended to step up the defense of southern Arkansas in order to protect the capital at Washington and buy time for Smith to defeat Banks in Louisiana. Once Smith defeated Banks, Price expected to receive reinforcements in order to complete the discomfiture of Steele.[52] Then, Price hoped, he would be unleashed for an invasion of Missouri. Richard Taylor had other ideas, as he wanted to finish off Banks once he had unhinged him in Louisiana. For Price to reenter Missouri, everything depended on his ability to delay Steele and use all the tact he could bring to bear in convincing his commander that the true field for decision lay in Arkansas and thence Missouri. Within a few days Price's large cavalry contingent — soon at seven brigades strong — would meet the Federal VII Corps on the field at the Prairie D' Ane in the first large-scale engagement of the Camden Expedition.

Notes

1. *OR*, Vol. 34, Part 2, 638; and Edward S. McLeod, "Frontier Division in the Camden Expedition," M.A. thesis, University of Northern Iowa, 2.

2. Edward S. McLeod, "Frontier Division in the Camden Expedition," M.A. thesis, University of Northern Iowa, 2–3; and *OR*, Vol. 34, Part 2, 253, 345, 394, 408, 443–448, and 617–618.

3. *Or*, Vol. 34, Part 2, 618 and 638; and McLeod, "Frontier Division in the Camden Expedition," 3–4.

4. Robert D. Black, *The Railroads of the Confederacy*, xxiii–xxix, and *OR*, Vol. 34, Part 2, 772 and 785.

5. Sperry, *History of the 33rd Iowa Infantry*, 59 and 67; and *ORN*, Series 1, Vol. 25, 774–775.

6. *OR*, Vol. 34, Part 2, 422–423.

7. *Ibid.*, 424; and *ORN*, Series 1, Vol. 25, 774–775.

8. *OR*, Vol. 34, Part 2, 432.

9. Steele "Papers," General Field Order #1 dated March 21, 1864.

10. Steele "Papers," General Order No. 11 dated March 5, 1864.

11. Richards, "The Camden Expedition," 15–16; and *OR*, Vol. 34, Part 2, 246, 368, and 646.

12. *OR*, Vol. 34, Part 2, 646 and 704, and Part 1, 657; and Richards, "The Camden Expedition," 16–17.

13. Riachards, "The Camden Expedition," 18; and *OR*, Vol. 34, Part 2, 706–707.

14. *OR*, Vol. 34, Part 1, 680; and Sperry, *History of the 33rd Iowa*, 70–73.

15. Mike Fisher, "The Camden Expedition," M.A. thesis, Pittsburg State College, 25; William L. Shea, "The Camden Fortifications," *AHQ* (Winter 1982), 319; and Bob Reeves, "Fort Lookout," *Ouachita County Historical Quarterly* (Fall 1998), 14.

16. *OR*, Vol. 34, Part 2, 1038–1039, 1077–1078, and 1102.

17. Fisher, "The Camden Expedition," 26; and *OR*, Vol. 34, Part 2, 1056, 1062–1063, and 1096.

18. *OR*, Vol. 34, Part 2, 1095.

19. *Ibid.*, Part 1, 672–673; and Sperry, *History of the 33rd Iowa Infantry*, 73.

20. Lothrop, *History of the 1st Iowa Cavalry*, 149; and *OR*, Vol. 34, Part 1, 672–673.

21. Castel, *General Sterling Price*, 161.

22. Johnson, *Red River Campaign*, 173; and *OR*, Vol. 34, Part 1, 821.

23. Lonnie J. White, ed., "A Bluecoat's Account of the Camden Expedition," *AHQ* (Spring 1965), 83.

24. Richards, "The Camden Expedition," 29–30; Wiley Britton, *The Civil War on the Border*, Vol. 2, 256; Wiley Britton, *The Union Indian Brigade in the Civil War*, 348–349; and *OR*, Vol. 34, Part 1, 661 and Part 2, 739.

25. *Ibid.*, 659; and McLeod, "The Frontier Division in the Camden Expedition," 4.

26. *OR*, Vol. 34, Part 1, 767–768.

27. *Ibid.*, 768–769.

28. *Ibid.*; and W. S. Burke, *Official Military History of Kansas Regiments*, 116.

29. W.S. Burke, *Orridical Military History of Kansas Regiments*, 117–118; and Amanda M. Dooley, *Autobiography of August Bondi*, 112, on microfiche.

30. *OR*, Vol. 34, Part 1, 770–771 and 776–777.

31. *Ibid.*, 769–770, 773, and 777–778.

32. *Ibid.*, 770.

33. Dooley, *The Autobiography of August Bondi*, 112.

34. Sperry, *History of the 33rd Iowa*, 75–76.

35. John Edwards, *Shelby and His Men; or, The War in the West*, 251.

36. Sperry, *History of the 33rd Iowa*, 76.

37. *OR*, Vol. 34, Part 1, 679.

38. *Ibid.*, Part 2, 784, and Part 3, 7.

39. *Report of the Joint Committee*, 383–385.

40. *OR*, Vol. 34, Part 1, 661, and Part 3, 77.

41. Samuel J. Crawford, *Kansas in the Sixties*, 109.

42. Sperry, *History of the 33rd Iowa*, 78.

43. Fisher, "The Camden Expedition," 38.

44. *OR*, Vol. 34, Part 1, 693–694 and 837; Sperry, *The History of the 33rd Iowa*, 77; and Edwards, *Shelby and His Men*, 252–253.

45. Richards, "The Camden Expedition," 38–39; and Shea, "The Camden Fortifications," *AHQ* (Winter 1982), 319.

46. Shea, "The Camden Fortifications," *AHQ* (Winter, 1982), 319–320; and Reeves, "Fort Lookout," *Ouachita County Historical Quarterly*, 13–14.

47. *OR*, Vol. 34, Part 1, 661.

48. *OR*, Vol. 34, Part 1, 710–712, 732, and 822; Lothrop, *History of the 1st Iowa Cavalry*, 152–155; and Francis M. Drake, "Campaign of General Steele," *War Sketches and Incidents: Iowa Commandery, Military Order of the Loyal Legion of the United States*, Vol. 1, 61–63.

49. *OR*, Vol. 34, Part 1, 661 and 721; and Sperry, *History of the 33rd Iowa*, 78.

50. Richards, "The Camden Expedition," 55; and *OR*, Vol. 34, Part 1, 674–675.

51. *OR*, Vol. 34, Part 1, 780 and Part 2, 728; Britton, *The Civil War on the Border*, II, 271; Roman

J. Zorn, ed., "Campaigning in Southern Arkansas: A Memoir by C. T. Anderson," *AHQ* (Autumn 1949), 242; and Henry Cathey, "Extracts from the Memoirs of William Franklin Avera," *AHQ* (Winter 1963), 101.

    52. *OR*, Vol. 34, Part 1, 780.

6

A Change in Plans

The Frontier Division finally made contact with Steele's column on April 5, but it would still take a few more days to complete the concentration at Cornelius' Plantation, three miles from Elkins' Ferry. While the unification of the army gave cause for relief to General Steele, it also brought with it a whole set of new problems in the realm of logistics. How much longer would the VII Corps be able to continue moving forward with only half-rations and sparse forage? Steele would have to decide. The Confederates now consolidated under Price were preparing to give Steele a hot reception the farther he moved south. His nondescript horsemen busied themselves by erecting breastworks on the wide Prairie D'Ane. The challenge for Price was to delay Steele long enough to allow Kirby Smith and Richard Taylor the time to complete the discomfiture of Nathaniel Banks' Army of the Gulf in Louisiana. Also on Price's mind was the protection of key locations in his district, Camden and the Rebel state capital, Washington. Loss of these nodes or a failure to adequately slow Steele could result in a disaster for the Trans-Mississippi Department. Could Price give Smith the time he needed and provide security to Confederate Arkansas? Based on the course of events so far, fate favored Price and his large cavalry contingent.

Having made contact with Steele, Thayer pushed south with a greater sense of purpose, but nature it seemed would do all in its infinite power to prevent the junction. Rain on the evening of April 6 once again turned the roads to mud holes. Moving out on the 6th from Rockport, it would take the Frontier Division three days to march to the Little Missouri. The bottomland bordering the rivers slowed movement to a crawl and Steele once more called upon his chief engineer, Junius Wheeler. Wheeler's tough pioneers had done much to improve the road for the 3rd Division's passage through the area only two days earlier. They had laid corduroy for several miles on either side of the Little Missouri and built a pontoon bridge as a hedge should the rising waters make Elkins' Ford untenable. To Wheeler's chagrin he discovered "that all the work of the day before was undone; corduroying and bridges were all afloat, the whole bottom nearly was under water, and the Little Missouri was no longer fordable." After making a quick assessment of the situation, Wheeler set his pioneers to work repairing the "worst places." The work parties performed miracles laying timbers over three miles of rain soaked road and emplacing a second pontoon 140 ft long reinforced by cable within 24 hours.[1] Without the effort of these determined engineers, it might have taken many more than three days to combine the VII Corps.

Thayer reported with his division late on the 9th bringing almost 5,000 men to raise Steele's strength to almost 12,000. The Frontier Division itself was a hodgepodge in organization and appearance. Divided into three brigades, it consisted of two infantry and one cavalry brigade. The regiments hailed from Iowa, Kansas, Indiana, and Arkansas. The Arkansans were from the high country of the Ozark Plateau and similar to mountain men across the south, their independent nature influenced their decision to remain loyal. Probably the most interesting units were the 1st and 2nd Kansas (Colored) Infantry Regiments. Raised immediately after Congress' authorization of recruitment of black troops, the 1st and 2nd had built an admirable combat record in battles on the frontier, including Honey Springs in Indian Territory. These regiments would play a fateful role in the expedition, but for now they were a curiosity to the white regiments of the VII Corps. Another oddity in the division was the regiments of Thayer's cavalry brigade. These had been recruited from Indian reservations in Kansas and contained a high number of native Americans and mixed bloods. Their unkempt hair presented quite a spectacle in the opinion of many of Steele's troops.[2] Sperry of the 33rd Iowa once again provided a vivid description of the arrival of the Frontier Division.

> While we lay here, the long-looked-for and much-talked-of, reinforcement of "Thayer's command" arrived from Fort Smith. A nondescript style of reinforcement it was too, numbering almost every kind of soldiers, including Indians, and accompanied by multitudinous vehicles of all descriptions, which had been picked up along the road.[3]

While their appearance gave way to much camp discussion, the fighting qualities of the men in the Frontier Division would soon win the respect and admiration of the better clad and disciplined soldiers of the 3rd Division.

When Thayer reported in he brought with him sad tidings of his own destitute supply situation. Based on this information, Steele decided to make his turn to Camden. In an April 7 update to Kimball, Steele described his situation and the reasons for the detour.

> Instead of [Thayer] taking the Caddo Gap road, as agreed upon, he went to Hot Springs, having turned off his road above Mt. Ida.... [As a result] He [Thayer] is entirely out of rations, and our delay has caused a consumption of the supplies which might have lasted us to Shreveport. I am now confident of having a sufficient force to walk over the rebels wherever they may meet us this side of Shreveport. I shall therefore, move straight on Camden after striking the prairie [D'Ane], and while supplies are reaching me from Little Rock or Pine Bluff will endeavor to clear your front, so that you will not be troubled with any considerable rebel force.[4]

In light of the failing logistics Steele intended to use Camden as a forward base to rebuild his strength before pressing on. In preparation for the army's arrival he issued a sheaf of orders to put his plans into motion.

He began by instructing Kimball "to furnish transportation for the following supplies: thirty days' supply of one-half rations of hard bread, one-quarter ration of bacon, and a full ration of salt and coffee for 15,000 men." Kimball would forward these from Little Rock to Camden or if unavailable there, Clayton would make up the shortages from Pine Bluff. The key was to ensure the desired supplies met him at Camden before his arrival with the VII Corps so the force would not have to waste time refitting. Steele intended the process of regeneration to be as short as possible so that the army would lose little time on the trip south.[5] Next, he dictated march orders for the advance, placing Carr in front with the cavalry followed by Salomon as the main body, and Thayer guarding the trains.[6] Once the corps had pushed Price back on Washington from Prairie D'Ane, the army would break sharply to the east under cover of a heavy screen. Having given Price the slip, the Yankees would march hard to reach Camden before the Rebels realized what had happened. All in all, Steele's scheme was competently planned and had a reasonable prospect of success. However, as events would show the enemy had a vote on whether Steele's plan would succeed in readying the army for a further advance southward, and they would demonstrate an uncanny ability to upset the Federals' ability to carry it out.

The 19th century appearance of the Prairie D'Ane has largely vanished as time has continually modified the topography. In the 1860s the prairie represented a prominent terrain feature for the casual observer as well as the military professional. The prairie is a circular plateau of land encompassing some 30 square miles. It lies approximately 100 miles southwest of Little Rock and about five miles south of the dank, forested bottomlands around the Saline, Ouachita, and Little Missouri Rivers. The open fields breaking out of the pine forest presented a refreshing change of scenery.[7] Lieutenant Colonel Adolph Dengler, commanding officer of the 43rd Illinois Infantry Regiment, left a vivid description of the prairie's appearance in April 1864.

> Like an oasis lies this beautiful prairie in midst of dense forests and almost impossible swamps, a relief for the eye of the traveler, who has for many days hardly seen anything but rocks crowned by dark pines or the gloomy cypress swamp. The prairie, elevated above the surrounding country, rises gradually toward its center. A ridge running along the northern edge, slightly covered with brush....[8]

Jo Shelby also found the change of scenery to have an energizing quality. "The broad prairie stretched away smoothly as a sea of glass," he recounted.[9]

As the VII Corps consolidated around Cornelius' Plantation, Price and his lieutenants chose their ground carefully to contest further advance down the Military Road. Marmaduke, who had sparred steadily with Steele since Arkadelphia, was still in close contact with VII Corps and would have the leading role in the coming fight. He decided to establish a line of defense flanking the Military Road on the ridge described in Dengler's narrative. The ridge lies about one mile south of the opening of the prairie with a small copse of trees known locally as Gum Grove adorning its center. Overlooking the entire prairie, it conveniently provided excellent observation of the surrounding area and also a superb field of fire to contest Steele's pres-

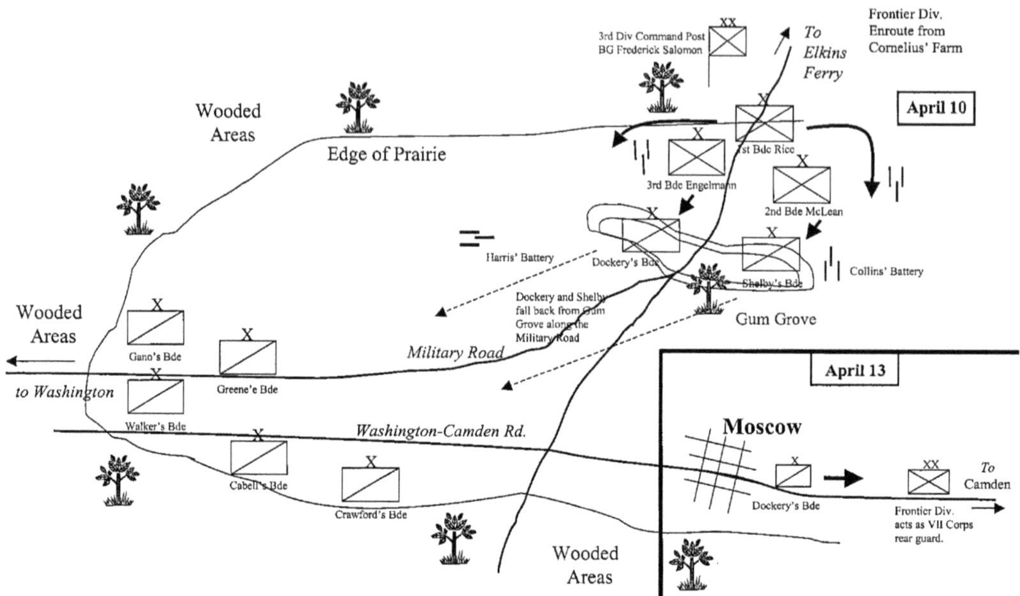

Engagement at Prairie D'Ane April 10-13. Price's converging army chose Prairie D'Ane as the ideal site to conduct a delaying action. He placed Shelby and Dockery's brigades forward at Gum Grove to contest the progress of the VII Corps. Steele's men discovered Price drawn up in force on the prairie on the morning of the 10th. After heavy skirmishing the Federals conducted an assault on the position late in the evening, carrying it after dark. For the next three days the two sides engaged in skirmishing, with the Federals advancing and the Rebels steadily giving ground. On the 13th after having driven Price from the prairie, Steele slipped to the east on the Washington-Camden Road before Price realized the Federals were gone. On the 13th Price sent Dockery in pursuit of the rear guard of the Union army catching them at Moscow. After initial success in breaking the rear guard, the Frontier Division reformed and drove off Dockery's Brigade closing the action at Prairie D'Ane.

sure. The Confederates had taken advantage of the lull in the action to improve the natural strengths of the position. They had thrown up a stout line of breastworks of dirt and timber to protect the dismounted cavalrymen from flying iron and lead.[10] Considering the fact that the Rebels had yet to dig in thus far in the campaign, their excavations at Gum Grove represent proof that they meant to give Steele a tough fight here on the prairie.

Marmaduke maintained vedettes forward under Lieutenant Colonel L. A. Campbell of the 3rd Missouri Cavalry in order to stay in contact with Steele's force at Cornelius' Plantation. In the meantime, he arrayed his forces at Gum Grove in the breastworks with Shelby's brigade on the right of the Military Road and Dockery's— recently arrived from Mt. Elba and temporarily under Marmaduke — on the left. The record appears to show that Marmaduke's mission was to staunchly contest the advance of the Union army without allowing his force to become decisively engaged or endangering his command. Price wanted time to marshal all of his converging brigades for a defense eight miles north of Washington. Marmaduke's defense would buy time for Price to construct a strong defensive line farther south. Price would then have Marmaduke fall back luring an unsuspecting Steele into a trap "where I [Price] felt confident if he advanced I could attack him [Steele] at a great disadvantage."[11] However, Price's haphazard style of command and management became manifest as he took personal command in the field making it doubtful he could form a coherent defense. The remaining brigades of Price's makeshift army were scattered about with seemingly little organization or scheme of emplacement other than Marmaduke's forces. As the commands arrived in the vicinity of the prairie, no one from Price's headquarters took charge to arrange them in any order. As a result, the individual brigades simply found a place on the field where they felt comfortable with little regard for defense or even divisional organization in some cases.

Price's army now numbered roughly 7,000 cavalry under a varying standard of discipline. This placed him at a 1.6 to one disadvantage in terms of force ratio, with Steele having about 12,000 men. This was a very favorable ratio for mounting a defense capable of delaying Steele and checking the rate of his advance, but with a determined effort by Steele, Price simply could not stop him. A closer look provides further insight as to why this is so. First, Price had virtually no infantry forces. Cavalry in the Civil War usually fought dismounted since firepower of massed rifles precluded making the glorious cavalry charge of a bygone era. When cavalry troops deployed for battle one in four men did not actually engage the enemy because they were assigned duty as horse holders for the other three troopers. This pared down Price's forces in combat to a 2.3 to one disadvantage. Another critical fact is that cavalrymen did not carry comparable arms as the infantry placing them at a firepower deficit. In the Trans-Mississippi Department, Rebel cavalry often had weapons varying from short carbine to shotgun, which were inferior to the weaponry of the foot soldiers. This further multiplied the challenges of defense for Price lowering his force ratio as a he prepared to give Steele battle. The advantage that Price did enjoy was greater mobility and a shorter line of communication. Since his entire force rode horses and these animals were considered in better shape than those of the Federals, Price had a distinct advantage in the ability to shift forces quickly.[12] He would have to rely on this to enable him to comply with Kirby Smith's guidance not to bring on a general engagement unless sure of his ability to win until Smith could defeat Banks. In light of Price's loose direction of affairs since taking personal command, he could very well lose what advantages he did have through mismanagement.

Steele was in more of a jam then Price realized and when he advanced toward Prairie D'Ane on April 10, he was not intent on advancing into Price's trap, but rather side stepping to the east. On the evening of the 9th Steele issued Field Order #8 to begin the advance at six in the morning. The army would march with Carr's cavalry in the lead, followed by Salomon's 3rd Division, the supply and pontoon train, and the Frontier Division as the rear guard.[13] Carr's cavalry would push forward to develop the situation while the infantry would fall in behind and deploy when necessary to push Price back.

Carr received his orders that night and made arrangements to carry them out as directed. But, at 5:30 A.M. on April 10 Carr had determined that his division was incapable of making the "strong reconnaissance" that Steele desired. One reason for this was the lack of forage required for the horses. This had forced Carr to dismount a large contingent of his overall strength. The 1st Iowa Cavalry, for example, had over 300 troopers on foot.[14] Compounding this problem, Carr reported that he could not account for part of his division that had not returned from a scout the day before. Combined this left Carr with only 600 mounted men to begin the march out of a total division strength of 2,600. Therefore, Carr requested that Thayer's cavalry brigade send help to make up for his shortage of horsemen.[15]

There is no record of Steele's reaction upon receipt of Carr's note, but the commanding general must have felt some irritation since Carr penned the dispatch only thirty minutes before start time. With Carr unable to carry out his orders at the appointed time the army would have to delay its movement until adequate cavalry was on hand. This inevitably caused the rest of the column some discomfort in waiting to move. The 33rd Iowa waited for hours standing by the road to take its place in march column. After a short delay Carr finally jumped off, but this gave little relief to the impatient infantrymen waiting by the road. The road was a narrow dirt path through the thick stand of timber winding to the prairie. All the units in front had to work their way forward before the rearward troops could file into the road. As a result, it was one o'clock in the afternoon before the 33rd Iowa lurched forward. Even then the maddening accordion effect caused the column to lunge by fits and starts. It took Private Sperry and his comrades almost four hours to march the four short miles to Prairie D'Ane.[16]

John B. Martin of the 1st Iowa Cavalry was among the dismounted horsemen sent forward with Carr's division on April 10. He recalled being deployed in skirmish order for the first time in the expedition. This was hard work, especially for cavalrymen, because the skirmishers had to fan out in the woods and move forward through the thick pine forest. Shelby had a token force of pickets in the woods to provide him early warning of enemy dispositions. Martin and his fellow troopers made contact with the fleeting Rebels in early afternoon. Bounding forward in small groups, the 1st Iowa "quickly cleared the woods and compelled the enemy to retire to their works."[17] As Carr's cavalry broke through the forest into the open, they got their first glimpse of Price's line at Gum Grove. Judging from the extent of the earthworks Carr knew that the infantry would have to come forward to push the Rebels out of their fortifications. He halted the division at the edge of the woods and continued to develop the situation while Salomon brought his division to the front for an assault.

Salomon had ridden at the front of his division that afternoon as the infantry struggled forward. Upon reaching the clearing Salomon realized that the Confederate earthworks would require more than cavalry skirmishers to push the Rebels off the ridge. Wasting little time he began deploying his division into line of battle. Lieutenant Colonel Adolph Dengler's 43rd Illinois Infantry Regiment led the advance of the 3rd Division and Salomon instructed Dengler to pass through the cavalry and file his brigade to the right of the Military Road. "Large numbers of the enemy cavalry and some artillery were deployed on the central ridge," Dengler reported of the hard work that lay ahead. William McLean's 2nd Brigade following Adolph Englemann's Brigade, filed to the left once the 3rd Brigade cleared the road. Samuel Rice, head bandaged from the fight at Elkins' Ford, was last in Salomon's column and would deploy to the rear of the front brigades, prepared to reinforce either Englemann or McLean. As the sounds of battle filtered through the woods, Rice sped the pace of his brigade at the rear of the division. The stop and go marching created the inevitable gap that occurs when troops move long distances in a narrow column. This forced the 36th Iowa to move at the double quick — a brisk jog with full equipment — over two miles to reach the prairie.[18] With these dispositions made, the soldiers would participate in an engagement that held much grandeur and as a pleasant bonus few casualties.

Once the infantry found their places the artillery of both sides commenced a duel that entranced the soldiers of both armies. The Confederates had two batteries, Collins' and Harris', in place to challenge three Federal batteries, Voegele's 9th Wisconsin Battery, Vaughn's 3rd Illinois, and Peetz' 2nd Missouri Light, that were busy emplacing on the north edge of the prairie. The artillery duel began at about five o'clock in the evening and lasted until after dark giving all observers quite a show of fireworks. Private Sperry, whose 33rd Iowa was ordered to support the 9th Wisconsin Battery, remembered "lying down flat on our faces" as the opposing batteries hurled iron at each other. Prairie D'Ane is one of the few battles of the Civil War where the antagonists could line up entire divisions in full view of each other. One writer described the scene as "the most imposing military display witnessed west of the Mississippi River during the war." The spectacle of parade ground formations spreading out in the open for battle awed many of the common soldiers who had the rare fortune to observe an engagement without fear for their lives. "The batter[ies] continued their vigorous and well-directed fire," Sperry noted. "The rebels responded actively; but their guns were of an old and inferior pattern, and their shot and shell, though very destructive to the trees in the rear, did not come very near us."[19]

While the artillery gave the troops a show, Salomon channeled his energies into pressing home an assault of the ridge held by Price's Rebels. He ordered a general advance of the infantry in the evening twilight to push the Confederates from Gum Grove. It must be noted that night attacks during the Civil War were extremely rare. Yet, bucking all conventions, Salomon resolved to carry out the attack. Skirmishers moved out to develop the strength of the enemy, followed by the main line of Englemann and McLean. Adolph Dengler stated that his regiment "rushed forward" at double quick time "not stopping till the height was won." The advance had been so rapid that the various regiments "vied with each other to be first to reach the ridge." Englemann credited Dengler's 43rd Illinois with accomplishing the feat, one that should have been far more difficult than it was.[20]

The Rebels expended a great deal of ammunition in the initial contact, yet inflicted few casualties — neither side suffered more than one hundred — and inexplicably put up a rather feeble defense of the dominating terrain feature in the area. With the open fields of fire the Rebels should have decimated the blue host as they advanced forward. The reasons for the hasty retreat require some explanation. First, as already elaborated upon, Price did not plan on making his stand at Prairie D'Ane. His intent was simply to delay Steele and draw the Yankees into a trap on ground he selected near Washington. Becoming decisively engaged at the prairie would jeopardize his ability to defeat Steele later since he did not quite have his army fully concentrated. Within a couple of days Price would have his force in hand to mount a more stubborn defense. Until then it behooved Price to conserve strength for the right moment. Second, as alluded to previously, the cavalry armaments were of uneven quality and lacking in range and accuracy against Steele's superior infantry small arms. Finally, atmospheric conditions exerted some influence on the outcome. The twilight assault combined with a nocturnal inversion held the smoke from cannon and rifles close to the ground making visibility problematic. This probably covered the approach of the Federals enabling them to move close to the entrenchments before the Confederates could bring aimed, massed fire to bear. These factors explain why the Confederates seemingly transferred possession of the ridge to the Federals at so small a cost.

Marmaduke ordered Shelby to retire from Gum Grove to a position about one mile southwest on the Military Road. Here the Rebels had prepared a second line of works to check the enemy.[21] Although flushed with success, Salomon decided to halt the assault as darkness now engulfed the landscape and the Federals needed to untangle units that became intermixed as a result of the attack. The Confederates had emplaced their batteries flanking their new position and the artillery duel ignited afresh "lighting up the very sky and making night hideous with screaming missiles."[22] The light show continued until around midnight when the fighting finally petered out. As the troops settled down with a watchful eye toward the enemy, they realized how cold it was that night. April 10 had been a warm day and the weary troops' exertions caused the men to swelter under their loads and wool uniforms. When the battle ended the sweat clinging to their bodies made the effects of the cold seem unbearable. Forced to lie on their arms in close proximity of the enemy, both armies had no fires to dry their clothes or warm up. The cold "compelled [men] to stay awake and shiver all night, and that without their accustomed supper." Yet, few of the suffering soldiers uttered a word of complaint as they waited for daylight to reopen the engagement.[23]

The "unclouded splendor" of the sunrise on Monday, April 11 promised to warm the stiff-jointed troops who lay cold and unsheltered on the open prairie. All those in line of battle expected an immediate advance that morning, but Steele had other plans. Rather than rushing pell-mell to the attack, he decided to assess the situation and then implement a course of action to satisfy his overall campaign design. The Rebels had pulled back from their positions at Gum Grove, but they still occupied a defensible location on the prairie. Before Steele could make his break to the east for Camden he had to push the Confederates completely off the open plain so they could not have direct observation of Federal movement. In order to give Price the slip he would resume operations in the afternoon with the cavalry leading, followed by a

solid two-brigade front of infantry. Once the Rebels relinquished their entrenchments the cavalry would continue to press the enemy beyond the prairie creating a
screen to allow the infantry divisions to turn left toward Camden.[24]

The soldiers of the Union army made the most of the morning respite while their
leaders planned for future operations. Details moved to the rear to obtain meager
rations of hard tack and salt pork from the wagon trains while others kindled cooking fires just behind the crest of the ridge. Hot coffee refreshed the soldiers as they
waited for orders. Following breakfast many of the troops took the opportunity to
snatch some needed sleep to make up for the restless night they had just come
through. The time seemed to drag as the men waited, but as soldiers are inclined to
do, they found ways to entertain themselves. Sperry recalled that some engaged in a
rabbit hunt in the thickets while others played cards, read novels, wrote letters home
to loved ones, or simply enjoyed the singing birds.[25]

Abruptly, around 2:30 P.M. the leisurely day ended when Steele ordered a general advance. Preceded by the blue cavalry, Salomon's division fell into line of battle
and lurched forward in a seemingly irresistible advance. As John Martin of the First
Iowa Cavalry turned back to gaze at the assembled 3rd Division, he regarded it as
"the most imposing spectacle I ever witnessed." Further, Martin stated that "we
advanced steadily and rapidly under a sharp fire ... but, nothing could stop us and
the Johnnies fell sullenly back." Sperry confirmed Martin's observations adding with
a bit of grandiose flare that when "Gen. Price saw us thus advancing, he threw up
his hands and exclaimed 'My God, they are coming in clouds,' and immediately
ordered a retreat."[26]

Staying within the framework of his plan, Price again drew off to entice the Federals south toward his planned ambush north of Washington. The Union men consolidated their latest gains and aggressively skirmished with Price's troopers until
night when they pulled back about halfway to their camp of the previous night. The
Confederates, unknown to the Yankees, quietly abandoned their latest positions in
a retrograde back to their fortifications just beyond the prairie. Price was still under
the impression that Steele wanted to continue on to Washington.[27] Steele's ruse had
worked to perfection as Price had done everything the Federal commander desired
to enable him to reach Camden in order to re-cock for the rest of the expedition.

After another uncomfortable night, the Union army proceeded at daylight on
the 12th to complete their mission to drive the Rebels away from Prairie D'Ane. Carefully advancing, the Union cavalry and infantry crept forward closing in on the empty
Rebel positions. Price had left only a small contingent forward to deceive the Federals into believing the Rebels remained in force. When the long lines of bluecoats
began their advance the thin platoons of gray troopers put up a lively show of skirmishing and then made a gradual withdrawal. Around nine o'clock the Union army
entered the line of breastworks. John Martin of the 1st Iowa Cavalry made a happy
discovery upon entry to the enemy works. One unfortunate Rebel had busily prepared his breakfast that morning when the Union line closed in on their position. In
his haste to escape the Reb failed to remove his corn "dodgers" from the fire. The

hungry Martin greedily appropriated the cakes, thus supplementing his diet of two hardtacks and giving him a full belly for the first time in two days.[28]

The Rebel line extended for about a mile and in spite of its hasty construction, the fortifications represented an admirable feat of engineering. "They [the Confederates] could have literally mowed us down in a direct assault," a veteran noted. But, the hasty retreat of the graybacks revealed their intent to bait a trap for the VII Corps. Adolph Dengler observed, nonetheless, that "General Price had been entirely deceived to the intent of our army."[29]

Steele immediately ordered Carr to take up a pursuit of Price's army to cloak his next move. After allowing VII Corps a short rest, Steele turned Salomon's 3rd Division to the east on the Washington-Camden Road to get a head start in a race for Camden. Steele split Carr's division, with the 3rd Brigade continuing to pursue the Rebels to the southwest while the 1st Brigade shifted to advance guard heading east. Thayer's Frontier Division would assume the rear guard to ward off attempts by Rebel cavalry to disrupt the march to Camden. The Yankees marched the rest of the afternoon and into the evening opening a wide gap between VII Corps and the unsuspecting Price. Salomon moved rapidly passing the small village of Moscow on the east edge of the prairie before dusk and camping on Terre Rouge Creek for the night. Carr and his 3rd Brigade made it to a Dr. Rook's Plantation and the Frontier Division settled in just west of Moscow.[30]

It must be noted that the point at which Steele turned to the east represents the zenith of Federal fortunes in the Camden Expedition. From Prairie D'Ane onward the entire Federal effort was a retrograde operation punctuated by unmitigated disasters to Union arms that threatened to outright destruction of the VII Corps. Steele intended the change in plan as simply a short breather to reconstitute a failing logistic situation. To his dismay the Confederates confounded every effort to resupply the army forcing Steele to make unpleasant decisions.

Early on the 13th the Union army started eastward, but the pace slowed precipitously as the troops began traversing the Terre Rouge Swamp bordering the creek of the same name. Once again the services of the Pioneer Corps proved invaluable. Captain Wheeler's stoic engineers repaired bridges over Terre Rouge and Cypress Bayou and corduroyed the intervening space to pass the army on to Camden.[31] In spite of their efforts, the work on the road dragged on in agonizing slowness giving the awakening Confederates an opportunity to recover from their malaise. Late on the 13th Price's cavalry began to pressure the rear guard.

Early that morning Price had waited patiently for Steele to advance "with his habitual caution" on the latest line of Rebel works. By mid-morning the bewildered Confederate commander discovered the error of his assumption. After sending out some patrols, Price realized he had miscalculated and that Steele had turned in retreat toward Camden at a hurried pace. One young Rebel trooper recorded that "the Yanks got scared and turned towards Camden" and his commanding general undoubtedly agreed.[32] Price now deduced that the Yankees intended to grab Camden for use as a forward operating base before continuing on to Louisiana. Price aimed to prevent this sensing that if Steele had begun a retrograde movement, his army must be in trouble. Accordingly, he hastily devised a plan to attempt cutting Steele off from Camden. He immediately ordered an all-out pursuit consisting of Maxey's Division from the Indian Territory and Fagan's Division. To Marmaduke Price assigned the critical mission to get in front of the Union army on its line of retreat to stop it short of Camden. Price trusted that Marmaduke, with brigade commanders such as Jo Shelby, would carry out his orders with great vigor to halt the advance of Steele's army.[33]

Marmaduke sped off at breakneck speed with Shelby leading the move around Steele's flank. While Marmaduke's wing executed the forced march to Camden, Price moved aggressively to attack Thayer. Dockery's Brigade led the pursuit of the rear guard and in late afternoon caught Thayer languishing east of Moscow waiting for the head of the column to clear the swamp. Dockery, who smarted for two weeks following the humiliation at Mt. Elba, went a long way toward resurrecting his reputation as he launched a vicious attack. Its sheer boldness on the open prairie carried great momentum that shattered Thayer's line of defense scattering regiments in every direction and enabling the screaming Rebels to snatch a section of artillery. Dockery's elated troopers now drove straight for the exposed Federal wagon train. Some elements of the gray brigade did reach the train, but the quick reflexes of Colonel John Edwards of the 18th Iowa Infantry restored order driving the Confederates away before they could cause serious damage. As the 18th Iowa pressed their counterattack, the 1st Arkansas (Union) and 2nd Kansas (Colored) along with fugitives of the broken units fell in line and pushed Dockery back to Moscow retaking the lost guns before being ordered back to the division. Skirmishing continued throughout the evening but the Rebels made no more serious attacks on Thayer that day.[34]

The losses for the day were low on both sides with Thayer losing 31 men; however, closer examination reveals a lost opportunity. This single Confederate brigade attack yielded impressive results, but had Price massed the two divisions at his disposal it is interesting to speculate about what he might have achieved. The Union army was in the process of attempting to cross a formidable barrier, the Terre Rouge Swamp, slowing its rate of movement and placing it in a vulnerable state. The swamp divided Steele's army into pieces, moreover, making it susceptible to destruction in detail by a massed assault from the rear. Yet, rather than assembling his full force Price allowed an individual brigade to make a headlong attack without coordination thereby wasting a superb opportunity to crush Steele. While Dockery's initiative is commendable, Price had once again failed to keep a rein on his subordinates and in the end allowed Steele to make the crossing with few losses. The action at Moscow is yet another sample of Price's haphazard leadership.

Thayer had regrouped his forces as the sun began to set and started moving through the swamp, continuing all night. Meanwhile, Shelby had moved throughout the night also and his hard-riding cavalry managed to get a scratch force to Poison Spring before Steele. The question now is whether or not he had an adequate force to actually stop the exhausted Federals. Eugene A. Carr had also been pushing

his men hard to reach Poison Spring before the Confederates. Steele had detailed
Rice's brigade and Charles Peetz' battery under the control of Carr to provide punch
for the cavalry should they encounter heavy resistance. In the early afternoon of
April 14, a patrol sent out by Carr made the discovery that the Rebels had won the
race to Poison Spring. After initially mistaking the Confederates for friends, the
Union troopers turned about to make their escape. A cross-fire decimated their ranks,
but the scouting party managed to get a report back to Carr informing him of the
presence of Shelby. Carr moved up more of his troopers to skirmish with the Rebels
while he assessed the situation. After interrogating prisoners taken in the engagement, Carr determined that he had elements of Greene's and Shelby's brigades to his
front, but was unsure if Price had moved his whole force around Steele's flank. He
conferred with Rice at 7:30 in the evening and together they determined to camp for
the night and assault the Rebel blocking position at daylight. If, as the two commanders believed, Price had only two small brigades of cavalry in the way, Carr and
Rice would have no problem driving the Confederates away.[35]

In addition to feeling out the enemy, Carr had sent out small detachments of
foragers to find subsistence for his hungry men. One of the parties met a pair of
Union men who informed them of the presence of a large quantity of corn that the
army could use to supplement their rations. The foragers brought off what they could
and reported this encouraging intelligence to Carr. The cavalry commander in turn
composed a note to Steele informing him of the existence of an ample store of corn.
He recommended that some arrangements be made to procure this forage to alleviate the growing supply difficulty.[36] While unable to act on the report immediately,
Steele filed the information away for future reference when the army reached Camden.

At daylight on the 15th, still about eighteen miles from Camden, Rice and Carr
rolled forward to clear the road of Rebels. Coming upon the junction of the Middle
Washington and Camden Roads, Shelby's troopers opened up a brisk fire on the
advancing Federals temporarily halting Rice. Carr and Rice now deployed left and
right of the road in an attempt to find the flanks of Shelby's Brigade. The ubiquitous
Sperry's 33rd Iowa moved around the Rebel left unmasking a battery that had pinned
down the main line on the road. Sperry reported that they rushed the guns forcing
the battery to cease firing. The charge enabled the advance to continue, as Shelby's
position became untenable. By 10:30 A.M. the column resumed a regular march punctuated by periodic skirmishing for the next three hours. The infantry would alternate between march column and line of battle as the Rebels took to harassing the
bluecoats. While the Rebels did all they could to impede the advance, Marmaduke
and Shelby knew there was little they could do now to prevent Steele's army from
gaining access to Camden. Accordingly, when the Confederates came upon the crossroads of the Camden and Lower Washington Roads, Marmaduke filed away to the
south to prevent his own force from becoming pinned against Camden.[37]

Mrs. Virginia McCullom Stinson had passed the morning with her normal chores
when the streets in Camden began to stir with excitement. Rumors raced through

town about the impending fall of the city to advancing Federal troops. For three years Camden had avoided the humiliation of occupation and maintained a semblance of prosperity in the midst of the war. Now all the citizens speculated as to their fate and that of their property when the Yankees came to town. They would not wait long to receive the answer to their questions. Shortly after noon, the lead elements of Carr's cavalry clattered into town having driven the final show of token resistance away. The plodding infantrymen would take considerably longer to close on the quaint city overlooking the Ouachita. Sperry reported that Rice's brigade, the lead infantry unit of the VII Corps, marched in around 6:30 in the evening. Elements of the corps continued streaming in non-stop until Thayer's division finally closed on Camden in the late afternoon of April 16.[38] Steele's army had gained Camden and with the exception of the troubling food problem had carried out its mission in admirable fashion. But, the challenge of feeding 12,000 men in enemy country with a tenuous supply line was causing the army to begin deviating from the plan. Already the army had diverted to Camden and would have to take several days to obtain forage before continuing on to Louisiana. Here is where the entire operation began to go awry.

Events in Louisiana had irretrievably changed the situation as well, yet the challenges of communication conspired to deny Steele full knowledge of what had happened to Banks on the Red River. Steele arrived in Camden late in the evening of the 15th and set up headquarters in one of the well-to-do homes in town.[39] Upon arrival in town the Federal commander heard a disturbing rumor that Banks had received a serious reverse in Louisiana. Steele had no way of confirming this intelligence since the "spies" — Civil War leaders used this word interchangeably with scout — he had sent to communicate with Banks had not returned.[40]

Unknown to Steele, on April 8 at Mansfield Banks was soundly defeated by the aggressive Stonewall Jackson protégé Richard Taylor. Taylor had sprung a large ambush with his concentrated army — including the divisions of Price's District of Arkansas — against a fragment of the Army of the Gulf as it trudged to Shreveport. After hitting and routing the head of Banks' column, Taylor advanced down the Mansfield-Pleasant Hill Road crushing individual divisions of the Federal army sending them tumbling south like dominoes. Only a determined defense by the 19th Army Corps under Brigadier General William Emory saved Banks from utter destruction. Taylor, his fighting blood at a fever pitch, drove after the retreating Union army the following day catching up with them a Pleasant Hill. After a severe contest the Federals checked Taylor's offensive when A. J. Smith's corps delivered a hammer blow. Taylor drew off, but a thoroughly shaken Nathaniel Banks decided to continue his retreat that night over the loud protests of several of his officers.

Kirby Smith's Fabian strategy had worked better than he could have hoped, but decisions now confronted him about how best to prosecute a counteroffensive. The influence of his two touchy subordinates would have great bearing on any decision he made as Price and Taylor had widely varying opinions on how to proceed. Taylor felt that the retreating Union army under Banks should be pursued relentlessly until destroyed. Further, he strongly believed that Steele would "commence retreating as soon as he hears the news from this quarter." The conditions certainly supported Taylor's assertion that he could destroy Banks since the rapidly falling Red River had trapped the Federal navy thus immobilizing the Army of the Gulf. With sufficient force Taylor believed he could pin Banks down, starve him into submission, and, by default, capture or force the destruction of the Union navy. Therefore, Taylor demanded action in Louisiana as the decisive field to attain far-reaching results. He was so adamant that he concluded a dispatch to Smith's chief of staff: "Should the remnant of Banks' army escape me I shall deserve to wear a fool's cap for a helmet."[41]

Smith disagreed with Taylor and he became extremely irritated by an increasingly sarcastic tone in Taylor's correspondence.[42] Kirby Smith had expressed a belief weeks earlier that "the only field for great results in this department is in the District of Arkansas."[43] The reason for this opinion was twofold. First, Smith knew that Steele was a professional soldier with a solid combat record. Steele's opponent was the erratic Price whose reliability was always the subject of debate in the Confederate high command. Banks, by contrast, was a politician-turned-soldier with a dubious record of achievement thus far in the war. Taylor's capabilities were well known and admired across the South. Therefore, Smith probably calculated that Steele in Arkansas was the more threatening of the Union commanders and Taylor his most competent subordinate. Second, Smith's Fabian policy was territorial in nature, placing a premium on retention of terrain over destruction of the enemy. Since this policy was in step with overall Confederate national strategy, he felt that it was his duty to ensure that his department remained under Rebel authority to the greatest extent possible. By mid-April Smith had not changed his mind about Arkansas and had actually become more adamant in advocating a pursuit of Steele. Smith states in an April 12 dispatch:

> Steele is bold to rashness: will probably push on without thought or circumspection. To win this campaign his column must be destroyed. Should you move below [in Louisiana] and Steele's small column will push on and accomplish what Banks has failed in ... we will ... be disgraced. Banks is certainly so crippled that he cannot soon take the offensive. Most probably he will fall back to Alexandria. The patient, uncomplaining spirit manifested by Arkansas, the prompt and unselfish behavior of Price in pushing on his whole infantry force to your support, merits a return. Great results are to be reached in that direction.[44]

Smith concluded by ordering Taylor to prepare three divisions of his command for service in Arkansas while Taylor would take the remaining division and cavalry to ensure Banks continued his retreat.

The decision infuriated Taylor causing him to launch a series of acidic dispatches at Smith criticizing its substance. Taylor's barbs failed to move Smith who continued resolutely on with preparations for a counteroffensive in Arkansas. Price's quiet strategy of providing full support of Smith's Fabian policy, in spite of his own objections to it, had worked in his favor. Price would soon receive three divisions of infantry, enough to turn the tables on Steele and eventually initiate his long sought invasion to liberate Missouri.

While Smith's strategy was sound in light of overall Confederate national policy, it would never achieve the sweeping results envisioned by Richard Taylor. Taylor stated at the time and in his memoirs that had he retained the force he had on-hand after Pleasant Hill, he could have destroyed Banks' army and Porter's fleet. This would have had a great effect on the entire Confederate war effort by "relieve[ing] the pressure on our suffering brethren in Virginia and Georgia." He also recognized the plausibility that a disaster in Louisiana combined with continued stalemate in the east would have a negative impact on public opinion in the North. With the presidential election in the offing, this could lead to the defeat of Lincoln at the polls, thereby repudiating his war policies and delivering victory to the Confederacy.[45] What Taylor was advocating was a bold move that could deliver a victory decisive in the outcome of the war. Smith, by contrast, supported stated Confederate policy to defend the territory of the Trans-Mississippi, which could never achieve anything beyond the borders of the department.

Smith would not change his mind and by April 14 had the wheels in motion to turn on Steele.[46] The unsuspecting Federal commander in Arkansas was still under the impression that Banks was moving according to plan. Steele therefore, continued to do his utmost to fulfill his part of the Red River Campaign even as Banks accused Steele of failing to support him in Louisiana. In an April 17 letter to Lieutenant Commander Thomas O. Selfridge of Porter's fleet, Banks had the gall to write, "General Steele fails to cooperate with us, as far as we can learn, and thus far renders no assistance."[47] This accusation is unwarranted and made with a dearth of knowledge about the situation in Arkansas. Steele had advanced deep into enemy territory against his better judgement, all the while feeding his men half-rations in country stripped of provender. Steele had certainly done this in full support of Banks and made every reasonable attempt to establish communication with him through the use of couriers.

Underlying Banks' assertions is an effort to shift full responsibility for the disaster at Mansfield from his shoulders to Steele. Banks simply had no way of knowing the extent of Steele's effort and therefore discounted it as insufficient. He also tacitly discounts the ability of the Rebels to utilize their own interior lines to achieve a concentration on his front. In light of the facts, Banks' accusation is off the mark and does disservice to Steele, who in spite of his own distaste for the operation made an honest effort to support the Red River Campaign from Arkansas. By doing so, Steele had surely saved Banks from ignominious destruction at the hands of a determined, yet ragged force under Richard Taylor. But, with an overwhelming force now moving north against him, Steele had to ensure that his own army would not suffer a sound defeat. The pressing issue of feeding the VII Corps, however, was plotting to deliver up the army without a fight unless he could obtain a reliable source of subsistence.

Notes

1. *OR*, Vol. 34, Part 1, 674–675.

2. McLeod, "The Frontier Division in the Camden Expedition," 6; and White, ed., "A Bluecoat's Account of the Camden Expedition," *AHQ* (Spring 1965), 85.

3. Sperry, *History of the 33rd Iowa*, 79.

4. *OR*, Vol. 34, Part 3, 77–78.

5. *Ibid.*, 79.

6. *Ibid.*, 104.

7. J. H. Atkinson, "The Action at Prairie D'Ann," *AHQ* (Spring 1960), 40–41.

8. *OR*, Vol. 34, Part 1, 732–733.

9. *Ibid.*, 838.

10. Atkinson, "The Action at Prairie D'Ann," *AHQ* (Spring 1960), 44; and *OR*, Vol. 34, Part 1, 824.

11. Richards, "The Camden Expedition," 58, and *OR*, Vol. 34, Part 1, 780 and 824.

12. Britton, *The Union Indian Brigade in the Civil War*, 351, and Williams, ed., *Military Analysis of the Civil War*, "Supply for Confederate Cavalry in the Trans-Mississippi," by Stephen B. Oates, 207.

13. *OR*, Vol. 34, Part 3, 104.

14. Lothrop, *History of the First Iowa Cavalry*, 159.

15. *OR*, Vol. 34, Part 3, 657 and 761.

16. Sperry, *History of the 33rd Iowa*, 79.

17. Lothrop, *History of the First Iowa Cavalry*, 160.

18. *OR*, Vol. 34, Part 1, 687, 707, and 722.

19. Burke, *Official Military History of the Kansas Regiments*, 427; and Sperry, *History of the 33rd Iowa*, 79.

20. *OR*, Vol. 34, Part 1, 722 and 733.

21. *Ibid.*, 838.

22. Edwards, *Shelby and His Men*, 219.

23. Sperry, *History of the 33rd Iowa*, 82; and *OR*, Vol. 34, Part 1, 687 and 838.

24. Lothrop, *History of the First Iowa Cavalry*, 160; Fisher, "The Camden Expedition," 60–61; Richards, "The Camden Expedition," 58–59; and *OR*, Vol. 34, Part 1, 661.

25. Sperry, *History of the 33rd Iowa*, 82–83.

26. Lothrop, *History of the First Iowa Cavalry*, 160; and Sperry, *History of the 33rd Iowa*, 83.

27. *OR*, Vol. 34, Part 1, 780; and Atkinson, "The Action at Prairie De Ann," 48.

28. Lothrop, *History of the First Iowa Cavalry*, 161.

29. Sperry, *History of the 33rd Iowa*, 83–84; and *OR*, Vol. 34, Part 1, 733–734.

30. Atkinson, "The Action at Prairie De Ann," 49; and *OR*, Vol. 34, Part 1, 687 and 761.

31. *OR*, Vol. 34, Part 1, 675.

32. Zorn, "Campaigning in Southern Arkansas: A Memoir by C. T. Anderson," *AHQ* (Autumn 1949), 242.

33. *OR*, Vol. 34, Part 1, 780–781.

34. McLeod, "The Frontier Division in the Camden Expedition," 8–9; Crawford, *Kansas in the Sixties*, 113; and Burke, *Official Military History of the Kansas Regiments*, 375–376.

35. Edwards, *Shelby and His Men*, 266–267; and *OR*, Vol. 34, Part 1, 762–763.

36. *OR*, Vol. 1, Part 1, 762.

37. *Ibid.*, 695; Sperry, *History of the 33rd Iowa*, 87; Edwards, *Shelby and His Men*, 268–269; and Britton, *The Civil War on the Border*, II, 275–277.

38. M. A. Elliot, ed., *The Garden of Memory*, Virginia M. Stinson, "Memories," 28–29; Sperry, *History of the 33rd Iowa*, 88; and McLeod, "The Frontier Division in the Camden Expedition," 10.

39. Steele would use two of the residences in Camden as his headquarters during his stay there. He would variously use the Graham House and the Chidester House, although the exact dates of his stay in either are not known.

40. *OR*, Vol. 34, Part 1, 661 and 676.
41. *Ibid.*, 530.
42. Jeffery S. Prushankin, "A Crisis in Command," 98–102.
43. *OR*, Vol. 34, Part 1, 494.
44. *Ibid.*, 531.
45. *Ibid.*, 541–543; and Taylor, *Destruction and Reconstruction*, 224–225.
46. *OR*, Vol. 34, Part 1, 212–213.
47. *OR*, Vol. 34, Part 3, 192.

7

"... a destroying mania
had seized the rebels"

As the Yankee army arrived in Camden many concerns had arisen to cause morale of the soldiers to wane. Food and forage to sustain the VII Corps was becoming ever more difficult to find. Failure to procure adequate quantities of either would certainly bring the expedition to a halt here at Camden or worse some place to the south where the enemy might trap the hapless army. The disturbing rumors of Banks' defeat also had an adverse effect on the spirits of the men. In sum, the time at Camden would prove a turning point in the expedition as Steele and his immediate subordinates pondered their next move. The Confederates under Price noticed a surge of confidence in their endeavors. Price's ragtag cavalry had not defeated Steele, but they had delayed his approach south and made it extremely hazardous and unrewarding to search for sustenance. Price and his subordinates had full knowledge of the disasters in Louisiana, which heartened their spirits. Further uplifting their morale was the fact that Kirby Smith was personally leading three infantry divisions northward to Arkansas for the purpose of destroying Steele's army. As Price's troopers cordoned off Camden with a thin picket, Price and his generals plotted their countermoves to bring about the destruction of their enemy holed up in the fortifications of Camden.

Upon closing his army within the earthworks surrounding the town, Steele sat down at his headquarters in the Chidester House to ponder what he must do next. He had to do two things immediately in order to enable his army to continue the march south. First, he had to establish communications with Nathaniel Banks to determine his next objective. If the rumors swirling about proved true, he might have to adjust his march route to affect a junction with Banks at a point other than Shreveport. Without knowledge of Banks' whereabouts or the condition of his army, Steele could find himself walking into a trap. Second, Steele had to do something to alleviate the supply situation. Without food for man and beast he could do nothing to support Banks.

Days earlier, Steele had written General Kimball at Little Rock ordering him to rush thirty day's rations to Camden where he would meet them by April 15 to refit his army.[1] Kimball went to work on this order preparing supply steamers to go by water to Pine Bluff and notifying Powell Clayton to outfit a wagon train to transport the provisions from there overland to Camden. In military operations there are times when seemingly anything that can go wrong will go wrong. Mid-April 1864 was one of those times as the supply steamers failed to reach Pine Bluff at the prescribed time. The steamers, *Adams* and *Chippewa*, had been carefully laden with supplies to succor Steele's hungry men and cast off from the docks at Little Rock on the evening of April 12. The boats had gone down river only twenty miles when they collided in the dark, sinking the *Adams*. The *Chippewa* sustained damage requiring repairs and a partial loss of ammunition and quartermaster stores. Kimball's assistant adjutant general attributed the cause of the accident to the carelessness of the pilot on the *Adams*.[2] The cause notwithstanding, Steele's men would have to go hungry a few more days waiting for relief since the wagon train did not arrive as the army pulled into Camden.

An unexpected incident occurred on the 16th that did temporarily alleviate the food situation. The Confederate steamboat *Homer* had moved up the Ouachita loaded with corn for Rebel soldiers in the area. The boat captain was not aware that Camden had fallen to the Federal army. As a result, the pilot moved the boat toward town oblivious of the danger ahead. John Martin of the 1st Iowa Cavalry had spent the 16th fanning out in small patrols from Camden to screen the main Union army as it consolidated in town. Martin and some of his friends had taken the opportunity to drop a fishing line in the Ouachita, in addition to the mundane duty of picketing. They "caught a fine lot of catfish and white perch which afforded an agreeable change to our bill of fare." The satisfied troopers had just finished filling their bellies with fried fish when they were ordered to "bring up the steamer Homer of Virginia [*sic*]." A mounted portion of the regiment had captured the hapless boat further down river and Martin's detail would take control of the *Homer* and direct it to Camden.[3] To the Federal quartermaster's surprise the boat contained a vast supply of corn amounting to over 3,000 bushels. Upon arrival of the ship the quartermaster had work details begin grinding corn in to meal at the still operating mills in town. This find would allay the food situation for a few days, but the army required more than this to continue offensive operations.[4]

As Steele contemplated his next move the Rebels began a systematic effort to destroy the available food supplies and mills in the region surrounding Camden. A veteran stated that "a destroying mania had seized the rebels" as they torched every source of food they could find.[5] Price was keenly aware of the desperate situation his antagonist found himself in and he sought to make logistics the Achilles' heel of Federal fortunes.[6] Camden itself had little to offer in the way of sustenance as the citizens themselves struggled to feed their families. In spite of Confederate efforts, Steele believed he knew a way to provide for his army after all. The Federal commander still had Carr's report of the availability of a large store of grain and meat west of Camden in the region known locally as Poison Spring. If Steele could procure this supply before the Rebels destroyed it, the effect might stave off further delay of the expedition. Captain Henry, chief quartermaster, suggested that the commander general assemble a forage train with an adequate guard to double back to Poison Spring. There the quartermaster department would requisition foodstuffs from willing Union families or appropriate it from the unwilling. This combined with the expected arrival of the train from Pine Bluff would place the army in good shape for future operations. Accordingly, Steele authorized the endeavor and Captain Henry made a request of John Thayer to supply the train guard for his wagons.[7] Unknown to all concerned, Steele had just set the wheels in motion that would result in arguably the biggest disaster to Union arms west of the Mississippi during the war.

Price established his headquarters at a place called Woodlawn southwest of Camden after the failure to cut off Steele. While he had not prevented Steele from reaching Camden he knew he would soon have an opportunity to pounce on his prey. After two meetings with Richard Taylor and tense correspondence, Kirby Smith had ordered three infantry divisions detached from the District of West Louisiana. The units he designated for service in Arkansas were Thomas Churchill's Arkansas Division, Mosby Parsons' Missouri Division, and John G. Walker's Texas Division. On April 11 the lead elements of this reinforcement had pulled back from Pleasant Hill, Louisiana, en route for Shreveport. From Shreveport the concentrated force would march north for Camden where Kirby Smith hoped to inflict a decisive defeat on Frederick Steele restoring the integrity of the Trans-Mississippi. The three divisions arrived at Shreveport on the 14th where Smith personally joined the assemblage for the movement. General Walker recorded that his division crossed the Red River by pontoon on the next day. While Walker felt there was an opportunity in Arkansas, he sided with Richard Taylor in believing that "the true line of action lay in Louisiana.[8] Price expected Smith to arrive within ten days thereby giving him a chance to finish off Steele.

Until the arrival of Smith, Price intended to institute a vigilant system to prevent Steele from obtaining food. Smith had ordered Price to torch anything of use to the Federals, which Price's eager troopers had done with great zeal. In addition to destruction of foodstuffs, Price detailed Marmaduke, Fagan, and Maxey to observe the major routes in and out of Camden. Should Steele attempt to send out for or receive any supplies, Price's wide ranging cavalry was to pounce on the relief column. This would either force Steele out of Camden or starve him into submission. Since no one expected VII Corps to submit to defeat by the humiliating method of siege, the Confederates felt that Steele would retreat to Little Rock. With enough early warning, the Rebels believed they could hit the Federal army on the retreat giving them the advantage of striking the Unionists in the open.[9]

In the early morning of April 17 Captain Henry's forage train and guard assembled in Camden for an expedition on the Camden Road leading west toward the Prairie D'Ane. The train consisted of 177 wagons to procure the estimated 5,000 bushels of corn available around Poison Spring. To protect this vast assemblage of wagons, John Thayer detailed Colonel James Williams with his First Kansas Infantry

(Colored) to lead the endeavor. Williams' command included his own regiment under command of Major Richard G. Ward and elements of three cavalry regiments—the 2nd, 6th, and 14th Kansas—and a two-gun section of the 2nd Indiana Battery. The entire task force totaled 670 soldiers of whom 438 were Negro troops. The column departed mid-morning for its destination about fifteen miles to the west.[10]

The Confederates of Colton Greene's Brigade had the proposed route of the Federals under surveillance. Greene immediately reported the departure of the train to his division commander, John Sappington Marmaduke. Marmaduke promptly relayed the developments to General Fagan, his fellow division commander, and suggested that with reinforcements he could destroy the train and escort. Fagan grasped the opportunity readily granting Marmaduke's request by sending William Cabell's Brigade to reinforce his division. As Marmaduke awaited Cabell's arrival, he hatched a scheme that aimed at the destruction of the Federal forage train.[11]

As the train and escort rumbled westward, Steele received at his headquarters positive confirmation of the disaster in Louisiana. Steele sent out several "spies"— scouts or couriers—at intervals during the expedition in attempts to keep Banks informed and obtain intelligence of Banks' progress in Louisiana. The intervening area between Steele and Banks, of course, was Rebel territory. This made it extremely time-consuming, not to mention downright dangerous, to get a message to Banks and return. Finally, after desperately trying to get reliable information for weeks, a scout arrived at Steele's headquarters. This man, while bearing no written communication from Banks, stated that the general had instructed him to say he had "defeated" the Confederates, but failing supplies compelled him to fall back. Steele was skeptical of this account, particularly the part about Banks having defeated the enemy. He could not see how Banks could lose 22 pieces of artillery and a brigade train, then retreat from the field and lay claim to a victory.[12] Since Banks had retreated Steele had two options left to him. He could retreat immediately or he could attempt to drive on to link up with Banks and salvage the operation. A retreat could leave Banks out to dry if he had major problems. An advance could expose Steele's corps to destruction because the Confederates may decide to mass against him. Without any written communication with Banks and no orders from the War Department, Steele was not quite sure of his next move. In the absence of guidance, Steele resolved that he must press on in order to aid Banks. To ensure he could reach the Red, he made a request of Chief of Staff Halleck to supply him via the Ouachita among his other efforts to open a supply route.[13]

The foraging party made good progress in its move west making fifteen miles. Colonel Williams camped by the road in the late evening as a central location for sending out smaller elements to gather corn. Williams knew that sizeable contingents of Rebel cavalry lurked nearby and that they would pounce on his small detachment as a lucrative target as soon as they could gather strength. Therefore, rather than allow the men to encamp he decided to press on with gathering food in order to get back to Camden before the Confederates could strike. Sending out wagons in all directions, the men quickly found the available stores of food. The Confederates, it seems, had not been as thorough as Price wanted in destroying foodstuffs that the Federals found useful. Around midnight most of the parties made it back to the rally point. After the rest of the foragers returned in the morning, the whole column would return to Camden, preferably by early afternoon. Williams estimated that he had nearly 5,000 bushels of corn along with a supply of meat and items confiscated from the local citizens by overzealous soldiers.[14]

Early afternoon of the 17th, General Thayer, fearing that Williams had inadequate strength, decided to reinforce the forage train with another infantry regiment. He quickly organized a combined arms force to go to Williams' aid consisting of the 18th Iowa, a small contingent of cavalry, and two howitzers. Captain William Duncan would command the 500–odd soldiers sent out to relieve Colonel Williams. This would give Williams a strength of about 1200 troops to defend the spoils of their little expedition. Duncan had his force assembled and on the move in the late afternoon.[15]

Amid a flurry of Unionist activity, the Confederates had busied themselves with assembling a force of their own to destroy the train. Marmaduke had his own division — minus Shelby[16] — and Cabell's Brigade were moving toward Poison Spring when one of his scouts watching the approaches to Camden reported another column departing town heading west. A disquieted Marmaduke halted his own column and again contemplated the situation. His hasty assessment told him that the force at hand was inadequate and he decided to ask Price for additional reinforcements. Reporting in person at Price's headquarters, Marmaduke laid out the situation and his belief that it would require a larger force to carry out the operation he had in mind. Eager to execute his aggressive subordinate's plan, Price assented to strengthening Marmaduke's strike force.[17]

In his haste, Price demonstrated his inattention to detail when he carelessly gave the mission to Samuel Maxey's Division. While this satisfied Marmaduke's need for additional troops, it also created a question of command. Maxey, by date of commission, outranked Marmaduke and by army protocol had the right and duty to assume command of the operation. While Marmaduke in all probability was not pleased with this turn of events, he nevertheless consented to offer up command to Maxey who quickly accepted. The magnanimity would not last as problems soon developed between the two senior officers. Maxey, now in charge, got things rolling immediately putting every unit in motion for Poison Spring. They would trudge through the night in order to get in position to ambush the unsuspecting Yankees.[18] Everything was now set for one of the ugliest engagements of the Civil War.

Over the course of the night all of the smaller Union foraging parties made their way safely back to the wagon train. This gave Colonel Williams reason to breathe easier for he knew he could get the train on the road back to Camden early in the morning. At dark on the 17th Captain Duncan halted his detachment about ten miles west of Camden on the Upper Washington Road. As his men prepared to bivouac for the night, Duncan dispatched a patrol to Williams to establish communication and inform the colonel of his mission to provide support for the train. The presence of reinforcements earmarked for Williams undoubtedly delighted the colonel as he worked to gather in his widely dispersed foragers. Williams told Duncan's courier to tell the captain to hold his position for the night. At dawn Duncan should then move to the train where his column would assume the mission as train rear guard.[19]

At daybreak Williams stepped off moving east toward Camden with Duncan simultaneously moving west to link up with the main column. As the sun rose in the eastern sky, Duncan and Williams effected a junction approximately a mile east of a place known by the locals as the crossroads. The united column now pressed on to the east in the following order: Williams' 1st Kansas under Major Ward in the lead, the trains in the center, and the Duncan detachment bringing up the rear. Shortly after restarting the march the Union troopers came into contact with Confederate skirmishers. Federal cavalrymen chased the Rebels east down the road until they encountered a roadblock. The surprised Federals quickly turned about and raced back to the main body to report. This development gave Williams pause as he realized he might have to fight his way back to Camden. Sensing the true nature of the danger, Williams stopped and closed the column into a tighter, more defensible formation and took stock of the situation.[20]

What Williams saw as he surveyed the ground troubled him greatly. The Confederates had selected an ideal location for an ambush and the force that Williams had on hand was not nearly enough to protect the entire length of the train. Therefore, Williams had the train park three wagons abreast on the north side of the road in a compact mass to enable his small force to better protect them. To the east on the Upper Washington Road, the Confederates blocked a portion of the highway bordered by dense woods on either side making it difficult for the Federals to flank the position. To the south of the road lay an open farm field — known as Lee's Plantation — that ascended in a gradual slope upward to a wooded ridge that dominated the lane below. The field was cut variously by a fenceline and meandering ravine that would act as obstacles to a Rebel advance. Conversely, the ravine would also offer cover to the greycoats as they moved to close with the train guard. All in all the terrain offered great advantages to the attacker and the Rebels had disposed their forces well to leverage its benefits.[21]

The Confederate command consisted of approximately 3,500 picked troops from Marmaduke and Maxey's divisions and Cabell's Brigade. The Confederates were in the saddle well before dawn in order to get into a strong position to contest the train's movement back to Camden. Marmaduke had nothing less than full destruction of the train on his mind as the grayclad troopers made their way through the pre-dawn darkness. The Rebels moved north from Woodlawn up parallel dirt farm paths that intersected with the Upper Washington Road east of the Federals. Marmaduke's Division led followed by Cabell and Maxey. While Maxey held nominal command, Marmaduke made all the dispositions for the coming action making him the *de facto* commander. This was a point not lost on the contentious Maxey especially when it came time to claim laurels from victory. As such, Marmaduke planned to move his own division and Cabell's Brigade on the Upper Washington Road and then turn west until he found an appropriate location for a blocking position. There they would deploy with Crawford's Brigade on the north side of the road, Cabell on the south side and Greene bringing up the rear giving Marmaduke the flexibility to move to the left or right as the situation required. Marmaduke placed Harris' and Hughey's batteries in line to sweep the road of Federals. Maxey would continue north up an adjacent path, but his division would diverge from the trail before reaching the Upper Washington. The division would then proceed cross-country through the woods south of the road to the ridge overlooking Lee's Plantation and the Upper Washington.[22] The Federals would run into Marmaduke's roadblock and halt the train. Then at the moment of confusion, Maxey would launch a flank attack from concealed positions on the ridge. Thus, Marmaduke would form an anvil, while Maxey acted as the hammer in the coming operation.

The endeavor contained inherent risks in execution that could undo all the careful arrangements made by Marmaduke. First, timing was a critical element to success. While Marmaduke held off the Federals in front, Maxey had to get into position to launch his attack before the Federal infantry overwhelmed the blocking position. If Maxey failed to reach the ridge in time, Marmaduke would suffer a serious defeat and the train would be able to reach Camden safely. A more serious danger was that Marmaduke's Division would have to fight with its back to Camden. Upon hearing a heavy engagement to the west, Steele could then decide to sally forth a relief force from town. Marmaduke would then be in danger of attack from the rear while engaged in front. In order to win this battle, the Confederates needed a combination of good leadership, impeccable timing, and a little luck. The Confederates would get all three.

By 9:30 A.M., Marmaduke had the blocking position set and his skirmishers were already sparring with the Federals. Skirmishing continued for a half-hour as the Federals who charged the roadblock were sent reeling back on their main body. About this time Maxey reined up to Marmaduke requesting a situation report. Marmaduke graciously reported to Maxey and suggested the course of action he had previously contemplated. Surprisingly, Maxey listened attentively and approved of his subordinate's plan. Maxey probably appreciated Marmaduke's obvious knowledge of the situation and, anxious for success, decided to accept an admittedly good plan. With the anvil set, Marmaduke now needed the hammer to make haste to its jump-off position located on the ridge. Maxey now quickly moved to execute his division's part of the operation.[23]

Maxey called in his two brigade commanders in order to give them a quick brief outlining their parts in the attack. Colonels Charles DeMorse and Tandy Walker commanded the two brigades of Maxey's undersized division. Numbering about 1,200 men, Maxey's Division was the most eye-catching and unusual unit in the entire Confederate army. Walker's Brigade consisted entirely of Choctaw Indians from the Indian Territory who cast their lot with the South. One observer noted upon their arrival in Arkansas that they were "mounted on ponies, dressed in all sorts of clothing, including buckskin with feathers in hats."[24] While some may have dis-

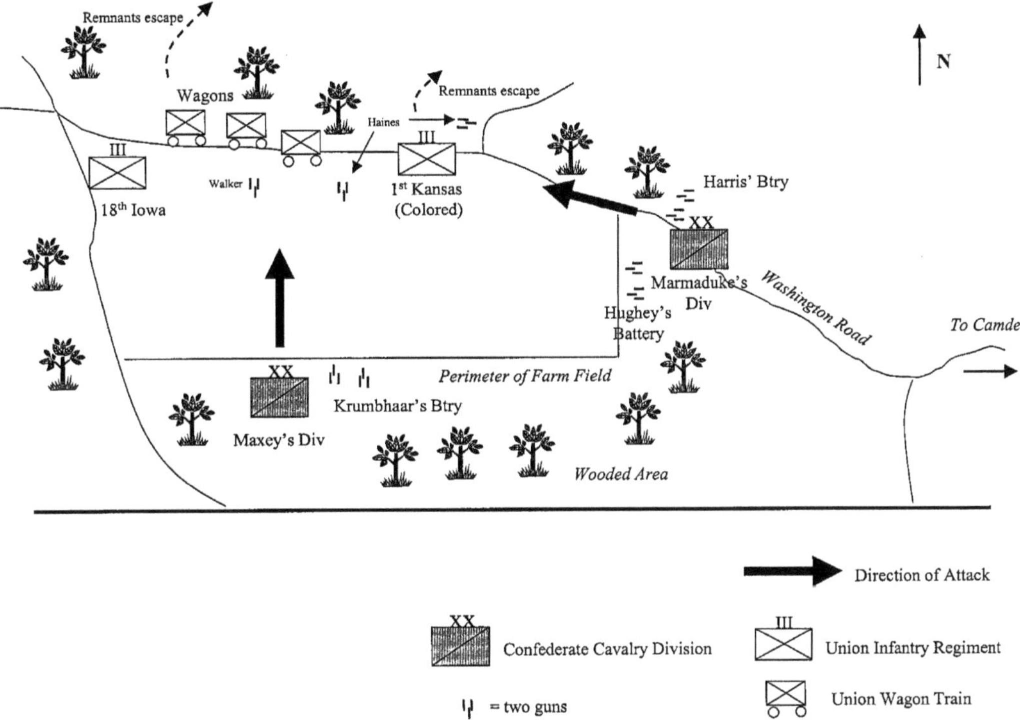

Ambush at Poison Spring. Confederate cavalry under overall command of General Marmaduke located the Federal forage train about 10 miles west of Camden. Marmaduke made a quick assessment of the situation and executed a well-placed ambush. Elements of two Rebel divisions routed the two Union regiments guarding the train resulting in loss of the entire train and a series of atrocities directed toward the men of the 1st Kansas (Colored) Infantry Regiment.

paraged their appearance, no one doubted their aggressive fighting qualities.[25] Maxey briefed his commanders that they would play a pivotal role in the coming fight. Nonchalantly whittling on a pine stick, Maxey instructed that the men dismount short of the Upper Washington Road and move on foot to the reverse slope of the ridge. Upon reaching their destination, DeMorse's Texans would form at a right angle with Cabell's left and parallel to the road. Walker's Choctaws would pass to the rear of DeMorse forming on the Texans' left in line. Captain Butler Krumbhaar's Texas Battery would form the center to provide fire support. As the dismounted cavalrymen filed into position the artillery would initiate a preparation lasting a half-hour to soften up the Federals, make them reveal their locations, and induce confusion. At the conclusion of the barrage, Maxey would advance in flank drawing Federal attention to the south. Once Maxey's attack produced its intended effect, Marmaduke would attack in front surprising the Federals and crushing them between the pincers.[26]

When the conference broke DeMorse and Walker immediately led their respective brigades off through the woods to their attack positions. The wiry Texans and

Indians took only thirty minutes to set their units for the assault. As Maxey's men approached the ridge, Harris' and Hughey's artillery opened on the Union column. The din of the cannonade was "the loudest and most terrific it has ever been my lot to listen to," one participant reported. While the crash of sound swirling about startled the Union soldiers guarding the train, the preparation failed to produce the effect Marmaduke desired. Major Ward commanding Williams' 1st Kansas ordered his men to lie down in order to prevent the Confederates from learning the exact locations of his regiment. The rest of the train guard followed suit and the storm of fire resulted in little more than thunderous noise as the Unionists suffered minimal casualties.[27]

Colonel Williams had maintained his faculties throughout the preparation and made his own dispositions to counter the Rebel moves. As Williams' own artillery attempted to reply, the colonel coolly surveyed the situation and noticed the dismounted Confederates filing onto the ridge to the south just as he had feared earlier they would. Williams ordered Major Ward to refuse his right wing to face south so that half of the 1st Kansas faced east toward Marmaduke's men and the other half fronted Maxey's Division. Williams had Captain Duncan likewise wheel a portion of his rear guard to the south and order the four cannons to orient in that direction as well.[28] These dispositions had barely been made when Maxey's Division came crashing off the ridge into the train guard.

Walker and DeMorse moved across the broken field in a rather ragged order due to the many obstacles that laced the field. The brigades were forced to halt at one point to adjust their alignment to maintain a proper battle line. This done the line lunged forward again only to run into a galling fire from the 1st Kansas. "I suffered them to approach within 100 yards of my line," Colonel Williams reported, "when I opened upon them with musketry ... and compelled them to fall back." The stunned Texans and Choctaws stumbled back to the protection of the ravine to reform for a second assault. Meanwhile, Krumbhaar's Battery had struggled to push the guns to the top of the ridge to support the attack. The dense undergrowth on the back side of the ridge conspired to prevent Krumbhaar from using the horses to haul the guns up the hill. Therefore, the gunners had to manhandle them up the hill. Krumbhaar made a request of DeMorse for assistance in moving the guns, but was rebuffed by the brigade commander. Undaunted, the battery commander used the numerous short saplings in the area to help him leverage the pieces forward.[29]

Krumbhaar now brought his guns to bear against the Union line with great effect as the Confederates reformed for a second assault. As Maxey's Division regrouped Cabell and Crawford pushed forward for Marmaduke's assault on the Union line. While Marmaduke made steady progress a potential crisis developed when Cabell failed to link his left flank with Maxey's right creating a yawning gap. In response, Marmaduke quickly called forward Greene's Brigade — the only one still mounted and uncommitted — to fill the gap.[30] The now massed Confederate force brought well over 2,500 men to bear against the thin train guard and this time the hapless Union soldiers would struggle to stop them.

Colonel Williams once again allowed the Confederate troopers to come in close before unleashing a devastating volley. The Rebel line staggered momentarily, but the sheer weight of the assault allowed them to recover in the face of galling fire from the blue line. A toe-to-toe firefight now ensued for the next hour as both sides fired volley after volley into each other at close range. The lines were so close together that the soldiers could hear the opposing lines talking. At one point, men from the 1st Kansas and the 29th Texas took the opportunity to become reacquainted. These regiments had met face to face before on the field at Honey Springs where the 1st Kansas had routed the Texans. Meeting again a year later, the Texans cast disparaging barbs at the Negro regiment and the 1st Kansas answered with a deluge of fire.[31]

The Confederates of Maxey's Division once again fell back a short distance to recover from the incessant fire of the Union troops, but now Cabell's Arkansans and Greene's Missourians closed in from the east. Williams' artillery, after firing continuously for well over an hour, had nearly exhausted all of its precious ammunition and gunners had suffered catastrophic casualties from Rebel cannon fire. With the Federal guns now falling silent, the infantry began to find their own situation deteriorating due to desperate shortages of ammunition. With these developments, Colonel Williams began to realize that he could no longer defend the train. His only hope of salvation was for the intense noise of the engagement to reach Steele at Camden. Maybe then Steele would send out a relief column to extract Williams from his predicament. He, therefore, resolved to fight it out as long as he could.[32] Ironically, Steele's men did hear the report of the fighting at Poison Spring, but never made an effort to relieve the beleaguered train guard.[33]

The Confederates advanced a third time with irresistible force and the Union line, too thin to cover the entire wagon train, began to bend back on the center. While Greene and Cabell pressured the middle, Crawford's Brigade on the Union left succeeded in outflanking the Federal line. As the Union left — the half of the 1st Kansas facing east — gave way it caused the rest of the line to melt away and Williams lost control of the fight. The 1st Kansas had fought heroically as long as it maintained a coherent line, but when the left gave way the regiment became gripped by panic. This uncovered the head of the train and Williams now turned his efforts to making an orderly retreat. He rode back to Captain Duncan of the 18th Iowa to inform him that he should form a line to allow the disordered elements to rally. Then he would attempt to retreat to the north by bounds to safely extract his force from the onslaught.[34] This decision, of course, meant that Williams intended to abandon the train and the booty it carried. However, to continue defending it with no hope of success translated into a loss of over 1,000 soldiers in addition to the train. In light of these facts, Williams made the only logical decision available.

The 18th Iowa barely had time to reform when fugitives from the 1st Kansas and screaming Rebels overwhelmed the regiment. The Confederates overlapped the Iowans' line by a wide margin and the white troops soon joined their comrades in beating a wild retreat in every direction. Jubilant Rebels swarmed the train, scooped up prisoners by the dozen and tore off in a ragged pursuit of the scurrying defenders. With little regard for unit organization, pockets of Union soldiers made a hasty retreat from the field by passing through a swamp bordering Lee's Plantation. The pursuing Rebels continued after the Federals to the edge of the swamp, but gave up in favor of easier pickings back at the abandoned wagon train. By about two in the afternoon the fighting had ended and the result was nothing short of a disaster for the VII Corps.[35]

As the remnants of the Union troops made good their escape, the rift in the Confederate high command began to take center stage. Marmaduke felt that too many Union soldiers had managed to escape and had unmercilessly driven his men to run down the fragmented command. Marmaduke had successfully managed affairs the entire day with tacit acceptance from Maxey up to now. At this point, Maxey decided to assert his right to command and recalled the scattered Rebels engaged in pursuit. Maxey preferred to round up the spoils of victory and directed the Confederates to begin gathering up the plunder to carry it back to Woodlawn. Also, he stated in his report, that he feared Steele would surely attack his rear and wanted to clear the area quickly. Marmaduke bitterly disagreed with this decision, yet he acquiesced in Maxey's insistence on calling off the pursuit.[36] A flap would later develop over who deserved the lion's share of credit for the victory. However, both men were careful in their reports to suppress a desire for laurels and for the most part stuck to the facts, a credit to both Maxey and Marmaduke. However, it must be stated that the concept and execution of operations at Poison Spring came from Marmaduke and therefore, he deserves credit for outstanding service.

While the battle had ended, the violence had not as some of the Rebels began committing atrocities against wounded and captured Negroes of the 1st Kansas. Eyewitnesses reported dozens of men were bayoneted and murdered by the hand of Maxey's men who hurled insults at the helpless prisoners as they carried out their ugly deeds. One Rebel observer was appalled at the sight "of so many dead Negroes." Further, there are accounts that some of the Choctaws even took scalps as trophies. The scene disgusted a burial detail from the 1st Iowa Cavalry and 18th Iowa Infantry sent to the field three days after the battle to give the fallen a proper interment. A Captain Rowland reported that "the white dead were scalped and all were stripped of clothing.... To add insult to the dead officers of the colored regiment," he added, "they were all laid on their faces, and a circle of their dead soldiers made around them."[37] A Confederate confirmed that "an uncounted number of dead negroes [sic]" littered the field.[38] Not all the Rebels agreed with this account of what transpired. One Confederate recalled that Maxey's men did indeed want to murder and "scalp the kill negroes [sic], but were not allowed" by their officers.[39]

Regardless of the opinions of witnesses, the statistics bear out that a disproportionate number of the 1st Kansas suffered a terrible fate as opposed to their comrades from the white regiments. Of the 438 men engaged from the 1st Kansas, 182 were listed as casualties, of whom 117 were killed — a very high ratio of dead to wounded. By contrast, of the 732 white soldiers from the train guard, 119 were listed as casualties. All total the Federals lost 301 troops, 175 wagons — 145 of which had highly prized 6–mule teams — four cannon, and an estimated 5,000 bushels of corn.[40]

As Maxey inventoried the days' spoils, his men discovered among the plunder articles of no military significance such as furniture, women's clothing, and farming implements.[41] As expected, the Confederates derisively criticized the Federals for carrying off such articles.

Poison Spring had a much smaller price tag for the victorious Rebels. While Confederate reports are incomplete, the record shows their loss at 114 men killed, wounded, or missing out of more than 3,000 engaged.[42] The figures confirm that Poison Spring was a signal victory for the Confederates. It raised Rebel expectations that they could force Steele to retreat or physically destroy his army. Conversely, the defeat demoralized the Federals in Camden, as the men would continue to struggle in their quest for food.

The ragged, defeated survivors from Poison Spring began straggling into Camden on the evening of the 18th and would continue in driblets for days to come. Inevitably, news of the debacle spread uncontrolled through all the regiments of the Union army. Soldiers gathered with their messmates around campfires to discuss the disaster and who could have been responsible. While opinions varied over culpability, the loudest complaints came from men who were desperately hungry. "We were now almost out of rations," a veteran recalled. "Hard-tack grew more rare and valuable, with each succeeding day." The Federals in Camden were certainly in a serious predicament as the regular ration issue for one day included only four ears of corn for each soldier.[43]

The supply situation was nearing desperation in Camden by April 19. The garrison was down to only three days' rations for the men and an incredible one day's forage for the 12,000 draft animals employed by the army. To make matters worse, there existed little forage in the valley of the Ouachita to offset the shortage of army provender.[44] Steele simply had to obtain a reliable source of supply or else the entire expedition would have to retreat back to Little Rock. Even if Steele could now emplace a workable system, the expedition might still prove unwinnable. This is because of the huge loss in transportation at Poison Spring. When the VII Corps arrived in Camden on the 15th it brought with it around 800 wagons to provide transport for the army's provisions. The loss of 175 wagons, complete with their teams, only three days later subtracted over twenty percent of the army's available haul capacity. A question now arose as to whether the corps still had enough transport to support the army even if it could build up a stockpile of rations.

While the leaders grappled with the challenge of feeding the army, the individual soldiers did what they could to take care of themselves. Soldiers reportedly "took possession of all the cows, sheep, and hogs" in town to supplement their rations. One feisty lady drove away some would-be cow stealers with a "big stick." Impressed by her spirit, the Yankees relented and left her cow. While the Union soldiers did not visit depredations on Camden, they were, nevertheless, unwelcome in town, especially the colored regiments. Most of the families in the city had close relatives in the Confederate army that lay just outside the limits of town. As a result, the Federal soldiers detected a quiet defiance among the citizenry. As Mrs. Stinson recorded in her memoir of the occupation, "I did not feel honored to have such people."[45]

On April 20 the supply difficulties were somewhat relieved with the arrival of a 150-wagon supply train "laden with subsistence, ordnance and quartermaster stores." The train contained 10-days half rations that included hardtack, bacon, salt and the Civil War soldiers' most prized issue, coffee. As happy as the soldiers were about the arrival of chow, they became ecstatic that the wagons also held a delivery of mail. Andrew Sperry recalled that the letters delivered that day were more prized than any others they had received during the war. Many a veteran would remember with fondness "the good old mail we got at Camden." This train was the one that had been delayed by the accident in the Arkansas River when the *Adams* and the *Chippewa* collided. Nathan Kimball had worked diligently to make up for the loss and within a couple of days of the accident pushed another supply package down the Arkansas to Pine Bluff. Here, Powell Clayton transloaded the cargo to wagons and sent them via Mt. Elba and Marks' Mills to Camden. In addition to providing succor in the form of supplies, as important was the arrival of the wagons themselves. These nearly made up for the losses incurred at Poison Spring.[46] If Steele could double this stockpile by making another trip to Pine Bluff for additional supplies, this would enable him to reach the Red and Banks' beleaguered army.

On the 21st Steele received Captain Dunham, bearer of dispatches from General Banks whose army was located at Grand Ecore on the Red. The VII Corps commander had wavered in recent days in his resolve to continue southward due to the intractable supply situation. Banks, however, expressed the belief that he could still take Shreveport, but needed Steele's assistance to do so. "The enemy is in larger force than was anticipated," Banks started his letter, "The lines," he continued, "upon which we operate are so far separated from each other that it is impossible for either of us to sustain effectively." But, if Steele could move down to the Red, Banks concluded, "I am confident we can move to Shreveport without material delay."[47] When Steele read Banks' dispatch dated April 15, he cast his very considerable doubts aside and strengthened his commitment to press on with the expedition.

If he had resolved outwardly to continue, privately he expressed shock at the "absurdity" of Banks' request.[48] In a letter responding to Banks, Steele reiterated his intention to march to the Red, but he also produced a full synopsis of the challenges that stood in his way. For one thing, Price had effectively stolen the initiative from Steele since the VII Corps had holed up in Camden. The Confederates had succeeded in delaying the VII Corps and prevented an early junction with Banks. Only three days previous Price's formidable mounted arm had created a crisis of sustainment in the area as VII Corps' supply and transportation assets were eviscerated at Poison Spring. Now a large reinforcement, numbering over 8,000 infantry, was moving north to join Price in order to counter any further progress by Steele. Nevertheless, Steele resolutely stated that "I desire to co-operate with you in the best manner possible."[49]

Before he could "co-operate," Steele had to open a line of communication free of enemy interdiction. He had laid out in great detail to Banks the inability of the VII Corps to forage or receive regular army rations. To remedy this, Steele suggested to Banks that perhaps he could assist in this vein by sending gunboats and transports up the Ouachita. Only days earlier, Steele had written to Halleck proffering the same course of action to open communication. This seemed a logical and easy to implement solution, but nature intervened to prevent this. Most of the Mississippi River Squadron under Admiral Porter had gone up the Red to support Banks' army leaving only a small force to patrol the long Mississippi. In ascending the Red River, the squadron had made a passage of the falls above Alexandria, Louisiana, a difficult obstacle in times of low water. Soon after running the rapids above the town, the Red River fell to levels not seen in years due to an unseasonably dry spring. As a result, the boats were trapped above the falls, as they could not descend the river without wrecking the ships in the passage. This meant that navy would not be able to offer any assistance to Steele in the form of transport or fire support. With the preponderance of Porter's naval forces involved in the Red River Campaign and regular patrols of the Mississippi, there were simply no naval vessels available that could open up a secure line via the Ouachita. Yet, Steele pledged to assist Banks in spite of all the factors that dictated calling off the expedition.[50] The unconvincing tone of Steele's reply to Banks reveals that he knew his promise was hollow and that he believed the whole endeavor represented nothing more than a forlorn hope. Further, the letter confirms that the initiative in the campaign had passed convincingly to the Confederates under Kirby Smith and Price in Arkansas.

To continue any march south, Steele would have to press on with the stockpiling of supplies at the depot in Camden for without them the army was immobile and vulnerable. Captain Henry, Steele's diligent chief quartermaster, made arrangements to supplement the stores at Camden in an attempt to ready the army for its advance south. While the Yankees busied themselves with preparing to push forward, the Confederates plotted the demise of their enemies. Large reinforcements were approaching Price's headquarters at Woodlawn with Kirby Smith at the head of the column. With these and the ever-watchful cavalry, Price would have adequate forces to inflict a disaster upon the VII Corps. Storm clouds were definitely gathering over Camden and would inexorably force the Union army back to where it originated.

Notes

1. *OR*, Vol. 34, Part 3, 77–79.
2. *Ibid.*, 147.
3. Lothrop, *History of the First Iowa Cavalry*, 161.
4. *OR*, Vol. 34, Part 1, 661, 668, and 680, and "The Federal Occupation of Camden as Set Forth in the Diary of a Union Officer," *AHQ* (Autumn 1950), 214. The estimates of the quantity of corn contained by the *Homer* run as high as 5,000 bushels depending upon the source.
5. Richards, "The Camden Expedition," 68.
6. *OR*, Vol. 34, Part 1, 661, 668, and 781.
7. *Ibid.*, 680 and 682.
8. John G. Walker, "The War of Secession West of the Mississippi River During the Years

1863–4–5," Myron Gwinner Collection, United States Army Military History Institute, unpublished manuscript, 56 and 60; *OR*, Vol. 34, Part 3, 766–767.

9. *OR*, Vol. 34, Part 3, 766–767, and 781.

10. Ira D. Richards, "The Battle of Poison Spring," *AHQ* (Winter 1959), 341–342; and *OR*, Vol. 34, Part 1, 680 and 743–744.

11. *OR*, Vol. 34, Part 1, 818–819; and Richards, "The Battle of Poison Spring," *AHQ* (Winter 1959), 342.

12. *OR*, Vol. 34, Part 1, 661–662.

13. *Ibid.*, 662.

14. *Ibid.*, 743–744; and Edwin C. Bearss, *Steele's Retreat From Camden*, 6–7.

15. Edwin C. Bearss, *Steele's Retreat from Camden*, 7–8.

16. Marmaduke allowed Shelby's Brigade to rest at Woodlawn since the brigade was spent from recent exertions on the trip from Arkadelphia to Camden.

17. *OR*, Vol. 34, Part 1, 818–819.

18. Richards, "The Battle of Poison Spring," *AHQ* (Winter 1959), 342; and Bearss, *Steele's Retreat From Camden*, 12–13.

19. Bearss, *Steele's Retreat from Camden*, 7–8 and 20–21; and *OR*, Vol. 34, Part 1, 748.

20. *OR*, Vol. 34, Part 1, 744; Burke, *Official Military History of the Kansas Regiments*, 414; and Bearss, *Steele's Retreat From Camden*, 21.

21. Britton, *The Civil War on the Border*, II, 282–283.

22. *Ibid.*, 282; and Bearss, *Steele's Retreat From Camden*, 15–18.

23. *OR*, Vol. 34, Part 1, 819.

24. Henry Cathey, ed., "Extracts From the Memoirs of William Franklin Avera," *AHQ* (Winter 1963), 102–103.

25. Annie H. Abel, *The Indian as Participant in the Civil War*, Vol. 2, 326–327.

26. Clement C. Evans, ed., *Confederate Military History*, X, 249; and *OR*, Vol. 34, Part 1, 819, 826, 841, 847, and 849.

27. Britton, *The Civil War on the Border*, II, 284–285; and Burke, *Official Military History of the Kansas Regiments*, 419.

28. Burke, *Official Military History of the Kansas Regiments*, 418; Britton, *The Civil War on the Border*, II, 285; and Richards, "The Battle of Poison Spring," *AHQ* (Winter 1959), 346.

29. Burke, *Official Military History of the Kansas Regiments*, 419; Richards, "The Battle of Poison Spring," *AHQ* (Winter 1959), 346; and *OR*, Vol. 34, Part 1, 846.

30. *OR*, Vol. 34, Part 1, 847.

31. Britton, *The Civil War on the Border*, II, 286.

32. Evans, ed., *Confederate Military History*, X, 249–250; Burke, *Official Military History of the Kansas Regiments*, 419; Britton, *The Civil War on the Border*, II, 286–287; and *OR*, Vol. 34, Part 1, 745.

33. Richards, "The Battle of Poison Spring," *AHQ* (Winter 1959), 345; and McLeod, "The Frontier Division in the Camden Expedition," 11.

34. Richards, "The Battle of Poison Spring," *AHQ* (Winter 1959), 347; and *OR*, Vol. 34, Part 1, 745.

35. *OR*, Vol. 34, Part 1, 745–746.

36. *Ibid.*, 820 and 842; and Richards, "The Battle of Poison Spring," *AHQ* (Winter 1959), 348.

37. Lothrop, *History of the First Iowa Cavalry*, 182.

38. Zorn, ed., "Campaigning in Southern Arkansas: A Memoir by C. T. Anderson," *AHQ* (Autumn 1949), 243; *The Sable Arm*, 176–177; Burke, *Official Military History of the Kansas Regiments*, 428; and Edwards, *Shelby and His Men*, 276.

39. Cathey, ed., "Extracts From the Memoirs of William Franklin Avera," *AHQ* (Winter 1963), 103.

40. *OR*, Vol. 34, Part 1, 746; and McLeod, "The Frontier Division in the Camden Expedition," 14.

41. Edwards, *Shelby and His Men*, 276; and Evans, ed., *Confederate Military History*, X, 250.

42. *OR*, Vol. 34, Part 1, 786.

43. Sperry, *History of the 33rd Iowa*, 90–91.

44. *OR*, Vol. 34, Part 1, 680; and Bearss, *Steele's Retreat from Camden*, 42–43.

45. Sperry, *History of the 33rd Iowa*, 90–92; Ira D. Richards, "The Engagement of Marks' Mills," *AHQ* (Spring 1960), 53; and Elliot, ed., *The Garden of Memory*, Mrs. Virginia M. Stinson, "Memories," 29–33.

46. *OR*, Vol. 34, Part 1, 680; Bearss, *Steele's Retreat From Camden*, 43; and Sperry, *History of the 33rd Iowa*, 91.

47. *OR*, Vol. 34, Part 3, 161–162.

48. *OR*, Vol. 34, Part 1, 676.

49. *OR*, Vol. 34, Part 3, 267.

50. *OR*, Vol. 34, Part 3, 267–268, and Part 1, 661–662.

8

"I decided to fall back at once..."

The situation in Arkansas was nearing a critical point for the Union army in the latter days of April 1864. Even as General Banks in Louisiana despaired of the lack of support from Arkansas, substantial Rebel reinforcements were, ironically, heading north to deal with Steele's small army. Steele had debated after the debacle at Poison Spring whether to continue south or pull back. If he retreated now the Confederates coming to Arkansas would achieve their purpose without a battle. This would leave open the prospect of Kirby Smith returning to Louisiana to finish off Banks and Porter. Richard Taylor would be most pleased by such a turn of events since he had clamored for Banks' destruction rather that making a "goose chase" in Arkansas. Steele's continuation of the expedition would further draw Smith northward and deny Taylor the opportunity to seal Banks' fate on the Red. Despite his conviction that any further advance was foolish, Steele had pledged renewed efforts to drive to the Red in support of Banks. This ensured that Kirby Smith would remain in Arkansas long enough to allow Banks to escape his predicament along with the Union navy. Steele's army would pay a heavy price at Marks' Mill in the coming days because of the commanding general's decision to press on.

On April 14 Thomas J. Churchill, Mosby M. Parsons, and John G. Walker staged with their respective divisions in Shreveport for a march north to Camden. The region between Shreveport and Camden, like most of southern Arkansas, lacked food and forage for man and animal. In order to subsist three divisions of infantry and draft animals, the army would require widely dispersed lines of march. As a result, Kirby Smith chose three separate avenues to move the army to Arkansas so that he could maximize the area from which he could obtain provisions. Churchill's Division would move on the Wire Road paralleling the Red River to Magnolia, where the division would turn east to Camden. Parsons' Division would take the Middle Road via Calhoun converging at Magnolia with Churchill and thence to Camden. Finally, Walker would strike out to the northeast to Minden and turn north to Camden.[1] It would take about a week to move the divisions, reassemble, and prepare for combat if all went well.

The column crossed a pontoon spanning the Red on April 15–16 for Arkansas, encamping just north of Shreveport. From here each division fanned out on its respective route to make the junction with Price's army in Arkansas. Sergeant Joseph Blessington of Walker's Texas Division was in the column that day and recorded the excitement that swept through the ranks as they stepped north. The officers chirped with pride at the recent victories in Louisiana over Banks and speculated as to their prospects in Arkansas. Over the next two days the Texas Division made over 42 miles before passing through the village of Minden. The citizens of Minden greeted the gray infantry with "enthusiasm [that] seemed to know no bounds." The pleasant welcome lifted the footsore soldiers' spirits many of whom "were thoroughly fagged out." Here the division halted to await orders for continuing the move.[2]

Kirby Smith rode ahead to establish contact with Price at Woodlawn in order to confer about what their combined force should do about Steele's army at Camden. Price informed Smith that Camden could not be taken by storm due to the impressive works erected by the Confederates the previous autumn and winter. The fortifications surrounded the city and were firmly occupied now by the Federals they were built to keep out. Rather than a direct assault that would cost many lives, Smith surmised that perhaps the army should take an indirect approach. If the army could slash around in the rear of the VII Corps operating on the line of communication, the Confederates would force Steele out into the open. This would enable Smith to engage Steele on his own terms defeating or possibly destroying the Federal army. Before the Confederates could do this, Smith would need the pontoon bridge over the Red, since they would have to span the Ouachita to move around Steele's flank. The delay in waiting for the pontoon train would cost the Rebels a few days in the move north.[3]

Rather than waste time with three divisions idle, Smith momentarily considered sending Walker's Division back to Taylor to assist in placing continued pressure on Banks in Louisiana. Elated, Taylor began to plan for the prospect of receiving his most reliable subordinate back for work against the Army of the Gulf. Smith dumbfounded Taylor on the 20th when he abruptly ordered Walker to continue the march to Woodlawn. Smith had opted to put in all available forces against Steele rather than making a piecemeal effort between Arkansas and Louisiana. After much deliberation, Smith declared that "the field for important military operations is opened by the capture or dispersion of Steele's force." In accordance with Smith's intent, Walker's Division took to the road again on the 22nd with the pontoon bridge slowly heading for Camden. All of this angered Taylor who could not understand Smith's seemingly indecisive process of decision-making.[4] The rift between these two talented commanders continued to widen with each passing day and the prospects of closing it seemed ever more remote.

Smith's first order of business in Arkansas was to push cavalry over the Ouachita to begin operations on Steele's lines of communication with Little Rock, Pine Bluff, and DeVall's Bluff. Smith, it seems, felt that Price's efforts in this facet of the campaign lacked appropriate energy. Smith aimed to inject some fire into Price and summarily ordered him to form a task force for the purpose of disrupting Steele's supply lines. Price now flew into action assigning Brigadier General James Fagan to command a four-brigade strike force consisting of the three brigades of his own division — Cabell's, Dockery's, and Crawford's — and Shelby's now rested troopers. For ease of command and control Fagan organized his unit into a small corps of two divisions. Shelby would command one division comprising his own brigade and Crawford's, and Cabell the other with his own brigade and Dockery's.[5]

Fagan started with his division to El Dorado Landing below Camden on April 22. Here Fagan planned to ferry his 3,000 troopers over the Ouachita. From there they would strike out to the northeast to cut Steele's ability to communicate with Pine Bluff. Shelby had moved on the 20th to Matlock's Ford above Camden. His brigade of about 1,000 men made a wide arc around Steele's army before dropping to the south to meet Fagan on the far side of the Ouachita opposite El Dorado. Shelby, always noted for vigilance and initiative, had scattered several scout detachments on the roads leading from Camden to keep watch on Steele. Shelby's alert troopers detected a long train moving out of Camden on the 22nd apparently destined for Pine Bluff. Upon receiving word of this development, Shelby quickly relayed the news to Fagan. Shelby's courier reached Fagan late on the 23rd, too late it turned out to act on the intelligence that day. Fagan allowed his men to rest for the night while he plotted the demise of the latest foray by the hungry Federals.[6]

Captain Henry was arguably the busiest man in the Union army during its repose in Camden. After the arrival of the train from Pine Bluff on the 20th, Henry had supervised the inventory, unloading, and preparations for the return trip. The train would obtain additional supplies from the depot at Pine Bluff and make an immediate turn back to Camden. Henry believed this would provide the army with just enough stores to make the trip to Louisiana for a rendezvous with Banks. To the 150 wagons from Pine Bluff, Henry added an additional 61 bringing the total to 211 to make the trek to Pine Bluff. Before the train left Camden it had to have an adequate guard to prevent another disaster such as that of Poison Spring. While Henry worked on the administrative details, Steele called together his division commanders to wargame a course of action that would ensure the safe passage of the train.[7]

Steele assigned the mission of train security to Frederick Salomon. Rather than providing for a reinforced regiment to guard the train, Steele wanted a brigade tasked to protect this one. In compliance with this guidance Salomon gave the mission to his 2nd Brigade commanded by the reliable Colonel William McLean. While this was an excellent selection, McLean on the 22nd of April was on the sick list unable to exercise command of the brigade. As a result, command of the 2nd Brigade devolved on the competent Lieutenant Colonel Francis Drake of the 36th Iowa Infantry who had turned in such a steady performance at Elkins' Ferry earlier in the expedition. Evidence of Steele's concern for the safety of the train is shown by his requirement that Drake personally report to the commanding general for further instructions.[8]

Upon reporting at headquarters, Drake found himself whisked into Steele's presence. Steele proceeded to issue some very specific instructions in a grave and serious manner. From Steele's tone Drake gathered how critical the mission was to not just the commanding general, but to the army as whole. Steele first introduced Drake to the guide he had assigned to help Drake find his way by the easiest route. Next, he described the conditions of the terrain along the road, specifically amplifying the Moro Bottom. The bottom was a nearly impassable swamp with only a narrow road traversing it. Steele believed this could serve as a possible ambush site for the Confederates due to its restricted nature. He told Drake that under no circumstances should he attempt to cross the swamp in late evening. In addition to Drake's own force, Steele stated that he was attaching the 1st Iowa Cavalry for the trip to Pine Bluff. From there this regiment would return to Iowa for a veterans' furlough owed it for reenlisting for the duration of the war. While Steele needed every soldier he could spare just now, he inexplicably decided to grant the 1st Iowa its leave. He seems to have feared breaching their contract more than the enemy. The commander concluded his meeting with Drake by telling the young lieutenant colonel that the train was ready for movement as soon as Drake could assemble his brigade.[9]

Drake's column contained several regiments of combat hardened veterans who had given a good account of themselves in many western battles. The guard included the 36th Iowa Infantry, 43rd Indiana Infantry, 77th Ohio Infantry, 1st Iowa Cavalry, detachments from the 1st Indiana Cavalry, 5th and 7th Missouri Cavalry, and Battery E, 2nd Missouri Light Artillery. Drake's command numbered some 1,200 infantry, 760 cavalry, and four guns for a total of about 2,000 soldiers. While this appears an impressive array, it would prove inadequate to protect the 200–plus wagons. When the train moved out it would stretch two to three miles down the road, far too long a frontage for Drake's brigade. Nevertheless, Drake rolled out of Camden in the early morning hours of April 23 bound for Pine Bluff.[10]

Drake arose early on the 23rd intent on stepping off at 5:00 A.M. As he moved through the assembled mass, he noted with pride the professionalism of the soldiers as they checked their equipment in preparation to move. Continuing down the column, he also ran into a sight that dismayed him as several hundred hangers-on were milling around at the rear of the train expecting to join the trek when the wagons lurched forward. The motley assemblage included an estimated 75 additional wagons belonging to the ever-present sutlers, cotton speculators, refugees, southern unionists, and 300 runaway slaves. Their presence unsettled Drake, as they would multiply the challenge of defending the train due to the disruptive effect the crowd would create. Although Drake objected to this development, he was powerless to prevent them from following the column. At best he could order them to keep their distance from the main body.[11]

The cavalry detachment led the advance as the sun rose, followed by the 36th Iowa, 43rd Indiana, the wagons, and the 77th Ohio as the rear guard. The 1st Iowa Cavalry would depart later in the day on foot catching up the column before it camped for the night. Drake found the going rough as the column swung into the Camden-Pine Bluff Road. The heavy rains of recent weeks had washed away sections of the road bringing the train to a halt periodically. This forced Drake to make hasty repairs to keep the column rolling. He decided to make use of the camp followers as a makeshift pioneer corps to shore up the roadbed. Consisting of about 75 contraband slaves, the small corps worked diligently, yet the damage to the road made progress agonizingly slow. This resulted in Drake making only twelve miles on the 23rd. With nightfall closing in late in the evening, Drake decided to encamp for the night and make an early start in the morning. During the night he would send the pioneers forward to corduroy portions of the washed out road and construct makeshift bridges over the many small streams to facilitate mobility the next day. As the soldiers prepared their bivouac, Drake took great care to post security around the campsite. Patrols fanned out in all directions up to five miles from the camp to provide early warning of any Confederate cavalry patrols that lurked in the area. He sent one to the junction of the Princeton and Camden-Pine Bluff roads to scout this critical point for Rebel activity.[12] Drake had certainly taken Steele's instructions to heart making an energetic effort to carry out his duty and protect the army's lifeline.

The pioneers moved out long before dawn with a cavalry escort and two guns from Charles Peetz' battery to cover their work efforts. The negro workers quickly repaired all washouts encountered enabling the empty wagons to make 18 miles on the 24th. The pickets and the main body still had no indication of any Rebels in the immediate vicinity — with the exception of finding an abandoned cavalry camp — and Drake was confident that he could get the train through to Pine Bluff in the next couple of days. Late evening on the 24th, Drake and company came to the head of the Moro Bottom. Remembering Steele's admonition to not attempt a crossing with night closing in, he stopped the column for a second night short of the swamp. Once again he sent patrols out in a wide pattern to prevent any possibility that the Confederates could surprise his encampment. Again, Drake had the pioneers work through the night to enable the passage through the bottom the next morning. The lieutenant colonel also took the precaution of sending a Lieutenant Schrum of Frederick Salomon's staff forward to Pine Bluff. The intent of this mission was to alert Powell Clayton of Drake's location and situation, and to have a mobile column ready to come to his assistance should the train run into problems. At early dawn the column would move out pushing through the swamp quickly so that the train would not be in an exposed position for an inordinate amount of time.[13]

Before dawn of the 25th the Union column was well on its way through the Moro Bottom with an advance guard and Peetz' guns providing security. The ad hoc pioneer corps had once again turned in a spectacular performance in improving the road. Thus far, the bluecoats had seen no Rebels, but this would change abruptly as the long train wound through the pine forest. Lurking ahead at a forgotten corner known as Marks' Mills were 4,000 tough Confederate cavalrymen waiting to pounce on a juicy target. General Shelby effected a junction with Fagan's Division as it crossed the Ouachita early on the 24th and immediately conferred with his superior. Fagan had formulated a plan for grappling with the Federal train after receiving Shelby's dispatch the day previous. Fagan knew that in order to destroy the wagon train he first had to stop it. To do this he decided to make a forced march along the Chambersville Road, which paralleled the Camden-Pine Bluff Road. He hoped that by hard riding the Rebel cavalry would cut the Federal route and halt the train somewhere near Marks' Mills. Then Fagan would coil around the train with assault units to hack up the defending train guard. Fagan believed the great length of the train would make it difficult for the Federals to defend. If the Yankees massed their infantry it would expose sections of the train to destruction. On the other hand, if they attempted to cover the whole length, the Union force would be thin, making the column vulnerable to a breakthrough at many points.[14] Everything portended another disaster for Federal arms and Fagan knew it.

As Fagan met with Shelby, he identified the objective point as Marks' Mills and sent him tearing down the road when the meeting broke. Fagan attached a guide to Shelby's staff to help him find the area of Marks' Mills with a minimum of navigational difficulty. The man, a private in Dockery's Brigade, proved a judicious choice, for William Marks was the son of the gentleman who owned the mills. Shelby was the right man to lead the van of Fagan's command because he drove his men relentlessly on the 24th. Setting a personal example, Shelby pushed the head of the column an astonishing 45 miles easily outdistancing the Federals as they approached Moro Bottom. Shelby decided to bivouac about eight miles short of Marks' Mills in order to rest his men after their grueling day in the saddle. At dusk Fagan — in camp a few miles behind Shelby — sent patrols throughout the surrounding countryside to pinpoint the location of the Federal column hoping they had not passed Marks' Mills. Much to Fagan's satisfaction, the Union train had not made it to the mills. During the night one of Fagan's scouts came in and informed the general that the Federals had halted on the evening of the 24th short of the Moro Bottom. This meant that they would have to cross it in the morning giving Fagan time to push his cavalry in front of the bluecoats. He determined to break camp for Marks' Mills at daybreak in order to set an ambush for the Union column as they emerged from the bottom.[15]

Fagan scarcely snatched any sleep on the 24th as he spent the night planning the attack of the next day. The scheme of maneuver called for Shelby and Cabell to launch simultaneous attacks on the head and flanks of the Union column. Shelby would move to a point between Mount Elba and Marks' Mills on the Camden-Pine Bluff Road. Upon reaching the road the division would make a left and ride in a southwesterly direction until encountering the train. Here, Shelby would act as the anvil and stop the train from proceeding any further down the road. Cabell's Division would at the same time move north on the Warren Road directly toward the mills. Just short of Marks' Mills, Cabell would dismount his division and deploy it in line of battle. When the head of the Union train ran into Shelby, Cabell would deliver the hammer blow crashing into the open flank from the south.[16] Fagan hoped the Confederates would achieve complete surprise and hence, thorough destruction of the train. The drawback to the plan was that it required precise timing to ensure the widely separated gray columns converged at the appropriate moment. If one of the divisions delayed in its movement, the Union infantry with the train could overwhelm one of the Rebel cavalry divisions before the other could arrive to help. Fagan, how-

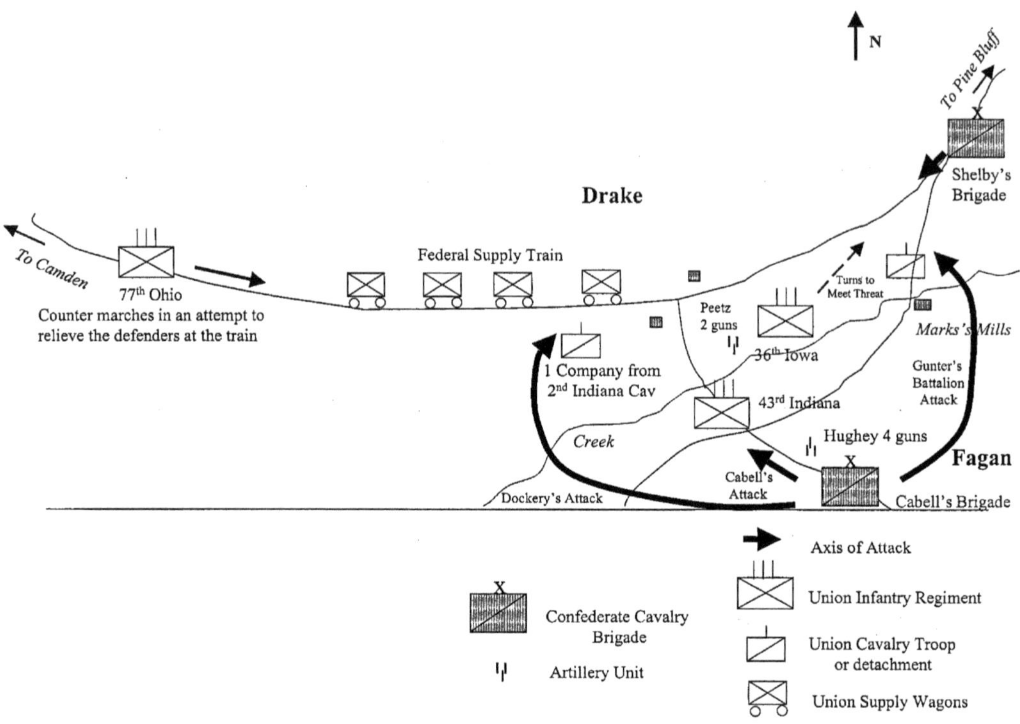

Engagement at Marks' Mills. General James Fagan discovered a train of 240 wagons on April 23 bound for Pine Bluff in an attempt to obtain food for the half-starving Union army at Camden. Fagan quickly marshaled his forces for a Poison Spring-style ambush on the train. The Union force guarding the train under Lt. Col. Francis Drake, numbering 1600, was overwhelmed as the head and flanks of the train came under heavy contact by Rebel cavalry. After a five hour struggle the wounded Drake surrendered to Fagan. The loss of the train forced Steele to abandon the Camden Expedition.

ever, had under his command some of the best subordinate cavalry leaders in the west and this went a long way toward minimizing the risk of precise coordination.

At dawn, according to plan, the Rebel troopers were in the saddle moving to their respective attack positions. When Shelby reached the Camden-Pine Bluff Road he sent the bulk of his force down toward Marks' Mills. He also detached a small force in the opposite direction toward Mt. Elba at the crossing of the Saline River to keep an eye on the road to Pine Bluff. Shelby worried that the Federals under Powell Clayton might come down from Pine Bluff to meet the train and threaten the rear of his column. Additionally, he wanted to seal off the crossing so fugitives from the ambush could not make it to Pine Bluff. Meanwhile, Cabell moved up the Warren Road to get in position for his assault. Cabell's movement went much slower as Dockery's troopers lagged behind creating a gap in the division. Cabell intended to place his own brigade on the right and Dockery on the left parallel to the road. The slow arrival of Dockery however, endangered Cabell to an attack on his own exposed left flank. To protect against this possibility, Cabell sent his own 7th Arkansas to guard his left until Dockery came up. As the brigade made its dispositions, Fagan, who had accompanied Cabell, peered over the ground catching sight of the train for the first time. Cabell stated that "the train was moving rapidly" as it jolted to the northeast toward Pine Bluff. The generals must have salivated at the sight of so many wagons moving in the open across their front. Just then shots rang out to the left as Federal patrols flanking the train made initial contact with Cabell's exposed flank.[17]

The Union column roused before daybreak on the 25th and as the sun rose the men fell in on the road to begin shuffling through the narrow path in Moro Bottom. Drake arranged the 43rd Indiana in the lead, followed by the 36th Iowa who moved beside the train on the right flank, while the 77th Ohio remained in camp until the train cleared in order to fall in as the rear guard. The 1st Iowa Cavalry still had not overtaken the train, but Drake expected them to join the column sometime that day. During the night the work party had done excellent service in corduroying the road through the swamp. Even so, the going proved difficult as "many wagons mired down and the mules floundering in seemingly bottomless slush holes." As the train struggled through the swamp, a courier from one of Drake's many patrols reported in with disturbing news. The patrol, it seems, had encountered elements of Rebel cavalry lurking on the Warren Road, but the courier did not believe it a serious threat.[18]

Nevertheless, Drake became somewhat apprehensive that the Rebels could make an attempt on the train as it cleared the swamp. He may have felt more at ease had Lieutenant Schrum made it through to Pine Bluff the previous evening. Schrum, however, barely proceeded beyond sight of the night's bivouac. As he trudged through the swamp on the 24th the ambulance he rode in became hopelessly mired in the muck. Schrum's arrival at Pine Bluff could have helped immensely the next day at Marks' Mills because Powell Clayton had taken the initiative to form a "flying column" in the event that the train needed assistance. He had even gone to the trouble to position the column forward to Mt. Elba to render quick support.[19] Altogether, Clayton's effort was intuitive and prudent, but without information on location or situation he could do little to help Drake.

As Federal infantrymen from the 43rd Indiana cleared the swamp they found unmistakable signs of heavy Rebel activity in the vicinity of Marks' Mills and sent a follow-up report to Drake. Now thoroughly aroused to the danger ahead, Drake decided to move to the front to have a look for himself. As Drake moved forward he found his stranded messenger, Lieutenant Schrum, and ordered him to take command of the train and move it to an appropriate point of safety while the infantry cleared the front of Rebels. Continuing on, Drake came across Major Wesley Norris of the 43rd Indiana conferring with a cavalry officer that he did not recognize. After further investigation, Drake found that a Major Spellman with 150 troopers of the 7th Missouri Cavalry had been in the area conducting a reconnaissance from Pine Bluff when his detachment bumped into the 43rd skirmishing with Cabell's Rebels. Spellman had immediately attached himself to Norris' regiment to fight the Confederates. Drake welcomed the reinforcements and then turned to Major Norris who reported that the Confederates in large force occupied a ridge on the south side of the road. This ridge dominated the road and would have to be cleared before the column could proceed. Drake ordered Norris to shake out a battle line and attempt to sweep the ridge. Norris was somewhat skeptical of his ability to carry the ridge because he believed the Rebels were in much greater strength than did Drake. Without arguing, however, Norris saluted and turned to execute the order.[20]

Norris' skirmishers had advanced one hundred yards when a volley sent them tumbling back: they had run into Cabell's 7th Arkansas Regiment. Drake finally realized that he had a serious fight on his hands and sent for the 36th Iowa and 77th Ohio to hasten to the front. As the 36th double-quick marched forward, Drake fed them into line on the left of the 43rd Indiana along with two guns from Peetz' battery. The struggle between Cabell's lone brigade and Drake's stiffening line continued for about an hour and a half with the Federal infantry slowly building to a point where it appeared they would overwhelm Cabell.[21] Fagan's dependence on precise timing was now threatening to upend the entire attack unless Dockery and Shelby could reach the scene.

Cabell had fought frantically at one point launching an impetuous charge with his outgunned cavalry that morning to hold the ridge overwatching the Camden–Pine Bluff Road. Feeding his men into the fight as they came onto the ridge, he simultaneously sent couriers dashing back down the Warren Road to encourage Dockery to come up more quickly. One account states that the reason for Dockery's delay was his insistence that his brigade halt to forage its animals since they had not had the opportunity to do so the previous night. "Neither orders nor cannon shots seemed to disturb the equanimity which he [Dockery] always carried with him in battle," one observer noted. In addition to Dockery's intransigence, nature intervened again in this campaign as a downpour drenched the battlefield. This further slowed Dockery's movement to the attack position. In the meantime, Cabell made judicious use of fire support to pin the blue infantry down and silence the 10–pound rifles of Charles Peetz' battery. Placing Hughey's Battery on the left flank, the guns were able to bring a devastating fire on the Union soldiers near the road and suppress Peetz' guns.[22] Just when Fagan and Cabell felt their ability to hold had culminated, Dockery swung into line on Cabell's left and the van of Shelby's Division threatened the unsuspecting Drake's own left flank.

Dockery's Brigade approached the rear of Cabell's line and then filed off the road to the left. Using the ridge to screen his deployment, Dockery moved around to form on Cabell's dangling left flank. When he had organized his line, Dockery moved forward on foot in consonance with Cabell. The combination of the two brigades allowed the Confederates to overlap Drake's right by more than a regimental frontage. This stabilized the Confederate line while conversely placing Drake in a perilous situation.

Shelby's Brigade had about ten miles to move that morning to reach the vicinity of Marks' Mills. The sound of heavy firing greeted Jo Shelby as his men trotted down the Camden–Pine Bluff Road. This assured Shelby that the prey had not passed his position, but also filled him with fear that Fagan, with the other half of the Rebel force, might get overwhelmed. Shelby put spurs to his horse and encouraged his men to pick up the pace of their march in order to save Fagan from disaster.[23]

The firing grew louder as Shelby drew closer to the field of action. When about one mile from the head of the Federal train, he formed his division for a mounted charge. Shelby deployed Crawford's Brigade —commanded by Colonel John C. Wright —on the right side of the road and his own brigade, under Colonel David Shanks, on the left. Two regiments— the 5th and 12th Missouri —would constitute a reserve that would follow Wright's force north of the road. Finally, Shelby called Captain Richard Collins' Battery to come forward. He wanted two guns to occupy a point in the center of the line on the road to fire two blank charges. The shots would signal to Cabell that Shelby had arrived and would represent the moment for a simultaneous charge by both divisions.[24]

Collins signaled for his cannoneers to pull the lanyards and two clear shots echoed across the landscape. At the signal, Shelby initiated his charge and Cabell, hearing the report of the cannon, threw his line forward. Together they crushed all resistance around the train. Dockery's Brigade passed around the flank of the 43rd Indiana crashing right into the wagons parked on the side of the road. From here, Dockery wheeled to the right to roll up the Union infantry. Cabell's charge ran headlong into the teeth of Federal resistance, but threatened on both flanks, the Union forces melted away. Cabell's dismounted men "drove him ... through the train, capturing two pieces of artillery." Hughey's Confederate battery had done excellent work cutting down the artillery horses of Peetz' battery immobilizing the guns. As Cabell's wild troopers bore down on them the Federal infantry supports abandoned the battery. This panicked Peetz' gunners who deserted their guns in a disorderly retreat. While Cabell and Dockery placed irresistible pressure on Drake's defense, it was Shelby's charge that thoroughly unhinged the Federal line precipitating a rout. The 36th Iowa attempted to refuse its left flank to meet Shelby's onslaught, but the strength and speed of the attack was simply too much for the Federals. As General Fagan moved through the wreckage of the fight he encountered a wounded Francis Drake and promptly demanded the surrender of the remaining defenders.[25]

Drake was pleased to see how Norris succeeded in pushing Cabell back believing he would soon continue his movement unabated to Pine Bluff. Just at the moment it appeared that Drake's men had won the day, Dockery's Brigade deployed on Cabell's left. Drake reacted by placing the 36th Iowa on the left of the 43rd Indiana to lengthen his line while directing Captain Peetz to the center of the line holding his fire "until they were in close range." When the Rebels came in range the battery opened with great effect and the infantry "poured in a deadly volley of musketry.... The contest raged with unabated fury," until Shelby appeared in Drake's rear. The 77th Ohio had still not made it to the scene and the two infantry regiments, Peetz, and the few cavalry troopers braced for Shelby's charge. Drake ordered five companies of the 36th Iowa to bend back to the left to meet Shelby, but as already discussed, this measure was wholly inadequate. Soon after giving this order Drake received a severe wound to his leg. A subordinate noticed blood spilling from Drake's boot and asked him

"[A]re you severely wounded?" Drake replied positively and continued issuing orders before he passed out from loss of blood. Leaderless, the Federal units disintegrated with fugitives fleeing in all directions.[26] When Drake revived Fagan was standing over him requesting his surrender. Drake remained quite groggy as he attempted to comprehend what had happened. One thing he knew for certain was that he exercised very little control over anything. To Fagan, Drake replied that he no longer held command and that the Confederates would have to refer to someone else to force a capitulation. Fagan politely acknowledged Drake's predicament and called for his surgeon while Shelby and Cabell scooped up the fugitives.[27]

The 77th Ohio Infantry and 1st Iowa Cavalry represented the only organized Federal units in the vicinity of Marks' Mills. The 77th Ohio had not moved forward with as much energy as Drake had requested due to a mix up in orders. When they did reach the field they threatened to upset the Rebel triumph. Captain Andrew McCormick commanded the 77th Ohio along with a section of Peetz' Battery E, 2nd Missouri attached to his rear guard. As he approached the field McCormick noticed that Cabell's Division was in disarray as a result of their victory and an opportunity for a counterattack presented itself. McCormick quickly formed the regiment in line of battle using the road as his axis of advance and with the two guns centered on the regiment. Once the regiment was formed, McCormick fixed bayonets and charged up the Camden-Pine Bluff Road landing a blow squarely on Cabell's flank sending the division reeling. The assault fell predominantly on Colonel James C. Monroe's 1st Arkansas Cavalry, who struggled to change front to face the enemy attack from an unexpected quarter. The momentary success of the 77th dissolved as Shelby's troopers bore down on the Ohioans. McCormick's men held solid for a few minutes until they received a surprise of their own. Major J. H. Harrell's Arkansas Battalion had been on rear security when his pickets caught sight of the newly arrived Federals. Grasping the situation, Harrell took the initiative to form his unit and swing it around to the rear of the 77th. When Harrell's men announced their presence with a shrill yell, the Ohioans lost heart and surrendered ignominiously. A dispute soon erupted between Dockery and Cabell's men over who should have the credit for taking Peetz' guns, but the engagement was largely at an end.[28]

The veteran troopers of the 1st Iowa had marched along in anticipation of their first furlough since enlisting three years earlier. As a part of their reenlistment contract, all veterans who signed up for another hitch would receive a 30–day veterans' furlough. These cavalrymen proceeded to Pine Bluff on foot because their horses were in no condition to make the trip to Pine Bluff and the army needed all its animals for transport. They left Camden on the 23rd and were to catch up with Drake's column before nightfall. The 1st failed to reach Drake in large part because of their being unaccustomed to making hard marches. Nevertheless, by morning of the 25th the veteran soldiers were closing in on the rear of Drake's column when they heard the unmistakable sounds of battle. As they approached the Moro Swamp "a most demoralized crowd of cotton speculators, sutlers, refugees, teamsters, etc., mounted on mules and horses dashed past." Close on their heels were elements of Confederate cavalry pursuing the defeated fugitives from Marks' Mills. Lieutenant Colonel Joseph Caldwell immediately placed his troopers, 520 battle experienced men, in line of battle to meet the onrush of Rebels.[29]

The Iowans held a decided advantage in that they held the far side of the Moro Creek bridge, which the attacking Rebels had to cross to come to grips with the Union soldiers. The Rebels from Shelby's command attempted to carry the bridge, but a concentrated volley prevented them from crossing. The Rebels did take some prisoners from the Union skirmish line including one Lieutenant Silas R. Nugen. The Confederates immediately interrogated the lieutenant in an attempt to determine the size and disposition of the Federal force at the bridge. In answer to their questions, Nugen stated that the 1st Iowa represented "the advance of General Steele's army." This revelation diluted the Rebels' enthusiasm for making another assault. Nugen's misinformation probably saved the 1st Iowa from a southern prison and happily ensured they would take their leave, albeit at a later date, for the Confederates called off their assault. Caldwell now countermarched back to Camden. Taking up successively strong positions as they reversed course, the 1st Iowa made it back to Camden without further incident. Charles Lothrop, regimental surgeon, remarked that the dismounted cavalrymen moved an astonishing fifty miles that day, an impressive march for men who normally had their mobility provided by horses.[30]

When the 1st Iowa encamped exhausted opposite Camden it was the first intimation Steele had of the disaster at Marks' Mills. The extent of the defeat exceeded the debacle of Poison Spring in terms of transportation and personnel and it cast a dark cloud over the high command and soldiers of the Union army. The Confederates brought approximately 4,000 soldiers to Marks' Mills of which about 2,500 were engaged when detachments for horseholders and flank guards are factored in. Of these, Fagan lost only 41 killed, 108 wounded, and 144 missing for a total of 293 casualties. The Federals, on the other hand, lost an estimated 1,500 men of approximately 1,800 engaged, most of whom were captured including the seriously wounded Francis Drake. In addition, Drake's train guard lost all its artillery and 240 wagons in a three-hour fight.[31]

As the Confederates inventoried the spoils, they took great delight in pillaging the contents of the sutlers' wagons. These contained sumptuous delicacies the Rebels had not seen for some time. Shelby's men made a "great haul" of Union greenbacks from the army paymaster and cotton speculators. The gray troopers were angered to find a great deal of personal belongings of families that lay along the Camden-Pine Bluff Road. These included furniture, bedding, jewelry, and family heirlooms. Many of the "women all along the road for miles back came on horseback to identify their belongings."[32] Together with Poison Spring, Marks' Mills represented a catastrophe for the Union army west of the Mississippi, one that would cause abandonment of the Camden Expedition.

Once again rumors of Confederate atrocities arose in official reports and memoirs as they had after Poison Spring. Francis Drake stated in his report that "a large number of negroes and Arkansas refugees ... were inhumanly butchered by the enemy, and among them my own negro servant." Confederate Major John Edwards, an aide to Shelby, confirmed that, "the battlefield was sickening to behold. No orders, threats, or commands could restrain the men from vengeance on the negroes...."[33] Such vindictiveness only added insult to the injury inflicted on Union arms. Worse than insult, the defeat at Marks' Mills had a demoralizing effect on the army.

Andrew Sperry recorded with disgust the fact that the outgoing Union mail became a casualty of Marks' Mills. The Federal soldiers at Camden had pored over their letters to loved ones in the days before the train pulled out. Now the Rebels "had a good time in reading over the words of love and hope, or the expressions of our opinions as to the situation." The stragglers from Marks' Mills trickled in over the next couple of days telling stories reminiscent of Poison Spring. Soldiers congregated around campfires discussing the latest disaster and the relative intelligence of their senior commanders.[34] One can imagine the caustic discussions that raced through regiments that evening. While the troops debated, Steele requested a report from his chief quartermaster to assess the possibility of sustaining a continuation of the expedition.

Captain Henry submitted a distressing estimate of the current situation and an assessment that the army could not stay in its present position or advance without an immediate infusion of forage and supplies. Henry stated that the army had lost the entire wagon train of 211 vehicles in the engagement at Marks' Mills. Further, the army had lost over 2,000 animals since the commencement of the campaign and those that remained were in poor condition. Henry counted 9,000 horses and mules in the transportation pool and estimated that he could secure forage for only 1,000 due to the "present impoverished condition in this part of the state." He concluded the report with a polite admonition that the commanding general must "give this question of supplying forage your immediate and earnest attention."[35] The crisis of the expedition had arrived and Steele knew it required an immediate decision to extract the army from pending disaster.

Frederick Steele decided to convene a council of his officers to solicit their opinions as to the possibility of continuing the campaign. Steele wasted no time in assembling his commanders, calling them together late on the evening of the 25th just hours after the engagement at Marks' Mills. One by one the generals arrived at headquarters and waited for the commanding general to enter. John Thayer, Frederick Salomon, Eugene Carr, and Samuel Rice were quietly discussing the army's predicament when Steele entered the room. Steele started the council by providing a synopsis of events over the past week and by reading Henry's analysis of the quartermaster situation. Next, Steele provided the latest intelligence to the generals.[36]

Steele had sent out numerous patrols and scouts to assess the disposition of Price's army and to confirm or deny the veracity of rumors racing through Camden about the arrival of reinforcements. Many of the local citizens had openly taunted the Union soldiers with statements about how inbound Confederate infantry divisions would soon turn the tables on the Federals and send them running or capture them outright. Several of the parties had succeeded in taking a number of prisoners from various Confederate outfits. From interrogation the Confederates revealed the fact that they belonged to at least three separate infantry divisions. Estimates placed Rebel strength at around 6,000 mounted men and between 8 and 10,000 infantry.[37] The Federal army by comparison had now less than 10,000 men of all arms, a severed line of communication, and currently only one line of retreat. The Rebels had them hemmed in on three sides in the fortifications surrounding Camden and the only way to continue south meant a climactic battle with a larger, fresh Confederate army. Further, the Rebels had high morale as a result of their stunning victories in both Louisiana and Arkansas and they were anxious to come to grips with Steele's emaciated force in Camden. Prospects for Union success, indeed, did not favor prolonging the campaign or continuing to the Red River.

Steele stated that he believed that the changed situation required an immediate retrograde movement to save the army. Steele understood that he did not have authorization to abandon the expedition, but he believed the circumstances dictated that he must preserve the army rather than continue on a forlorn hope. The Federal commander must have known that tremendous criticism would come his way from such a decision inside and outside of the army. This may have been why Steele wanted the opinions of his officers in a public forum. If they all agreed that continuing south was hopeless, Steele could then deflect some of the expected barbs. Therefore, in addition to requesting a public statement, Steele had each man submit his thoughts in writing for the record. His generals did not let him down and provided full support in an admirable show of loyalty.

Fred Salomon started by expressing in positive terms that the VII Corps "must fall back to the line of the Arkansas, and that the movement should commence at once." He added, "[T]o go out and fight the enemy would only cripple us, and if supplies are exhausted we have no means to get more." The conversation now moved to Eugene Carr, the feisty cavalry commander. Up front he concurred with Steele and offered that "Kirby Smith has evidently no further fear of General Banks." Therefore, he was now concentrating on Steele in order to "pass to our rear and cut us off." In essence, Salomon and Carr believed that Smith intended nothing less than the destruction of the VII Corps. Further, he had the Federal army in a box that he would soon enough close the lid on if the Unionists did not move quickly. Thayer stated that he favored "falling back ... at least by tomorrow night" lest the Rebels encircle the army and force its capitulation.[38]

The only dissenting opinion came from Samuel Rice, Salomon's First Brigade commander. Rice had a reputation of being perhaps the most combative general in the army. Rather than commencing a retreat, Rice wanted to move to the east to Hampton destroying the bridges over the Ouachita and taking up a strong position to draw the Rebels into a disadvantageous battle. Rice seems to have believed that the Union army could still rebuild its strength and break through to the Red River. However, he said that should this prove impractical the army should then "go toward the Arkansas."[39]

Steele did not take long to deliberate for he delivered a verdict before the meeting broke. He wrote in his report:

> If we had been supplied at Camden I could have held the place against Kirby
> Smith's entire force, but on learning that my communications were effectually
> [*sic*] interrupted, and that the line of the Arkansas was threatened by so large
> a force of the enemy, I decided to fall back at once.[40]

Based on his decision Steele issued verbal orders for the army to make preparations for a retreat. All baggage and ammunition would be quietly loaded during the 26th on the remaining transport assets. The troops would stay in position until nightfall and then commence a crossing of the river under cover of darkness. The decision to retreat gave Steele a great deal of consternation, yet under the circumstances there is little else he could have done without losing his army. Besides, his effort had already saved Banks' army to fight another day when it most certainly should have perished.

The key subordinates dutifully supported their commander publicly, but privately an undercurrent of disapproval became evident in writings after the war. Mid-level officers recorded most of these memoirs and their criticisms of Steele are scathing. While the senior officers—Salomon, Thayer, and Carr—suppressed any criticism of the commanding general, one may surmise that the musings of their subordinates at least in part reflected the opinions of the division commanders. The two most prominent examples of dissension arose from the pens of Captain Frederick Heineman, staff officer to General Salomon, and Colonel Samuel J. Crawford, regimental commander in Thayer's Frontier Division. Heineman in his war diary goes out of his way to accuse Steele of hard-headedness, sloth, and cowardice. After Poison Spring he ranted that "Steele ... doesn't appear to know anything about Arkansas, where he is or what he thinks of doing. Damn these regulars!" The debacle at Marks' Mills moved him to say, "I think Steele will realize ... that some of our citizen soldiers know more at times than a West Point book." Finally, he alleges that "we all join without a dissenting voice" in condemning Steele for his conduct of the Camden Expedition.[41]

The fiery commander of the 2nd Kansas (Colored), Colonel Crawford, minced no words in his assessment of Steele's generalship. He alternately described the expedition as "disgraceful" and "humiliating." In a final summary of the campaign, Crawford pronounced it a "gigantic failure. Had General Thayer, General Carr, General Rice, Colonel Cloud or any one of a dozen officers in the corps been in command, he would have been thundering at the gates of Shreveport before a gun had been levelled [*sic*] at General Banks's army."[42]

The assessments of Heineman and Crawford are simply emotional ravings that stand empty of intelligent analysis of the true situation. Both men ignore the reality that the army could not feed the men or animals. No amount of determination or outpouring of emotion could make up for the fact that the army had inadequate transportation, operated in a country denuded of forage, and had an aggressive enemy in front and rear. It is very likely that if Steele had attempted what Heineman and Crawford proposed, the VII Corps would have been destroyed in detail. These men in subordinate positions, while certainly not on the inside at corps headquarters, must have known the army's predicament. Yet, they chose to discount the significance of the logistical problems for their own purposes. Thayer, Carr, and Salomon may have shared the opinion of their officers, but did not leave anything to the record. This is of great credit to each officer for loyalty is an intangible of unit cohesion that sharpens the fighting edge, especially in times of great stress. Had the division commanders publicly adopted the stance of their underlings, it would have had a corrosive effect on the army. This did not happen and although the army lost much in material and personnel, the VII Corps, on the whole, remained intact when the expedition ended only days later.

The Union army at Camden would now begin an ignominious retreat that mortified many in the ranks. However, the worst of the expedition was yet to come. The VII Corps would fight a major battle — the biggest of the entire campaign — march through rain and knee-deep mud, and suffer acute hunger that would test the hardiest of souls. What these men did not know was that their efforts had extracted the 30,000 men of the Army of the Gulf and the Mississippi Squadron from a tight situation. The continuing exertions of Steele and his army ensured that Kirby Smith would not return to Louisiana in time to fulfill Richard Taylor's fondest wish, the destruction of General Banks and his army.

Notes

1. *OR*, Vol. 34, Part 3, 768–771.

2. Joseph P. Blessington, *Walker's Texas Division*, 242–243.

3. Bearss, *Steele's Retreat From Camden*, 49 and 51 and *OR*, Vol. 34, Part 1, 481.

4. *Ibid.*, 534 and 541 and Blessington, *Walker's Texas Division*, 244.

5. *OR*, Vol. 34, Part 1, 581 and 788.

6. *Ibid.*, 789 and 835 and Bearss, *Steele's Retreat From Camden*, 51–52

7. *Ibid.*, 55–56; *OR*, Vol. 34, 680, 688, and 712; F. M. Drake, *War Sketches and Incidents of Iowa*, I, "Campaign of General Steele," 66; and Richards, "The Engagement of Marks' Mills," *AHQ* (Spring 1960), 54–55.

8. Drake, *War Sketches and Incidents*, I, "Campaign of General Steele," 66.

9. *Ibid.*; Lothrop, *History of the First Iowa Cavalry*, 162–163; and *OR*, Vol. 34, Part 1, 663.

10. *Ibid.*, 712.

11. *Ibid.*, 721–713.

12. *Ibid.* and Lothrop, *History of the First Iowa Cavalry*, 163.

13. *Ibid.*; Drake, *War Sketches and Incidents*, I, 67; and Richards, "The Engagement at Marks' Mills," *AHQ* (Spring 1960), 56–57.

14. *OR*, Vol. 34, Part 1, 788; Bearss, *Steele's Retreat From Camden*, 62–63; and Richards, "The Engagement at Marks' Mills," *AHQ* (Spring 1960), 55–56.

15. *OR*, Vol. 34, Part 1, 788–789 and 835.

16. *Ibid.*

17. *Ibid.*, 793.

18. Drake, *War Sketches and Incidents*, I, "Campaign of General Steele," 68–69.

19. *Ibid.*; *OR*, Vol. 34, Part 1, 772; and Bearss, *Steele's Retreat From Camden*, 61.

20. *Ibid.*, 61–62 and *OR*, Vol. 34, Part 1, 713.

21. Drake, *War Sketches and Incidents*, I, "The Campaign of General Steele," 68–69 and Richards, "The Engagement at Marks' Mills," *AHQ* (Spring 1960), 58.

22. *Ibid.*; *OR*, Vol. 34, Part 1, 793–794; Evans, ed., *Confederate Military History*, X, 254; and Edwards, *Shelby and His Men*, 278.

23. *OR*, Vol. 34, Part 1, 793 and 835; Evans, ed., *Confederate Military History*, X, 254; and Edwards, *Shelby and His Men*, 278.

24. *Ibid.*, and *OR*, Vol. 34, Part 1, 835–836.

25. *Ibid.*, 789, 794, and 836; Edwards, *Shelby and His Men*, 279; and Drake, *War Sketches and Incidents*, I, "Campaign of General Steele," 70.

26. *OR*, Vol. 34, Part 1, 713–714 and Drake, *War Sketches and Incidents*, I, "Campaign of General Steele," 70.

27. *Ibid.*, 71–72.

28. *OR*, Vol. 34, Part 1, 717 and 796 and Bearss, *Steele's Retreat From Camden*, 73–74.

29. Lothrop, *History of the First Iowa Cavalry*, 163.

30. *Ibid.*, 164.

31. *OR*, Vol. 34, Part 1, 665 and 787. Confederate reports noted in the *OR* are incomplete and the Federal totals are estimated by Colonel Powell Clayton two days after the fight.

32. Evans, ed., *Confederate Military History*, X, 260 and Bearss, *Steele's Retreat From Camden*, 78.

33. *OR*, Vol. 34, Part 1, 714–715 and Edwards, *Shelby and His Men*, 279.

34. Sperry, *History of the 33rd Iowa*, 91–92.

35. *OR*, Vol. 34, Part 1, 683.

36. Bearss, *Steele's Retreat From Camden*, 87–89.

37. *OR*, Vol. 34, Part 1, 676–677.

38. *Ibid.*, 671.

39. *Ibid.*

40. *Ibid.*, 668.

41. Elliot, ed., *The Garden of Memory*, "Diary of Capt. Heineman, U. S. A.," 76 and 78.

42. Crawford, *Kansas in the Sixties*, 113–114 and 134.

9

"There was no dry place to lie down"

The Union army began to make preparations to evacuate Camden on April 26. The retrograde to Little Rock was the point at which the Yankees were most vulnerable to annihilation during the Camden Expedition. The Rebels had successfully stymied Federal attempts to reach the Red River in support of Banks' army in Louisiana. They did this by capitalizing on the major liability of the Union army, the rickety logistics situation. Having forced the VII Corps to turn back to Little Rock, the Rebel high command had two possible courses of action. First, Kirby Smith could attempt to destroy Steele as his haggard column struggled northward to the line of the Arkansas. Or, he could merely shadow Steele with a small force and turn back to Louisiana with the bulk of Price's army to finish off a cornered Nathaniel P. Banks on the Red River. Smith's decision would have far reaching effects beyond the confines of his remote department and was heavily influenced by the dispositions of his primary subordinates, Sterling Price and Richard Taylor.

Following the council of war, Steele issued instructions for the army to prepare to retreat on April 26th after dusk. The poor condition of the public animals required that the army would have to abandon much of its supplies. Rather than leave valuable stores to the enemy, Steele ordered the destruction of all wagons and supplies that the army could not move. Steele's headquarters sent out orders in the early morning hours of the 26th to all divisions to prepare for movement that evening. Captain Henry received details of soldiers from the several divisions to assist in the business of destroying excess baggage.[1] Imperative to their efforts on the 26th was operational security. The Federals had to go to great lengths to conceal the purpose of their activities. With the large Rebel army hovering outside the Camden fortifications, any sign of a hasty evacuation could bring about an attack, upsetting Union plans.

Captain Henry and the rest of the VII Corps expertly handled their instructions as the citizens of Camden failed to perceive fully the purpose of Federal work details that day. To deceive the town folk Captain Henry moved the army trains in small packages across the Ouachita rather than massing them for movement. Additionally,

139

he assembled those wagons earmarked for destruction at different locations. Just prior to the time of movement, he would commence destruction so the citizens would have little time to relay word to the Confederates outside the city. The chief quartermaster also issued what rations he had available in a manner that appeared as the normal routine since the army arrived in Camden. This scanty fare amounted to two pieces of hardtack, a half-pint of cornmeal, a small portion of meat, and a few beans of coffee per man. This would have to suffice the soldiers for the entire march to Little Rock.[2]

The ruse the Federal soldiers created worked beyond all expectation, as many of the populace had no inkling that the occupying army was preparing to leave. "I was not wise enough to know that General Steele's whole army was going that very night," recalled one resident.[3] Private Sperry stated that word of the retreat was withheld from many in the ranks as well. The 33rd Iowa received orders for a night march in the early afternoon and began quietly packing up.[4] In spite of Federal efforts to keep the planned retrograde a secret, a few observant residents did take note of unusual activities in town on the 26th. Steele had foreseen that word would leak out and took the precaution of closing Camden to civilian movement for the day in order to prevent anyone from alerting the Confederates. Nevertheless, one man attempted to slip through the lines to notify the Rebels. Union pickets shot him on the spot for violating Steele's order.[5]

The deception continued into the evening as the army went about its normal routine. Regiments conducted changing of guards, sounded tattoo and taps, and kindled cooking fires. Meanwhile, the business of destroying excess supplies and baggage started shortly after dusk. Details of soldiers fired ninety-two wagons, tents, mess kits, and astonishingly, a large quantity of meat and hardtack. Obviously, some provision should have been made to distribute the remaining foodstuffs in light of the dire lack of rations prevailing among the ranks and the hard march in the offing. Regardless, the chief quartermaster managed to systematically liquidate everything of value while simultaneously moving the army trains over the Ouachita. Once the trains and rear echelon troops had cleared the river, the combat units began to fall in for the start of the march.[6]

Shortly after taps at about 9:00 P.M., the army commenced its movement. Steele assigned Carr's cavalry division to lead the march providing a screen forward of the army to protect the main body from Fagan's cavalry. Thayer's Frontier Division would follow Carr as soon as his troopers had cleared the pontoon bridge over the Ouachita. Salomon's division would constitute the rear guard. Critical to success of the retrograde was the security provided by Salomon to the very last minute. During the entire rearward movement Salomon would show himself more than equal to the task of protecting the rear of the army. On this night he initially doubled the picket posts to ensure no lapse of security. Second, he assigned the recently attached 2nd and 6th Kansas Cavalry Regiments to conduct patrols in Camden to prevent any depredations against the local population. Finally, he assigned Adolph Englemann the mission to contract the perimeter as the rear guard covered the final retreat across the river. All in all, Steele's choice of Salomon was a wise one, as the army evacuated Camden without tipping its hand to the Confederate sentries outside the city.[7]

Carr's cavalry intended to reach a point well beyond the range of direct observation of the town, easily defensible, and with forage and water in immediate proximity. The crossing of the cavalry was completed in the early evening hours of the 26th. Thayer's division began crossing the pontoons within minutes of Carr's unit and had cleared the bridgehead just before midnight. At this point, Salomon started Rice's brigade over the bridge and the efficient colonel pushed his four regiments to the far side of the river in a timely manner. Meanwhile, Salomon left the 40th Illinois on the near bank of the river to protect Junius Wheeler's pioneers as they broke down the pontoons. This was the most agonizing process of the whole evacuation as the engineers had to pull up and load planking, and stringers, and deflate the India rubber rafts that provided buoyancy to the bridge. Englemann and Salomon worried that the Rebels would attempt to rush the bridgehead while the engineers worked to clear the area.[8]

Nevertheless, the evacuation came off "to its last soldier without confusion or accident."[9] However, the precautions Salomon took to safeguard the population was not entirely successful. The inevitable stragglers would give Salomon's provost guard fits in preventing them from visiting outrages. Mrs. Stinson reported that after dusk the Yankees revealed their intent to pull out. As these revelations came out troublemakers "threatened to burn the town before they left." Further, "the Yankees began shooting my chickens and they kept it up until they had killed every chicken.... What a night of terror it was."[10] Even with such incidents, Camden survived the evacuation relatively unscathed in contrast to the destruction Banks' army perpetrated when they pulled out of Alexandria, Louisiana.[11] More importantly the Federal VII Corps evacuated literally under the nose of a larger Confederate army that failed to discover the occurrence.

Kirby Smith assumed direct command of the Confederate army only days before the Federal evacuation. One reason he took direct control of the army was his dissatisfaction with Price's handling of affairs thus far. While Price had stopped Steele's advance, a lack of energy marked his operations and Smith found this unacceptable. To step up the pressure on Steele, Smith had personally ordered Fagan on his raid that resulted in the victory at Marks' Mills. Yet, Smith's effort to instill greater vigilance failed as the entire VII Corps pulled out of Camden without the Rebels suspecting anything was afoot. Price reported hearing word of the evacuation sometime before 9:00 A.M. as his advance guard "liberated" the town at that time. By the time Price's men arrived there, Steele's army was already over an hour up the road to Little Rock. Further, the Confederates had no way to cross the Ouachita. As mentioned earlier, Smith had ordered his pontoon bridge north angering Richard Taylor. However, by some mismanagement the engineers had received orders to halt and return to Shreveport.[12] The error was not discovered until it was too late on the morning of the 27th and the Rebels were immobilized on the south side of the river.

The Confederates now attempted to improvise a crossing as Steele's army increased its lead over the hapless graybacks. Smith, upon learning of Steele's escape, immediately ordered a pursuit of the Federal army. In response, Price's men began construction of a rickety raft bridge using timbers from the scuttled steamer *Homer*. Orders went out to the infantry divisions to move to Camden and await completion of the bridge preparatory to conducting a vigorous pursuit. Dr. Junius N. Bragg of the 33rd Arkansas, Churchill's Arkansas Division, recorded the excitement that raced through the Rebel camp that morning. At noon, "a citizen came out and brought the information that the enemy had evacuated Camden." Immediately the camp was bustling with activity as the division prepared for a forced march to catch Steele. The 33rd Arkansas cooked three days' rations and loaded a minimal number of wagons with supplies of ordnance and foodstuffs to accompany the unit. By early afternoon Churchill's men had left their bivouac and marched into Camden to assemble for the river crossing.[13] Construction of the raft bridge proceeded at a snail's pace since all the materials were improvised. Interminable delays occurred as Price's men scrounged for logs, planking, and stringers. Price's ad hoc pioneers did not complete the bridge until late that night forcing the Confederates to delay the pursuit until the next morning.

Walker's Texas Division had just arrived in the vicinity of Camden on the 26th as Steele's army was making preparations to leave. The soldiers had hoped to spend the day resting and recovering from the long march from Shreveport. The sudden evacuation of the Federal army dashed these hopes when orders arrived to pursue the fleeing Yankees. Sergeant Joseph Blessington remembered hastily cooking three days' rations and packing his gear for yet another forced march. About mid-afternoon the Texans moved out arriving in Camden at four o'clock. Since they could not press on Walker's men assembled near Churchill's troops by the Ouachita waiting for completion of the floating bridge. Knowing it would take all night to complete the bridge, Blessington and his comrades used the respite to gather some much needed rest before commencing the pursuit. However, some troops milled around the town inspecting the fortifications surrounding Camden. Blessington was so impressed with the apparent strength of the earthworks that he stated "we should have had some difficulty in taking it [Camden]."[14] Indeed, a direct Rebel assault on Camden could have only resulted in a long casualty list.

As the infantry huddled around the bridgehead on the Ouachita, Smith sought to mobilize the cavalry for immediate pressure on the retreating Federals. The most promising possibility was for Fagan's large contingent to get in front of Steele on the Military Road blocking his way back to Little Rock. Fagan's men had spent the 26th clearing the battlefield at Marks' Mills and scouting the Saline River crossings. As Fagan policed the battlefield, he pondered how he could find food for his force. The captured wagon train contained very little booty in the way of foodstuffs and Fagan had not made provisions to sustain his division beyond the ambush at Marks' Mills. Following the successful action at the mills, Fagan had orders to proceed to Little Rock to harass Steele's logistics base. However, Fagan felt that the pressing supply situation demanded that he place first priority on finding sustenance for his troopers and mounts. Having no inkling that Steele was preparing to leave Camden, Fagan resolved to move west to Princeton on the Military Road in search of forage, ironically in perfect position to block Steele's retreat up that route.[15] Jo Shelby was quite disturbed by what he perceived as a distinct lack of drive in Fagan. According to his biographer, Shelby believed the disaster at Marks' Mills would force Steele to retreat back to Little Rock. Thus, he believed that Fagan should either attempt to move closer to Camden to establish communication with Kirby Smith or aggressively cross the Saline and emplace blocking positions on possible crossing sites Steele might use in a retreat.[16] In spite of Shelby's effort, Fagan opted to search for food around Princeton.

Kirby Smith recognized these possibilities and attempted to send a dispatch to Fagan ordering him to block the crossings over the Saline. The problem is that Smith had no idea where to have the message delivered since he had lost contact with his subordinate. The only alternative was to send several couriers in various directions hoping to catch Fagan in time to counter Steele's retreat. Meanwhile, Smith set Marmaduke's well-rested troopers into action telling him to proceed to a place called White Hall, a known ford site, and from there proceed with all possible speed to cut off Steele's flight. Marmaduke's Division, with Colton Greene in the lead, reached White Hall around 5:00 P.M. and attempted to ford the river. The river was running at a high stage due to the incessant rains of late and the process took longer than expected. To speed the movement up, Greene obtained two small boats to ferry his troops and artillery to the far shore. The animals were forced to swim to the opposite bank. The combination of ferrying and swimming took all night to complete and Greene's troopers did not begin an all out pursuit until 6:00 A.M. on the 28th.[17] Yet, another unit spent the day hung up by the formidable obstacle of the Ouachita providing Steele precious time to widen the gap between his fleeing corps and the anxious Rebels.

In addition to Smith's efforts to marshal his forces for pursuit, he issued a curious order that weakened his army at a time when he needed every man he could lay his hands on. On April 28 Smith instructed Maxey's small division to return to the Indian Territory. Allegedly, the Federals under Major General James G. Blunt planned an operation to wrest control of the region from the Rebels once and for all. Talk of Blunt's thrust into the Indian Territory proved false, but Smith nevertheless persisted in sending away one quarter of his mounted force as he simultaneously attempted to catch Steele. Pursuit is a mission best suited for a cavalry division and yet Smith issued orders returning them back to their district. It seems plausible that a sound defeat of Steele would have arrested any offensive in the Indian Territory since the Federals would have had to consolidate strength to stop an inevitable counteroffensive. Edwin Bearss points out in his narrative that it is hard to imagine anything in the backwater Indian Territory "important enough to justify this drastic reduction" of the cavalry.[18] The order returning Maxey westward represents one of a series of blunders committed by Kirby Smith as he assumed command in Arkansas. As the pursuit progressed the effect of his decisions would only compound as the Rebels struggled to come to grips with the Federals.

By 9:00 A.M. on April 27, Steele had made a clean break unfettered by the pursuit of any Rebels. To enhance his getaway, he had a major obstacle in his rear that would delay Kirby Smith for another 24 hours—the Ouachita River. The Federal commander had slipped away with an entire army corps without alerting the Confederates of his intent, which is no small feat. Steele's management of the movement thus far had been nothing short of brilliant as he had stolen a full day's march on his opponent. The opportunity to catch a retreating column on the march often portends destruction for the fleeing army and is a rare occurrence and the Confederates seemed intent on frittering away their chances. Kirby Smith's management of affairs was dismal to the point of incompetence. First, by an unexplained mix up his pioneers had sent the precious pontoon bridge back to Shreveport where it was useless. Second, despite an effort to encourage more vigilance from Price's command, the Rebel pickets had allowed the Federals to escape from under their very noses. Third, after sending Fagan in pursuit of the Federal supply train, Smith had lost all contact with half his cavalry. Fourth, while desperately grasping for any way to place pressure on the fleeing Yankees, he ordered Maxey's mounted men back to the Indian Territory effectively reducing his cavalry force by one quarter. This left Smith with only Marmaduke's single brigade under his direct control, not nearly enough to slow Steele. Finally, the agonizingly slow process of improvising a floating bridge served to delay the army as effectively as if they had attempted a contested crossing. So far, Smith, a highly competent commander in earlier campaigns in the Civil War, had not lived up to his reputation. However, nature would intervene once again allowing the Rebels to make good their earlier mistakes.

As Smith's Arkansas contingent struggled to catch Frederick Steele, events in Louisiana were quickly reaching a climax. Following the Battle of Pleasant Hill on April 9, Banks pulled his army back to his advanced supply base at Grand Ecore. Admiral Porter's fleet received word of the reverse near Loggy Bayou about thirty miles short of Shreveport. Distressed, Porter ordered the navy to turn about and rendezvous with Banks at Grand Ecore. At this time Richard Taylor and Kirby Smith held their conferences and quarreled about the next phase of the campaign. Taylor favored an immediate pursuit of Banks aimed at the destruction of the Union army and by default the navy. Smith leaned toward allowing Banks to retreat unmolested from Louisiana and instead proposed shifting the bulk of Taylor's forces north to stop Steele's advance. Smith believed Steele represented the true threat to the Trans-Mississippi and Taylor's tone had undoubtedly irritated Smith. Price, on the other hand, had given Smith cheerful cooperation throughout, encouraging the commanding general to reciprocate support. As a result, on April 14 Smith ordered three of Taylor's four infantry divisions north to Arkansas without Taylor.

As Smith proceeded to Arkansas, the reeling Army of the Gulf presented Taylor with three distinct opportunities for destruction or capture. First, Taylor invested Grand Ecore with a loose cordon temporarily trapping Banks against the Red River. But, Banks outnumbered Taylor by a margin of over five to one and the Army of the Gulf easily brushed the Rebels aside as they retraced their steps to Alexandria. The next chance occurred on April 23rd as the Union moved through a narrow strip of land ensconced by the Cane and Red Rivers. The unique geography of this region served to pin the Federals into a trap if only Taylor could engage the spring. He did manage to move his paltry force into position to command the potential escape routes, but the Federals simply overpowered him. By the 25th — the same day of the disaster at Marks' Mills— Banks was back at Alexandria manning the city defenses. This was the final opportunity that Taylor had to destroy Banks and it was a major chance to discomfit the Yankees. This is because the Union navy could not proceed below the falls due to low water. In contrast to the incessant rains in Arkansas, Louisiana was experiencing a prolonged period of dry weather that caused the Red to drop far below seasonable levels. The army therefore, could not continue the retreat lest the navy fall to Taylor's Confederates. However, Taylor's infantry-starved army handcuffed him at this juncture.[19]

Taylor once again attempted to hem in the Army of the Gulf with a loose investment on the 28th of April. While he made these dispositions, he began a written campaign to plead for more troops for his command to ensure Banks' destruction. Taylor wrote to General John B. Magruder, District of Texas, Governor Henry W. Allen of Louisiana, and Kirby Smith describing his want of adequate troops. From the tone of his dispatches it is obvious that Taylor was irritated by his inability to finish off Banks. His letters are laced with barbs at Smith, despair at sparse resources, and requests for more troops. Taylor knew that Alexandria was a golden opportunity and that as the loose siege protracted Banks would have time to extricate Porter's boats— work had already begun on a dam to raise the level of the Red — and proceed south in retreat.[20] Taylor simply had to have more troops to break up Banks' work in the river and seal him in without hope of an escape.

The only real hope Taylor had for realizing an accession to his force was for Smith to dispatch some of the precious infantry that he took from Taylor after Pleasant Hill back to Louisiana. For this to happen, Taylor would have to change the fundamental thinking of his commander. As we have seen, Smith fervently believed that Frederick Steele was the main threat to his department. Further, he seemed perfectly content to have Banks leave Louisiana unmolested while he and Price pummeled Steele to destruction. Therefore, it is extremely doubtful that Taylor could have altered Smith's course given his propensity to insult Smith while arrogantly offering his own alternative course of action. The question then arises, should Smith have continued to chase Steele after he left Camden or, should he have shifted forces for an attempt to run down Banks. Perhaps, John Walker answers this question best in his account of the campaign.

> Banks' army was no longer capable of offensive operations and such was the demoralization [of] the battles of Mansfield and Pleasant Hill.... Doubtless it was to have been expected that the whole Confederate force would have thrown itself upon the track of his flying army, but unfortunately for the Confederates, General E. K. Smith was not the leader to comprehend the true line of action ... against the opinion and advice of all his principal subordinates [obviously referring to Taylor and his entourage], he unwisely deter-

> mined to leave the pursuit of Banks ... and to dispatch Walker's Div., and the Missouri Div. of Parsons, and the Arkansas Div. of Churchill against the Federal army still at Camden under Steele.[21]

Taylor would not receive reinforcements because Smith had hardened in his resolve to close with Steele. There are three reasons for Smith's fixation on the much weaker VII Corps. First, and most significant, is that Grant's order forced Steele to commence the expedition and it had the intended effect. The threat the northern prong of the Red River Campaign posed forced a Confederate counteraction that relieved pressure on Banks. While the Camden Expedition did not ensure that Banks' thrust would be successful, it certainly saved Banks from disaster. Second, is Taylor's complete inability to exercise tact and good judgment in his relationship with his superior. Taylor's penchant for acerbic, direct criticism of Smith caused the commanding general to disregard Taylor's sound advice and a desire to distance himself from Taylor. Finally, Sterling Price had masterfully brought Kirby Smith around to his vision of present and future operations in the Trans-Mississippi Department. Price's willing cooperation with Smith and good-natured suggestions for the defense of Arkansas and the utility of a Missouri expedition made Smith amenable to Price's ideas. As a result of these factors, the Federal effort in Arkansas had accomplished its purpose by diverting attention away from Banks in Louisiana and ultimately saving the veteran Army of the Gulf from destruction.

The Federal army spent the 27th of April putting distance between themselves and the immobilized Confederates at Camden. Eugene Carr led the van of the Union army and he pressed the march with unrelenting fury fanning out on the flanks and front of the main body to protect it from Price's ever present mounted forces. By 10:00 A.M. Carr had already made about sixteen miles giving the army a good head start. Among his responsibilities this day was to maintain a keen eye out in search of forage to supplement the meager rations carried by the soldiers. Around midday Carr's scouts reported that they had discovered a large cache of corn about thirteen miles south of Princeton. Further, the area had "two or three small spring branches" making the place ideal for obtaining food, water, and some much needed rest after an exhausting 24 hours spent evacuating Camden. Carr quickly penned a note to Steele informing him of the find and recommending it as a spot suitable for a bivouac. After closing the dispatch he added a post-script stating succinctly, "no enemy seen or heard of."[22] This was indeed good news.

At the rear of the Union army were indicators of a precipitous withdrawal as the infantry jettisoned unwanted equipment as they tramped forward. Private Sperry reported that the hungry soldiers found their loads too much to bear and began littering the roadside. As the day progressed, knapsacks, coats, and articles of every description marked the path of the retreat. Luckily, the weather cooperated with the bluecoats as the 27th had dawned clear promising good conditions for a march. Nevertheless, many of the Yankees found the going hard. Though the march was a challenge, the rank and file were happy that the Rebels had so far failed to make a foray on the column on the move. But, even this seemed to set the men on edge as it spawned "rumors that the rebels had got between us and Little Rock."[23] The soldiers reasoned that since the Confederates did not hit the rear they must have moved to the front to block their route to Little Rock. The discussion continued throughout the day as the army arrived at the campsite Carr had selected earlier in the day.

The sun was beginning to descend on the western horizon when the tired army pulled into the bivouac. Upon arriving Carr turned over control of an estimated 1,500 bushels of corn that his cavalrymen had carefully gathered from local farmers. Captain Henry received the precious forage from Carr and quickly set priorities for distribution. Before any of the men received a kernel, Henry ensured that the draft animals were fed first. The animals were already in a weakened condition having suffered from the shortage of forage in southwest Arkansas. If Henry had lost control of the corn before feeding the animals it is quite likely they would not have been fed and would then have been unable to haul the artillery, pontoons, and supply wagons. After feeding the animals, Henry issued the remaining corn to the soldiers, a quantity quite inadequate for the need.[24]

Most soldiers were more content to get some sleep and forget about their hunger. While the soldiers went about their business, Steele issued strict orders that evening to wake the army at 4:00 A.M. on the 28th in order to continue north maintaining the considerable distance gained on the previous day. Promptly before dawn the buglers sounded reveille rousing the army for another day of hard marching. In contrast to the 27th, storm clouds began to gather in the west threatening to make the movement a miserable affair. It did not take the army long to assemble on the road and step off toward Little Rock. One soldier reported that it took an astounding 26 minutes for his brigade to form for the march. "Never before," he recalled, "had we seen such haste when a whole column was moving."[25]

The army retained the same divisional order of march as it continued to Little Rock. During the retreat Fred Salomon emphatically demonstrated his value as a division commander. Keenly aware of the strain of conducting a rear guard action, Salomon shuffled the march order of his division to ensure he could keep his brigades as fresh as possible. Englemann — who commanded the rear guard on the 27th — would lead the division while Samuel Rice would assume duty at the rear covering the retreat.[26] Salomon's judicious management of his unit throughout the retreat paid huge dividends for Frederick Steele only a couple of days later at Jenkins' Ferry. The corps made only eight miles on the 28th as they went into camp north of Princeton. It was about one in the afternoon when the Yankees swung through the quiet, "pleasant looking little town." The reason for the short march was the discovery of a herd of cattle that Captain Henry quickly appropriated for the army's consumption. The men happily filled their bellies that afternoon for the first time in several days. Unfortunately, the public animals did not fare as well since Henry failed to find a sufficient quantity of forage for them.[27]

As the bluecoats enjoyed their supper, a few wild-eyed survivors of the Marks' Mills fight wandered into camp. Their arrival touched off another round of rumors that the Rebels were surrounding the army and hovering for the kill. While the stories were not true, the Confederates were closing the gap the Yankees had opened on the 27th.[28] Further, Fagan's detached cavalry division was within a stone's throw of the VII Corps, just to the north on the Military Road, yet neither Steele nor Fagan knew of each other's presence. The lack of information and reliable intelligence available to the Confederates continued the comedy of errors that began with the graybacks' failure to ascertain the Federal evacuation of Camden. However, the early halt of the 28th allowed the hard driving Rebels to right their earlier mistakes and in retrospect it appears that Steele made a grave blunder by stopping for food rather than driving forward with the cattle in tow. If Smith could catch Steele on the move, block him, or catch him at a point of disadvantage — such as in crossing the Saline — there was the real potential that Smith could destroy the VII Corps. Such a turn of events would lay Missouri open to invasion and possibly mollify a disgruntled Richard Taylor in Louisiana.

The Rebels made it over the Ouachita at two points at around 6:00 A.M. on the 28th with Greene's cavalry and Churchill's infantry effecting crossings. Greene's mounted men swung into the road setting a torrid pace in an attempt to close the gap. Marmaduke's orders to Greene were to proceed by a circuitous route to a crossroad known as Buck Snort. From there Greene would place his brigade across the Military Road blocking it long enough to allow the slower infantry divisions to make contact with Steele's rear. Unfortunately, the Yankees had too much of a jump on the Rebels. Greene pushed his tired brigade hard for the next thirty hours pressing on through the night of the 28th. Greene reached a position north of Princeton on the 29th — just after an early departure by Steele. Signs of the recent passage of the Union army greeted Greene and his men. Discarded articles of every description littered the road and abandoned campsite. Aware that he had lost the race, Greene sent a short dispatch to Price informing him of the situation and pressed on now in pursuit of the Federal rear.[29]

Churchill's Division began crossing the floating bridge at Camden nearly simultaneously with Greene and his brigade. The crossing took an inordinate amount of time due to the flimsy nature of the bridge construction. Dr. Bragg reported, "the men could only walk in single file and ten feet apart" in order to prevent the bridge from giving way. "The crossing was tedious and slow," and as a result, it took several hours to complete the transfer of Churchill's men to the far side of the river. The Arkansans finally began moving up the Military Road at about noon bound for Princeton.[30] Parsons' and Walker's divisions followed Churchill closely coming over the bridge in the late afternoon. In order to achieve maximum speed, Kirby Smith restricted the impediments that could slow the infantry. He ordered only enough wagons to haul ordnance for battle and that each man would carry adequate rations and ammunition for three days. All the Confederates were confident of catching the fleeing Federals as they set a fast march pace that afternoon. In spite of the late start, the Confederates made seventeen miles on the 28th camping at the same point the Union army had used the previous night.[31] Since Steele had moved a mere eight miles on the 28th, the Confederates were miraculously within striking distance of the Federal VII Corps. It seems that Steele's decision to stop and feed his men north of Princeton had nullified the considerable head start he had achieved by the brilliant evacuation two days earlier.

As Smith's main body started rolling north, Fagan was moving west toward the Military Road from Pratt's Ferry. He struck the road in the early evening hours of the 28th and immediately sent out forage parties. Fagan reported after the expedition that he was astride the Military Road about 25 miles north of Princeton that night. This placed him only a few miles from Steele's army squarely across the enemy's route of escape. Fagan, however, was not aware of this important development and when his foragers failed to procure adequate provender for his horses he was unsure of his next move. Having not heard from Smith in several days and completely oblivious of Steele's plight, he decided to continue westward to Arkadelphia. Here, he hoped to communicate with Kirby Smith and obtain forage for his animals and troopers.[32] Fagan's move to Arkadelphia is arguably the pivotal tactical decision of the expedition. Shelby's biographer lamented that Fagan chose to continue westward rather than acceding to Shelby's suggestion that he close off "the only two roads open to Steele."[33] Had Fagan consented to block off the Military Road and Pine Bluff Roads, Steele would have found himself in a very tight predicament changing the entire dynamic of the retreat. When Fagan moved to the west on April 29 he unwittingly opened Steele's line of retreat. Only the weather could slow Steele now.

The Federals moved out at 4:00 A.M. on the 29th once again retaining the same order of march per General Steele's directive. Salomon continued his method of rotating brigades so that his rear guard would remain as fresh as possible under the circumstances. Englemann pulled rear guard preceded by Rice's brigade. As the Iowa troops moved north away from Princeton they found the country of the same pleasant character as their Iowa farms. The terrain "was more striking" than any "we had ever noticed in the South." The region provided the jaded Yankees with a much-needed change of pace. However, by noon the scenery was changing as well as the weather as the army began moving into the Saline Bottom. The Saline River is a sluggish stream that branches off the Ouachita. It is bordered on either side by an impenetrable bog extending a couple of miles from its banks. Carr's troopers reached the low swampland first and soon after rain began to fall, becoming incessant within minutes, slowing the march to a crawl. The cavalry and the trains began to churn up the road until it was indistinguishable from the swamp. This forced Junius Wheeler's pioneers to deploy forward to make the road passable.[34]

The Confederates started two hours earlier than the Federals in their attempt to close the final eight miles. Kirby Smith issued orders dictating that the army should rise at 2:00 A.M. to commence the pursuit. The groggy infantrymen rolled out of their blankets in the predawn darkness and it took about an hour to get the column rolling, but once they started the Confederates set a torrid pace. Sterling Price reported that the army marched 28 miles in spite of the fact that the rain turned the road into a quagmire. Blessington recorded that while his division made no contact with the enemy, they saw innumerable signs of recent enemy activity encountering "blackened ruins" and discarded gear. Obviously, the Federals were in a rush to escape the rapidly closing Rebels.[35]

The infantry divisions failed to engage, but Smith's cavalry finally made contact in the early afternoon. Marmaduke, with Greene's Brigade, had narrowly missed Steele's column the day before. He knew that without a force to block the head of the Federal column, the Confederates had to reach the rear guard or the Yankees would make good their escape. Therefore, Marmaduke assigned the 8th Missouri and Wood's cavalry battalion in the lead followed by the 3rd and 4th Missouri regiments. About mid-morning the Rebels finally caught sight of the fleeing bluecoats. The 8th Missouri began exchanging shots with the 6th Kansas, attached to Salomon's division, as the rain began. A running skirmish developed lasting all afternoon as the feisty Confederates attempted to break through to the Union main body. The efforts of the Missourians would go frustrated as Englemann deployed his brigade to stiffen the resistance of the Kansas troopers. The 40th Iowa, 43rd Illinois, 27th Wisconsin, and Springfield Light Artillery formed a line of battle that arrested the advance of the lightly armed Rebel cavalry. Greene attempted to throw in the 3rd and 4th Missouri along with Harris' Battery to bull through the determined Federals, but he drew off after a sharp engagement. Greene now called for additional help before he became involved in a battle he could not handle.[36]

Greene's disengagement ended the fighting for the day as each side took stock of the situation. Things did not look good for the Federal army at this juncture. Carr's cavalry reached Jenkins' Ferry on the Saline around 2:00 P.M. where the advance was arrested by the raging river. The level of the stream had remained high in recent weeks because of the heavy rains. Compounding the problem was the deluge that started shortly after midday and continued all afternoon into the evening. A quick reconnaissance by Carr convinced him that the Union army could not ford the Saline. The army would have to build a pontoon to effect a crossing and this would take time. Further, once constructed it would require several hours to push the force over the single span bridge.[37] The time required to construct the bridge would stall the retreat for about 24 hours and now the process would have to take place under Rebel pressure.

Carr reported his findings to Steele who made a quick assessment of the situation and began issuing orders for the next several hours' operations. Steele now realized that he had squandered the huge lead the army had built up on the 27th. The Rebels had closed a seventeen-mile gap with hard marches and now stood poised to land a hammer blow on the Federals pinned against a raging river. Nevertheless, sound deliberations and the energetic action of Steele would once again extricate the Federal army from a dangerous situation. First, he ordered Carr to proceed to Little Rock "as rapidly as possible by the shortest route" as soon as the pioneers completed the pontoon. The purpose of this was to sweep ahead of the main body to intercept Fagan's cavalry that was rumored to be lurking on the far side of the Saline. Next, he dictated that the army would consolidate the trains at the ferry in readiness to cross over the moment Carr cleared the bridge. Thayer's Frontier Division would provide near side security to the bridgehead and act as a reserve for Salomon. To Salomon fell the arduous duty of providing security for the army by deploying his division away from the river to enable the force to cross free of enemy action. Salomon understood that if required he would have to fight a full-scale engagement against the entire Confederate army to protect the Federals.[38] Steele assigned the right officers to each mission, particularly Salomon with the rear guard.

The Federal army began concentrating around Jenkins' Ferry in the Saline Bottom as scattered skirmishing continued in the early evening. Some of Captain Wheeler's engineers were busily corduroying the approaches to the ferry while the remainder toiled in constructing the vital pontoon bridge. Carr's cavalry fidgeted while awaiting the completion of the bridge so they could carry out Steele's latest order. Thayer's hardy Frontier Division cordoned the bridgehead and assembled strike columns for quick reinforcement of Salomon if required. Finally, Salomon supervised the emplacement of a solid, coherent defensive line to fend off the Rebel assault everyone expected the next morning. Regardless of where they stood, the soldiers of each unit found the conditions universally poor. The rain continued to pelt the hapless troops as they struggled to carry out their assigned duties. This compounded the already atrocious situation in Saline Bottom. There were no tents for shelter, and further, there was no place to erect one if anybody had the time or inclination. Many of the Union soldiers reported that the swamp stood at depths ranging from knee to waist deep and the road was a thick, soupy mass of clinging mud. Attempts to start fires to warm and dry soldiers were thwarted by an obstinate mother nature that extinguished the flames. As the evening twilight gave way to a dark night, the rain droned on and some soldiers ate a miserable and meager dinner while others searched for a suitable place to get some sleep. All were destined for a sleepless night though, as the standing water frustrated their efforts. The soldiers simply stood at their posts all night since "there was no dry place to lie down; and if there had been, the rain was too cold." Thus, the Federal army passed a miserable night, a "fit[ting] prelude for the bloody morrow."[39]

Notes

1. *OR*, Vol. 34, Part 1, 680.
2. *Ibid.*; Bearss, *Steele's Retreat From Camden*, 90; and Sperry, *History of the 33rd Iowa*, 95.
3. Elliot, ed., *The Garden of Memory*, Mrs. Virginia McCullom Stinson, "Memories," 33.
4. Sperry, *History of the 33rd Iowa*, 95.
5. Ira Don Richards, "The Battle of Jenkins' Ferry," *AHQ* (Spring 1961), 4.
6. Sperry, *History of the 33rd Iowa*, 95; and *OR*, Vol. 34, Part 1, 680.
7. *OR*, Vol. 34, Part 1, 668, 677, and 688–689.
8. *Ibid.*, 677, 689, 697, and 723.
9. *Ibid.*, 689.
10. Elliot, ed., *The Garden of Memory*, Mrs. Virginia McCullom Stinson, "Memories," 33.
11. The Army of the Gulf left a path of wanton destruction in its wake during the long retreat from Mansfield. This culminated in the burning of Alexandria as Banks' army embarked on the final leg of its escape from the Red River Valley in the second week of May.

12. *OR*, Vol. 34, Part 1, 782; Bearss, *Steele's Retreat From Camden*, 93; and Richards, "The Battle of Jenkins' Ferry," *AHQ* (Spring 1961), 5.

13. Dr. Junius N. Bragg, "Chasing Steele through Jenkins' Ferry," *Ouachita County Historical Quarterly* (Spring 1998), 9.

14. John G. Walker, "The War of Secession West of the Mississippi River," Myron Gwinner Collection, US Army Military History Institute, 61; and Blessington, *Walker's Texas Division*, 246–247.

15. *OR*, Vol. 34, Part 1, 790.

16. Edwards, *Shelby and His Men*, 290.

17. *OR*, Vol. 34, Part 1, 826–827, 829, and 834; and Walker, "The War of Secession West of the Mississippi River," 62.

18. *OR*, Vol. 34, Part 1, 846–847; and Bearss, *Steele's Retreat From Camden*, 100.

19. Forsyth, *The Red River Campaign of 1864*, 89–108.

20. *OR*, Vol. 34, Part 1, 583–591, and Part 3, 791, 795–796, and 822–823.

21. Walker, "The War of Secession West of the Mississippi River," 56.

22. *OR*, Vol. 34, Part 1, 763.

23. Sperry, *History of the 33rd Iowa*, 96–97.

24. *Ibid.*, 680, 763; and Bearss, *Steele's Retreat From Camden*, 96–97.

25. Sperry, *History of the 33rd Iowa*, 97.

26. *OR*, Vol. 34, Part 1, 723.

27. *Ibid.*, 680 and 723; and Sperry, *History of the 33rd Iowa*, 97.

28. Sperry, *History of the 33rd Iowa*, 97.

29. *OR*, Vol. 34, Part 1, 829.

30. Bragg, "Chasing Steele through Jenkins' Ferry," *Ouachita County Historical Quarterly* (Spring 1998), 9–10.

31. *Ibid.*; and Blessington, *Walker's Texas Division*, 247–248.

32. Evans, ed., *Confederate Military History*, X, 261–262.

33. Edwards, *Shelby and His Men*, 290–293. Edwards is referring to the Military and Pine Bluff Roads.

34. *OR*, Vol. 34, Part 1, 677, 723, and 764; and Sperry, *History of the 33rd Iowa*, 97.

35. *OR*, Vol. 34, Part 1, 782; and Blessington, *Walker's Texas Division*, 248.

36. *OR*, Vol. 34, Part 1, 723–724, 826, and 829; and Burke, *Official Military History of the Kansas Regiments*, 141.

37. *OR*, Vol. 34, Part 1, 669, 677, and 764.

38. *Ibid.*, 669; and Britton, *The Civil War on the Border*, II, 299–300.

39. *OR*, Vol. 34, Part 1, 726; and Sperry, *History of the 33rd Iowa*, 97–98.

10

"There was nothing of the romance of war..."

As the Union army made its preparations for battle and worked on the Saline bridge, the Confederate high command met to etch out a course of action for April 30. At dusk on the 29th only Greene's cavalry had made contact with the Federal army. Greene's Brigade currently occupied positions on the ridge overlooking the bottom with skirmishers maintaining observation of the Federal rear guard. But, the Confederate infantry was still several miles from Saline Bottom. Price's divisions were about fourteen miles from Jenkins' Ferry and Walker another six behind Price. While Smith had finally caught up with Steele, he did not yet have an adequate force to prevent him from crossing the Saline. If Smith did not move quickly the fleeting opportunity to deal a severe blow would vanish. Determined not to let Steele elude him again, Smith issued orders to bring him to battle early on April 30.

As Smith and his staff set about penning written orders, a courier arrived bringing news of Fagan's whereabouts. One of Smith's scouts finally caught up with the wayward cavalryman on the 29th when he was 34 miles from Jenkins' Ferry. Fagan instantly perceived the enormous opportunity that had slipped through his fingers over the past 24 hours. The cavalry commander instantly ordered his column to countermarch back to the ferry in order to assist Smith's effort to destroy Steele before he could reach Little Rock. He would commence at dawn on the 30th in the hope that Steele would still be attempting to cross the river.[1] Fagan's dispatch greatly disappointed Smith for he also saw that a rare chance to bag an army had passed. Nevertheless, he redoubled his own effort to close with Steele. If he could engage Steele on the 30th and prevent his crossing of the Saline, then perhaps Fagan would cut across the route of retreat and trap the haggard Federal army. Therefore, Smith decreed that the army would wake at midnight and move no later than 1:00 A.M.[2] This would give the weary Rebel infantry very little rest before they had to hit the road again. However, the Rebels, like their Yankee antagonists, would have no respite as the weather made it impossible to find any comfort.

Churchill's Division, leading Price's command, reached the small town of Tulip after dark on the 29th. The incessant rains and long march had exhausted the men as they moved north. The dreary night also had a somewhat demoralizing effect on the ranks as well. Dr. Bragg reported that "the night was so black that one could almost feel the darkness with the hand. Sounds of distant thunder," he continued, "fell upon the ear, which as it came nearer, swelled into a roar." Price ordered a halt for the evening here and the men immediately sought a place of shelter from the rain. Some soldiers tore up fences and laid the rails down so they would not have to lie on the wet ground. In spite of their efforts, the Rebels found it difficult to get a fitful sleep as the rain came down in sheets interspersed with thunder and lightning.[3] Walker's Division shared the misery of their comrades in Price's command. Many a Texan was awakened by rising water as the rain "partly overflowed" their bivouac site. What rest the Rebels did get was cut short by Smith's orders for an early march. Throughout the camp officers and non-commissioned officers roused their soldiers to form ranks and move shortly after midnight. After a hardtack breakfast, Smith's army fell in at 1:00 A.M. and began trudging north to ensnare the Yankees at Jenkins' Ferry.[4]

Though it seemed inconceivable, the march from Tulip to Jenkins' Ferry was worse than the movement on the 29th. The rain continued endlessly as the Confederate column slogged through the mire. Many a weary infantryman found himself ridden over by mounted officers hustling up and down the column. Each time an officer trod upon a hapless soldier the column issued a stream of curses at him for his indifference to their plight. At one point, a clumsy horseman knocked down three men as he trotted forward. The angry soldiers cornered the officer threatening him at bayonet point to know his name and business. The gentleman "replied that his name was E. Kirby Smith, and that his business was to command the army." The stunned soldiers sheepishly acceded the commanding general the right of way and fell back into ranks.[5]

Walker's Texans had a very difficult time in moving forward considering their place in the order of march. Steele's entire army and Price's command had preceded the "Greyhounds" and the tread of thousands of men and animals had churned the road into a thick mire. Blessington conceded that in spite of their enthusiasm for pursuing the enemy, "the severity of the march" had broken down a vast number of troops leaving them "in a wretched condition."[6] Troopers from the recently dismounted 28th Texas Cavalry found the pursuit especially difficult. "Lack of sleep and terrible marching conditions so fatigued the men" that many fell out of ranks due to exhaustion.[7] This, of course, reduced the strength of the 28th Texas and other units as well. The straggling would have a detrimental effect on the Rebel army as it lost important striking power while preparing to launch a major assault.

The Federals had remained busy that night as the rain continued without ceasing. After issuing orders for the evening, Steele proceeded to the ferry where he could exercise direct supervision of operations at the bridge. Perhaps the real hero of the expedition and Jenkins' Ferry was the hard working chief engineer, Captain Junius Wheeler. Once again, as he had done on the Little Missouri and Ouachita, Wheeler bore down to task and improved the approaches to the river and constructed the pontoon bridge before dark. Elated by Wheeler's effort, Steele immediately sent Carr to the far side to begin his mission of preventing Fagan from blocking the route to Little Rock. Carr quickly hustled his men clattering over the wooden planking and occupied the high ground above the Saline Bottom for the remainder of the evening. Shortly before midnight in the driving storm, Steele had successfully crossed all of his cavalry and half of the hundreds of wagons that comprised his supply and ordnance stores.[8] Considering the atrocious nature of the weather this is an amazing testament to the perseverance of the Federal soldiers.

The Federal infantry passed an uncomfortable night by snatching the little rest they could grab and improving the defensive dispositions. A seemingly indefatigable Frederick Salomon worked feverishly all night supervising his line for the morning. The immediate vicinity of the battlefield where Salomon's line stood consisted of the inundated bottom cut by the Military Road and a tributary of the Saline running parallel to the road known variously as Cox or Toxie Creek. The area was heavily wooded with thick undergrowth in all directions except for three small farm fields that broke up the monotonous terrain. From west to east they were the Jiles' Cornfield, Cooper's Field, and Kelly's Field. None of these was more than 300 yards by 100 yards in area. Initial contact on the 29th had occurred just west of Jiles', but during the night Salomon contracted his defenses centering them on Cooper's. Thayer's Frontier Division assembled around Kelly's Field providing a reserve for Salomon. Salomon moved down his line ensuring coherence of his defense in the early morning hours and was quite pleased with what he saw. The hearty Federal infantrymen had dismantled all the fences in the vicinity and stacked the rails to make crude breastworks for protection.[9] The Union division held a formidable defensive position with its right anchored on Cox Creek and left resting in a thick swamp, and to its front an open Cooper Field that stood with one to three feet of water. This did not bode well for Rebel success in the morning.

As the first gray streaks of dawn began to break through, the Confederate army was already in motion. Leading the advance was Greene's cavalry brigade of Marmaduke's Division. Marmaduke sent him forward shortly after daybreak to reestablish contact with the Yankees to prevent an easy escape, and determine the disposition of the enemy. Colonel Greene started forward personally leading the 3rd and 4th Missouri Regiments. The troopers moved gingerly feeling for bluecoated infantry in the thickets of the Saline Bottom. Due to Federal repositioning during the night the Confederates found the battlefield of the previous day abandoned. Upon reaching the Jiles' farmhouse Greene decided to deploy skirmishers and dismount as they continued forward to avoid an ambush. Now on foot the cavalrymen pressed on in a light rain until they reached the Jiles' Cornfield. Here, scattered shots greeted the Rebels as Salomon's pickets from the 33rd Iowa fired the first rounds of the Battle of Jenkins' Ferry.[10]

Greene now shook out a regular line of battle in an attempt to develop the situation. The 3rd Missouri moved off the road into the muddy field taking the left,

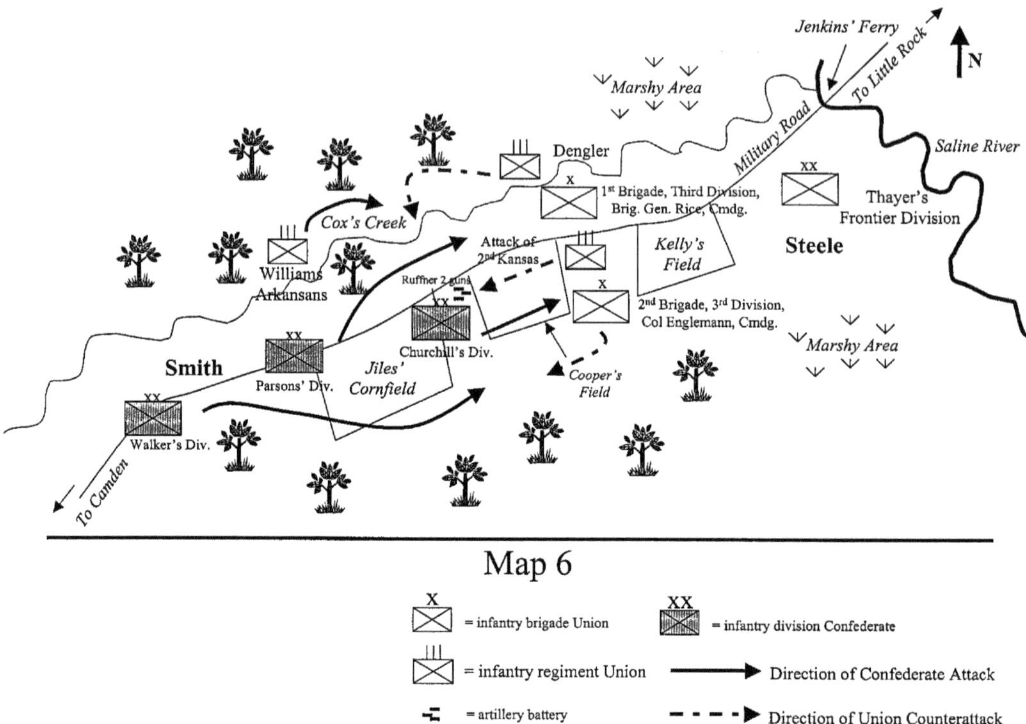

Map 6

Battle of Jenkins' Ferry. Smith caught up with Steele at Jenkins' Ferry and immediately prepared to attack. His efforts quickly went awry as he fed individual brigades and divisions into the fight piecemeal. The Federals were able to parry every thrust and launch successful counterattacks allowing the beleaguered Union army to escape to Little Rock.

and the 4th Missouri followed moving up on the right. As the line drew near the edge of the woods outlining the field, a volley of musketry halted the advance. Greene's men returned fire and a steady din of musketry echoed throughout the bottom for the next half-hour. The 3rd Missouri took advantage of cover offered north of the road and threatened to flank the Iowans as the 4th Missouri occupied their front. The combative and competent Union brigade commander Colonel Rice moved to the scene of the action to assess enemy intentions and to provide Salomon with a picture of the situation. Realizing the skirmish line would soon find itself outflanked, he ordered a slow withdrawal back toward the main line of Federal resistance. Simultaneously, he ordered the rest of his brigade forward to the edge of Cooper's Field where the 33rd would form a solid line with the other regiments to halt the Rebel reconnaissance. This would deceive the Confederates about the true location of the main Federal line, thus drawing the unsuspecting Rebel main body into a Federal firestorm in Cooper's Field. Greene followed the retreating skirmishers until stopped by Rice's improvised line believing he had located the main Union defensive belt. The plucky Confederates traded shots with the Federals as Greene rendered a report to Marmaduke setting the stage for the infantry assault.[11]

As Greene had worked to regain contact with Steele's army, the Confederate infantry divisions struggled forward against bottomless roads and relentless weather. Price's command led the way with Churchill's Arkansas Division, 2,000 strong, in front and Parsons' Missourians close behind. Next in line, but farther back, were Walker's Texans pushing forward in the same nasty conditions as their counterparts. Churchill pulled up on the ridge overlooking the Saline Bottom about 7:30 A.M. and allowed his division a much needed rest. The exhausted soldiers quickly broke ranks to find an appropriate place to snatch a short nap as the sounds of heavy skirmishing echoed up from the valley below. Moments after Churchill turned his men out Price and Smith arrived to confer with him at the Tyra Brown farmhouse. Smith was well aware that his opportunity to crush Steele against the Saline was slowly slipping away unless he could strike a blow immediately. Therefore, he ordered Churchill into the fray lest Steele use any respite to complete the extraction of his army from the trap in the Saline Bottom.[12]

Smith's hasty decision to throw in Churchill in an uncoordinated attack began a pattern at Jenkins' Ferry that would continue until the engagement concluded in the early afternoon. Churchill's Division set in motion a series of piecemeal, brigade-sized attacks that did little more than produce a lengthy casualty list for the Rebels. While Smith's desire to close with Steele is understandable, the lack of thorough reconnaissance, failure to formulate a coherent plan of attack, and refusal to mass his larger army demonstrate a rather incompetent method of command. With poor information about the enemy, Smith deployed each Confederate unit forward on a narrow front as it arrived on the field. This gave the Federal division under Salomon, reinforced by Thayer, the ability to defeat each Confederate thrust in detail while never becoming seriously threatened. The result of Smith's impatience is that he lost an excellent chance to destroy Steele. Had he consolidated his forces and sought out an assailable flank — which did exist — odds favored Smith in his endeavor to finish Steele.

Churchill formed his groggy division at 8:00 A.M., placing Tappan's Brigade in the van, followed by Hawthorn, Gause and elements of Dockery's Brigade dismounted. James C. Tappan's Brigade soon formed a line of skirmishers and passed through Greene's cavalry as they closed with Salomon's defenses in the vicinity of Cooper's Field. Dr. Bragg stated in his account that the brigade found the going very tough since the thick undergrowth and inundated ground served to throw the formation into disarray. The brigade made frequent halts as Tappan worked to realign his skirmish line. Finding his line too long to properly control, Tappan detached the 33rd Arkansas and assigned the regiment as the reserve. Tappan then led the remaining regiments forward as the 33rd watched and listened attentively. The 19th and 24th Arkansas (Consolidated) and 27th and 38th Arkansas (Consolidated) broke into the open on the west side of Cooper's Field preceded by a group of Rebels dressed in blue frock coats. Tappan hoped that he could trick the Federals into believing that this group was a wayward foraging party returning to friendly lines. The Union soldiers would hold their fire upon seeing the blue coats enabling Tappan's Brigade, following closely behind the imposters, to get in close before the Unionists opened up. But, the deception failed as Churchill's men met a firestorm coming from Salomon's skillfully deployed defense.[13]

The beleaguered Confederates took cover in a swale at about the mid-point of the field and found themselves pinned down under heavy fire. Colonel Hiram Grinstead and his 33rd Arkansas had waited in reserve about twenty minutes when they received orders from Tappan to come forward to assist the brigade in continuing the assault. Dr. Bragg recorded that his regiment dutifully moved forward as the rain slackened slightly. "There was nothing of the romance of war" as they marched into a torrent of fire from the Union line that gray morning. The "cold, wet and hungry" Rebels were greeted in the same way that their sister regiments had been only minutes earlier. However, the 33rd advanced farther, moving to within "30 paces" of the Federal line before their assault collapsed with the survivors running for cover in the swale with their comrades. Among the 92 casualties from the 33rd was the regimental commander, the respected Colonel Grinstead.[14]

Churchill now called Hawthorn's Brigade to the front while placing Gause in reserve. Hawthorn fared a little better than Tappan. His left became entangled with Tappan's in the swale, but the right made some progress as Colonel R. G. Shaver found an unprotected flank on the Federal left. Passing around the 50th Indiana, Shaver for a time threatened to unhinge the whole Federal defense. Shaver's success quickly turned sour when the ubiquitous 33rd Iowa and 12th Kansas reacted on their own initiative to halt the advance. Shaver now withdrew back to the main line taking shelter in the ditch with the rest of the division. For the next two hours Churchill's Division traded shots with Salomon unsupported in a ditch barely 150 yards from the well-protected Federals. "The struggle," Churchill described in his after action report, "was desperate beyond description."[15] Finally, after what must have seemed an eternity to the miserable soldiers in the Confederate line, Parsons' Division arrived on the field. Unfortunately, the same lack of planning and coordination that characterized Churchill's attack awaited Parsons' as Kirby Smith fed this division piecemeal into the fight.

Elements of Rice's Federal infantry brigade manned the forward positions on the gray April morning. As dawn broke revealing another dreary day ahead, the Union soldiers pulled what food they had from their haversacks, if any. For most this consisted of a hardtack cracker and an ear of corn, not nearly enough to subsist exhausted, wet infantrymen poised for a fierce day of fighting. While the Union soldiers munched on their sparse breakfast, Salomon made his way around inspecting the defenses. He felt that Rice's brigade constituted an unnecessary bulge in the division line and ordered the aggressive brigadier rearward to present a seamless front. Rice's commanders were in the process of assembling when Greene's skirmishers broke the morning stillness with the intermittent pop-pop of muskets. Posted on the east side of Jiles' Cornfield, the 33rd Iowa slowly withdrew from their exposed position drawing Greene's dismounted troopers after them. The firing became quite hot at times, but the competent Colonel Cyrus Mackey commanding the Iowans, skillfully thinned his lines with few losses.[16]

Rice's 1st Brigade initially halted on the west side of the Cooper Field to leave the impression on Greene that here stood the Federal main defense. Upon running up against this line Greene halted and sent back his report that he had located the Federal defense and would maintain contact until the infantry arrived. In the meantime, Rice pulled back passing through Salomon's division posted in the thick woods fronting Cooper's Field and took up a strong position to the left rear in echelon of Englemann's 3rd Brigade. Englemann had heard the sounds of heavy skirmishing to his front and prepared his men to receive the forward outposts. Simultaneously, his regimental commanders steeled their line for a Rebel assault while the sound grew louder as it approached the brigade. The van of Churchill's Division, Tappan's Brigade, had just arrived and passed through Greene in preparation for its assault. Fearing a sudden burst of fire as they crossed the open field, Tappan outfitted several men with blue jackets hoping the Yankees would spare these "foragers" as they got in close to the main line. Englemann would not allow the Rebels to beguile him, and his double line of riflemen unloosed a sheet of flame staggering Tappan. The graybacks quickly scrambled into the ditch midway into Cooper's Field to return fire. Pinned down, the grim Rebels banged away at the puffs of smoke emanating from the woods while awaiting the arrival of Hawthorn's infantry.[17] Elated by breaking up this weak assault the Federals gained confidence in their defensive position. However, stiffer challenges would test the Federal army as Parsons' and Walker's stout divisions would soon hit them in front and begin curling around their flanks.

Parsons' arrived on the field at about 9:00 A.M. shortly after Churchill's Division shot its bolt against Steele's improvised breastworks. Parsons met with Price on the ridge overlooking the bottom as he allowed his men to rest in the Tyra Brown field. Price had just received word that Churchill's assault had failed and that if support did not arrive quickly the pinned down attackers might suffer a serious setback. Accordingly, Price briefed his subordinate as to the situation and sent the Missourians forward into a firestorm. While Churchill had attempted piecemeal brigade attacks, Parsons decided to deploy his division as a massed two-brigade front with artillery accompanying the line of battle. He pulled his brigade commanders together for a quick huddle to discuss the dispositions. Colonel Simon Burns would take the left extending from Cox Creek to Cooper's Field. Lesueur and Ruffner's batteries would move up the Military Road and deploy just off the road on the west side of Cooper's Field to deliver supporting fire. Brigadier General John Clark's Brigade would tie in with Burns' right in Cooper's Field while extending his own right flank deep into the woods on the south end of the field. Parsons hoped his line would then overlap the Union left exposing it to a wheeling movement, thus turning Salomon out of his position.[18]

It took Parsons about an hour to get his worn out men into line for the assault. As Parsons worked to deploy his division, Kirby Smith met with Price to confer about Churchill's situation. As Smith learned the fate of the Arkansans, his own disgust for Price's lack of frontline leadership began to rise. However, instead of taking Price to task for not moving forward to command the fight, Smith decided to move to the front himself to provide the guidance that Price seemed unable to provide. Smith knew that Parsons' assault would probably meet with the same results as Churchill's and wanted to await the arrival of Walker before launching another attack. But, several factors pushed him to commit Parsons prematurely. First, Walker was still several miles from the field and would not arrive for at least another two hours. This could possibly give Steele the respite he needed to make a clean withdrawal from the Saline Bottom. Second, Churchill was making periodic and ever more desperate requests for support as his division struggled to hold its position in front of Salomon's division. Therefore, rather than exercising tactical patience, Smith concluded that he must throw in Parsons immediately lest Salomon annihilate Churchill, or worse, Steele once again escape relatively unscathed. Following the precedent set by Churchill's earlier forlorn assault, Smith assented to launching another major unsupported attack against a determined Federal defense.[19]

As Parsons' 2,000 men rolled forward, Smith decided to accompany the assault to oversee the execution and assist in any way he could. As events would show, his presence only seemed to muddle the tactical situation as he began to give individual units orders bypassing the established chains of command. As Smith rode forward he encountered some of Churchill's broken regiments streaming to the rear after their abortive attack. Realizing that another purely frontal assault would result in another thrashing at the hands of the obstinate Federal resistance, Smith began to organize a second strike column. A part of Dockery's cavalry had recently been attached to Churchill's command as the pursuit got under way at Camden. These men, now dismounted and commanded by Lieutenant Colonel Horatio Gates Perry Williams, had done little more than listen with disinterest as Tappan and Hawthorn's brigades had been mishandled in Cooper's Field. Williams had put together a solid combat record over the course of the war, serving recently as Dockery's second-in-command. The erratic Dockery was currently riding with Fagan's Division and Williams found himself in command of the 400–odd dismounted and ragged soldiers left behind when Fagan left for Marks' Mills. This skeleton unit was suffering from poor morale, but if anyone could restore this sad lot to fighting trim, Williams seemed the right choice based on reputation.[20]

The newly minted 19th Arkansas was now standing by idly as Parsons' Division strode forward. When Smith came upon Williams and his motley assemblage he struck on an idea for a flanking assault across Cox Creek using these idle troops from Churchill's Division. The decision to assign Williams' regiment such a critical task is highly questionable given the condition of the unit at this juncture. Nevertheless, Smith met with Williams briefly in the Saline Bottom and ordered him to cross to the north side of Cox Creek. Once on the left bank of the stream, Smith told Williams to take control of some high ground that dominated the Union line of defense. This point, perpendicular to the Federals, would provide the Rebels with an ideal location to enfilade the bluecoats. This fire, combined with the frontal assault by Parsons, might force the Federals to abandon their strong position. Then Smith could pour in Walker's Greyhounds to finish off the cornered Federals at the bridgehead.[21]

The plan had promise, but once again Smith's haste doomed the endeavor. For one thing, the combined strength of Williams and Parsons numbered barely 2,500 men while Salomon had about 4,000 muskets in line. Second, as already touched upon, Williams' regiment suffered from a host of problems, notwithstanding the horrible conditions of the battlefield and exhausting marches. Had Smith waited another two hours he could have weighted the flank attack with elements of Walker's Division. Patience on Kirby Smith's part could have delivered the results the departmental commander so desperately sought. Longer casualty rolls, instead, would accompany this lack of foresight.

Smith assigned his aide-de-camp, Lieutenant Cunningham, to act as a guide for Williams and then departed to observe Parsons' frontal assault. Williams promptly assembled his regiment and moved out toward the overflowing creek. Perhaps the most difficult aspect of the mission was to find an appropriate crossing site. Cox Creek, like the Saline, was out of its banks at several points making any attempt to cross a challenge. Lieutenant Cunningham searched diligently for a ford and his efforts paid off as he located a suitable site under the circumstances. Williams pushed his men into the swirling water with cartridge boxes and muskets raised above their heads in the chest-high creek. The regiment got across quickly and scrambled up the slick opposite bank. After a short break to catch their breath and realign the regiment for movement forward, Williams again stepped off. The Arkansans' progress was agonizingly slow as thick undergrowth on the north side of the stream held up the struggling regiment.[22] The slow pace ensured that Parsons' assault would proceed unsupported meeting the same fate as Churchill's hapless brigades only an hour earlier. As Lieutenant Cunningham and Lieutenant Colonel Williams struggled along to deliver the flank attack, they soon heard the unmistakable sound of heavy musketry swell on the south side of the creek confirming Parsons' men had engaged.

Thomas Churchill had not sat by complacently as Salomon pummeled his division in Coopers Field. He had held Colonel Lucien Gause's Brigade in reserve while Tappan and Hawthorn made their individual attacks. Therefore, Gause had a relatively fresh brigade awaiting orders to join the fight. Churchill sent word back to Gause to come up immediately to the support of Hawthorn's hotly engaged men in the muddy field. Gause promptly complied setting his men in motion shortly before 10:00 A.M. When Gause arrived, the Federals greeted his brigade in a similar fashion to the way they had greeted his comrades. A hail of fire slammed into his butternut infantrymen as they emerged from the woods. Gause's men quickly made for the muddy ditch where Churchill's other brigades had found shelter from the Federal musketry. Everywhere Gause's men passed they could observe the fury of the earlier fight in the field as it was strewn with dead, wounded, and the inevitable debris that littered a contested battlefield. Gause's arrival, however, allowed Tappan to make an organized withdrawal while giving heart to Hawthorn's flagging men. This stabilized the situation enough for Churchill to hang on in the swale until Parsons arrived.[23]

Shortly after Gause came to the relief of his fellow brigade commanders, Parsons' line of battle came up in the rear of Churchill's hard-pressed troops. Along the way Parsons happened upon Churchill's command post where he quickly received a brief of the situation ahead. The Arkansan told him that the Union defense had devastated his center and that it would likely fall back in the next few minutes. Churchill informed Parsons of Shaver's limited success and from it surmised that the Federal defense did not extend very far into the swamp south of the field. Churchill suggested that Parsons could possibly overlap the Federal line and that he would assist this endeavor by attaching Gause's Brigade to Parsons for the renewed attack. Since this coincided with Parsons' own plans he readily accepted Gause and thus, had more force to land the attack as well as a longer line to threaten the Federal left flank. Accordingly, Parsons ordered Clark and the artillery to maintain the original course while having Burns pass to the rear of Gause in order to form on his right. This gave Parsons a three brigade front that extended beyond the Federal line for a considerable distance. As soon as the division had made its adjustments, Parsons ordered it forward for the attack.[24]

The combined strength of the Missourians and Arkansans represented the only real opportunity the Confederates had at Jenkins' Ferry to defeat the Union army. It was the time on the field when the Rebels brought the greatest strength to bear at a single moment. With Parsons' three brigades—including Gauses—the grayclads had a little over 3,000 men. If Williams' flanking column north of the creek is added to the tally, the Confederates had about 3,500 men in action. However, this gave them only a one-to-one ratio for the attack and Salomon could, and did, readily call forward the Frontier Division from their position in reserve. Therefore, even this assault stood no realistic chance of success.

Clark and Gause had not proceeded far across Cooper's Field before the sustained fire of Salomon's solid ranks arrested any movement beyond the swale, which by now was filled with the human wreckage and wild-eyed survivors of the earlier attacks. One aspect of Clark and Gause's assault that differentiated it from those previous is the fire from the artillery. Lesueur and Ruffner pushed their respective guns far to the front to support the infantry. In the process, they enabled Clark and Gause to make the farthest sustained advance of the day in this quarter, moving at one point to within 50 paces of the Union line. However, both battery commanders had placed their guns a little too far forward for when the infantry assault petered out the mud conspired to leave them stuck in an exposed position. Colonel Samuel Crawford, commanding the Union troops in this sector, recognized an opportunity to snatch the guns from the struggling gunners and formed a strike column from his 2nd Kansas (Colored) Infantry to take the guns. The boldness of the 2nd Kansas' counterattack and a surprise showing by Yankees north of Cox Creek prevented the Rebels from cracking the Federal defense in Cooper's Field.[25]

On the right, Burns' Brigade came closer to achieving success. Burns' Missourians had a hard-earned reputation for embodying the image of warriors, having fought in some of the hardest battles in the Confederate west. As they moved forward to engage the Federal left Dr. Bragg noted that "this brigade was one of the best the Confederacy ever had." Further, the doctor recorded the regard the men in his regiment held for the Missourians as they passed. The Arkansans raised a cheer for their comrades and encouraged them to "get even" when they closed with the enemy. This is exactly what they intended to do.[26] Pushing on through intractable undergrowth and standing water, Burns' men soon happened upon the 33rd Iowa and 12th Kansas Infantry regiments that had so roughly handled Shaver's regiment. A hot firefight quickly developed as the opposing lines traded volleys at point blank range in the woods. Battle smoke began to blanket the dank forest and soldiers from the 33rd Iowa "soon learned to stoop down" to dodge choking from the pungent odor and to avoid the deadly missiles emitting from hundreds of Rebel muskets. After about a half hour of firing, Burns' Brigade soon pressed ahead having gradually worked their way around the Federal left. This turned the outnumbered Yankees out of their position forcing a retreat. Colonel Mackey called for his 33rd Iowa to pull back and the 12th Kansas conformed to his movements. As Mackey coolly sat on his horse managing the retrograde, a stray ball shattered his arm forcing the indomitable commander to leave the field. Command now devolved upon the steady Major Cyrus Boydston, who guided the regiment through the rest of the fight.[27] Although the Iowans and Kansans made an orderly withdrawal, the rearward movement rendered the whole Union line vulnerable since an entire Rebel brigade was lurking in the woods off the Federal left. The situation required initiative and prompt action and this is exactly what John Thayer delivered at the precise moment Salomon needed reinforcements, just as he had on other fields such as Fort Donelson.

When Shaver's Arkansans inadvertently slid around the open Federal left, the Union commanders suddenly realized that the swamp to the south did not provide the security that they had expected. John Thayer had spent the early morning hours listening intently as the sound of heavy musketry emanated from the west. He placed his regiments in a state of high readiness in Kelly's Field, prepared to advance in any direction at a moment's notice. Thayer's foresight enabled the Union army to quickly plug Shaver's incursion on the left flank before the situation became serious. As the tumult moved closer Thayer called for the 2nd Kansas (Colored), the 14th Kansas Cavalry, and the 1st Arkansas (Union) to form for movement. As they began to fall into ranks a courier arrived informing Thayer of Salomon's need for reinforcements to shore up the left. Promptly, Thayer put the regiments in motion toward the troubled sector. Marching to the sound of the guns, Colonel Charles Adams commanding Thayer's 2nd Brigade, sent the 1st Arkansas and the 14th Kansas to the left while dropping off the 2nd Kansas (Colored) in the center. The arrival of the Frontier Division troops extended the Federal line far beyond Shaver's flank forcing him back.[28]

Salomon had also shifted some of his own regiments to meet the threat, as well as accepting the arrival of the reinforcements from Thayer. The 27th Wisconsin Infantry marched rapidly behind the line out to the sagging flank and was soon joined by the Frontier Division troops. The Wisconsin men and the 14th Kansas Cavalry moved far out to the left in order to extend the front further to the south. Together they would provide a screen to protect the main defense from being surprised by any further attempts to use the swamp as an avenue to the left flank. Colonel John Garrett's 40th Iowa Infantry of Salomon's division had busied themselves in the rear with refilling depleted cartridge boxes when a captain from the 12th Kansas Infantry sent an urgent request for support. Garrett curtailed his replenishment and hastily pressed his regiment back into line. In a twist of good fortune, the 27th Wisconsin arrived at almost the same time as the 40th Iowa. Garrett and Colonel Conrad Krez, commanding the Badger State troopers, agreed to cooperate in launching a spoiling attack on Burns' advancing Rebels. Soon the Wisconsin and Iowa troops swung into line for an assault with the Frontier Division troops. The advance heartened the 33rd Iowa and 12th Kansas regiments, which now halted their retreat and conformed to the movements of their benefactors. The suddenness of the Federal recovery astounded Burns and his Missourians, as they believed victory was in their grasp. Moving ahead "with a shout" Garrett reported that the Union put the Rebels to their heels soon passing "over the enemy's dead."[29] This turn in momentum reestablished the pattern of failed Rebel assaults as Burns' deflated Missourians returned to their jump off positions.

As the Federals on the left repulsed Burns' Brigade another drama was unfolding in the center as the 2nd Kansas (Colored) got a measure of revenge for their fallen comrades of Poison Spring. Colonel Samuel Crawford literally chafed with impatience as his regiment waited to enter the fray in Kelly's Field. As part of the Frontier Division, the 2nd Kansas had been forced to sit in a reserve position as the fight in Cooper's Field reached a crescendo. Finally, orders arrived from the front for Crawford to move to the relief of Salomon's hard pressed line. The aggressive colonel put his crack regiment in motion at double quick time and soon reported to General Rice whose brigade was in the thick of the fighting. Rice was unimpressed with the appearance of the 2nd Kansas at the front. When Crawford went to ask Rice where to enter the line, the general sneered and asked Crawford if he believed the regiment would really fight. In addition to his reputation for hard fighting, Crawford was also a staunch abolitionist who had unwavering confidence in his men. Insulted by Rice's question, he snapped back with a sarcastic tone that "I can take my regiment where any live regiment will go." Taken aback, Rice smiled and told Crawford to "move over on the right and relieve the 50th Indiana," which was running short of ammunition.[30] Crawford's regiment would soon have an opportunity to show their mettle.

The 2nd Kansas found a place at the south end of Cooper's Field where the forest met the open area. They had no sooner closed the unit in line when a Rebel charge came bearing down on the 660 newcomers from the 2nd Kansas. Elements of Gause's and Clark's brigades came on with the notorious Rebel yell ripping the air. Crawford's regiment stood unperturbed by the raucous Confederates as their colonel prepared them for combat. Crawford allowed the Rebels to approach within 150 paces before giving the command to fire. According to Crawford, the "balls went crashing through ... bringing [them] to a standstill." The Rebels traded shots toe to toe with Crawford for some time as the batteries that accompanied them brought their fires to bear on the bluecoats. For a time it appeared that the Rebels could have overcome the firestorm and overrun the Federal center. Then, from out of the blue, an enfilading fire began to tear holes in the compact ranks of Clark's Brigade. The Rebels were astounded to find that their flanking force north of Cox Creek had foundered and a Federal regiment was pouring fire into their midst.[31]

The fire was too much for Clark and he ordered his brigade to fall back. The haste of their withdrawal left the Rebel batteries exposed in the open field with no support. The incessant rains of the past 24 hours had created a quagmire that was nearly impossible for heavy guns to maneuver through. As the Rebel gunners struggled to free their cannons, Crawford seized on an opportunity to deal a hard blow. Realizing that the Confederate guns were ripe for capture, Crawford sent his adjutant to Rice to appeal for permission to charge and bring the guns into Federal control. Rice, impressed by the 2nd Kansas' performance thus far, consented to Crawford's request. When Adjutant Playford arrived back at the regiment, Crawford issued the command to "fix bayonets" before stepping off. Next, the adjutant called for "forward, at the quick step" and the 2nd Kansas rolled forward with a cheer. "A third of the way across," Crawford stated, "I leveled one volley at the battery, which brought down horses enough to hold three of the guns and sent the other three flying from the field."[32]

With the horses of three guns down, the Federal infantry now quickened the pace to take control of the cannon. Upon reaching the remaining guns a hand-to-hand struggle developed for control between the outnumbered Rebels and determined Federals. The Kansas troops, caught up in the emotion of the melee, shouted "Remember Poison Springs" in honor of their fallen comrades. The 2nd Kansas is reputed to have reciprocated the Rebel atrocities of Poison Springs in kind by taking no prisoners. Crawford admitted to using the bayonet freely and "terroriz[ing] the Rebel line of infantry." The colored troopers successfully captured three guns and dragged them back to Federal lines. While they were more than happy to capture the cannon, they took only one Confederate soldier alive, reportedly killing or mortally wounding 150 Rebels near the battery.[33] Crawford decided to release this hapless lieutenant, but before sending him back the colonel dictated a message to deliver to his generals. After a dissertation on the evils of Confederate conduct with reference to Negro soldiers, Crawford got down to the point. He stated:

> I want you to tell General Price, General Churchill, General Parsons, General Hawthorn, General Clark, General Dockery, Colonels Gause and Burns what regiment it was that held the pass south of Toxie [Cox] Creek, from 8:30 in the morning until their lines were broken and their artillery captured at half-past twelve. Tell them further that I accept their new flag with all that its colors imply; and from this day forward, so long as they bear it aloft, by their action on the battlefield, I shall simply tell the men to *remember Poison Springs.*[34]

Crawford's men, in spite of alleged atrocities, had performed in an outstanding manner helping stabilize the Federal center and capturing three cannon as well. The 2nd Kansas had "fought its most distinguished action of the war" and contributed immeasurably to a solid victory at Jenkins' Ferry.[35] Frederick Steele agreed with this assessment stating in his after action report that "the conduct of the colored troops of my command proves that the African can be made as formidable in battle as a soldier of any other color."[36]

The 2nd Kansas was not the only regiment that had blunted Parsons' fierce assault. Men from three other units delivered an unwanted surprise on the unsuspecting Rebels. Williams' 19th Arkansas had struggled through thick undergrowth north of Cox Creek when Parsons crashed into the Federal line. Kirby Smith had intended for Williams to gain an enfilade position before Parsons landed his blow. However, the difficult nature of the terrain prevented the Arkansans from reaching the position. In addition, Salomon had taken the precaution of placing a thin line of two companies from the 29th Iowa and the scattered survivors of the Marks' Mills debacle to act as skirmishers north of Cox Creek. Their purpose was to provide early warning of any Confederate attempt to use the area beyond the creek as an avenue to flank the Union army. As Williams and his regiment drew near the position they desired to occupy, the sharpshooters from the 29th took them under fire. This temporarily halted Williams as he attempted to determine the strength of these unseen snipers.[37]

Captain Marmaduke Darnall in command of the Union detachment, made his own assessment and recognized that Williams' regiment represented a serious effort to flank the Union line by fire. Should Williams gain the enfilade position, it would destabilize the integrity of Salomon's line. Darnall also realized that his own sparse force north of the creek was inadequate to stop the Arkansans from taking their objective. Therefore, Darnall sent an urgent note to Salomon describing the situation and requesting immediate reinforcement. Upon receiving Darnall's message, Salomon flew into action. Grasping the gravity of the situation, Salomon found Adolph Englemann and ordered him to send a regiment across Cox Creek and drive the Rebels back.[38]

Englemann passed the mission on to his dependable subordinate Colonel Adolph Dengler. The colonel formed the 43rd Illinois and hastily turned his regiment toward the creek. On arrival at the south bank the troops showed "some hesitancy" to wade into the stream due to the depth and current. Dengler angrily ordered his men into the creek and in his haste did not take the precaution to remove cartridge boxes. As a result, many of them filled with water fouling the black powder in their boxes, effectively neutralizing many of his men. Reaching the far bank, Dengler turned left and drove toward the sound of skirmishing from Darnall's detachment. "The Forty-third," one observer reported, "was soon briskly engaged" and finding many men unable to fire, Dengler called for help. Salomon responded with two companies from the 2nd Kansas (Colored) under Captain Frank Kister and the other four companies of Garrett's 40th Iowa commanded by Major Sherman G. Smith.[39]

Meanwhile, Dengler and Darnall's detachment engaged in a hot fight until the needed reinforcements arrived. Shortly, Smith reported to Dengler who had him form the right wing. Together, the two units plunged forward through the underbrush. Dengler moved frontally while Smith executed a turning movement on the Rebel left flank. This maneuver convinced Williams that he could not hold his position and he began a steady withdrawal. Now, Captain Kister arrived and likewise reported to Dengler for instructions and the colonel told him to place his unit on the left anchored on the creek. Having gained the upper hand, Dengler sought to push Williams from the north side of the creek and then wheel to assist his comrades on the south bank. Kirby Smith helped Dengler at this point by ordering an astonished Williams back across the creek to assist the hard-pressed Rebels in Cooper's Field. With the Confederates pulling back, Dengler executed his left wheel until his line paralleled the stream on a rise overlooking the left flank of Clark's Brigade. Once set, he had the men from these three regiments pour a devastating fire into the stunned Rebels to the south.[40] Dengler's initiative staggered Parsons' assault, ending the second major attempt to destroy Steele's force against the Jenkins' Ferry bridgehead.

It was now about 11:30 A.M. and the rain had finally subsided. Salomon's Federal division reinforced by Thayer's Frontier Division had completely frustrated two uncoordinated attempts to destroy the VII Corps, buying time for the Federals to evacuate the remainder of the trains and artillery from the west bank of the Saline. Steele, who had been curiously absent from the fighting, now ordered the unengaged regiments of the Frontier Division to begin filing down to the river. Simultaneously, Salomon took advantage of the lull in the fighting to adjust his lines by ordering Dengler to recross the creek, effecting an extension of the line further south, and replenishing cartridge boxes that were running low after over three hours of continuous fighting.[41] The Federals had used their time wisely because the battle was not yet over. As Parsons' assault began to falter, Walker's Texans finally started to assemble on the ridge overlooking the Saline Bottom.

Walker's Division made an exhausting 23-mile march through driving rains and atrocious road conditions to reach the field. Walker, like his predecessors, allowed his men to snatch a much deserved rest upon arrival. As his men filed by to find a suitable spot to halt, Walker could be seen on the side of the road offering them words of encouragement. The hardy Texans responded with "cheer after cheer" for their respected leader. Walker reciprocated their affection, yet the mask of command could not hide the concern he felt for them now. For Walker knew that he would soon have to lead many of them to their deaths in the dank woodland of the Saline.[42] Indeed, Kirby Smith was already planning a third assault that he hoped would deliver the destructive blow he had sought throughout the morning.

The failure of Parsons' attack disheartened Smith greatly, but the Rebel commander was not ready to give up. As he had observed the assault, Smith realized that the Federal left was in the air and that Burns' Brigade had come very close to turning Salomon's line. Smith believed that the only thing that had stopped Parsons' assault was the lack of weight on the Confederate right as they attempted to outflank Salomon. If Smith could properly array Walker's Division for another drive, exploiting the vulnerability of the Federal left, he believed he could drive through to the Ferry. Walker, however, was skeptical of this assessment for he saw a much different situation. Walker had fought recently at Pleasant Hill and this battle on the Saline looked remarkably similar. At Pleasant Hill Richard Taylor had committed division after division piecemeal into the teeth of bristling Union defenses. Now only two and a half weeks later, Kirby Smith was about to commit "the same fatal blunder."[43]

In spite of his reservations, Walker, a consummate professional, would do his duty and lead the third attack. Smith had studied the topography closely over the past couple of hours and found a little used farm track that he hoped would lead to the exposed Federal left flank. Smith wanted to send two brigades on this path while Walker's third brigade used the Military Road to approach the Federal front. Meanwhile, Parsons' two brigades, along with elements of Churchill's Division, would provide support to bolster Walker's attack. Once the flanking brigades were in position, Walker would launch his assault seeking to gain the Federal rear cutting Salomon off from the bridgehead.[44] This plan had promise if the farm branch actually led beyond the Federal flank.

In accordance with Smith's orders, Walker began forming the 4,000 men of his division after rousing them from their short repose. Walker told Brigadier General Thomas Waul to take his brigade and advance straight up the Military Road. While Waul did this Walker would accompany his other two brigades down the farm lane with Colonel Horace Randal in the lead followed by Brigadier General William Scurry. Walker hoped that Waul's Brigade attacking on the left in Cooper's Field would distract the Federal line drawn up there. Then, Walker would land a two-brigade blow on the unsuspecting Federal flank. Accordingly, Walker lurched forward with a division of worn out Rebel infantrymen sometime after 11:30 A.M. Around noon Waul's lone brigade emerged from the timber surrounding Cooper's Field and made ready for a charge. When Waul believed that Walker's column was in position to attack the Federal flank he gave the order for his own unit to plunge into the open field. Waul reported that his brigade came "under a continuous and destructive fire" upon entering the field forcing him into the same ditch that had sheltered a succession of Confederate units. As Waul's tenacious Rebels held on in the midst of a murderous fire, Randal and Scurry were attempting to untangle themselves in the densely wooded area west of Cooper's Field.[45]

Unfortunately for Thomas Waul and his men, Walker's column was nowhere near their proposed assault position when he attacked. The isolated farm track that Kirby Smith had placed his hopes for success upon proved disappointing. Randal's and Scurry's brigades trudged through a morass of mud in pressing toward what they believed was the exposed Federal left. Yet, when they finally emerged from the path in the timber Walker discovered that the lane led to the southeast corner of the Jiles' Cornfield, far from the intended objective. As the Confederates emerged into the field they suddenly realized the error of their advance. About the same moment, Walker could distinctly hear the rumble of musketry signaling Waul's now unsupported attack. The division commander valiantly redirected his two brigades toward the sound of firing to extricate Waul's lone unit. This required Randal and Scurry to shake out a line of battle and then advance through the dense belt of timber separating the Jiles' Cornfield from Cooper's Field. The task brought about an interminable delay in deploying the flanking column and pressing into action.[46]

Salomon's division had once again easily repulsed a piecemeal, uncoordinated brigade attack and was waiting in readiness for Randal's and Scurry's struggling Rebels to appear. It took about a half-hour for the Confederates to reach the battle area. A portion of Randal's Brigade was the first to arrive and they appeared behind Waul's hunkered down men in the swale. This meant that instead of attacking an open flank, Randal and Scurry would actually have to assault frontally. Walker attempted to shift the hapless Rebels further to the right so that Randal would not become entangled with Waul in his charge. Yet, even with this adjustment the Confederates did not overlap the Federal line. On the contrary, Salomon's division extended beyond Walker's flank, and, making matters worse, Major Smith and Captain Kister had their pesky bluecoats in position north of Cox Creek to pour a deadly crossfire into the Rebel left.[47] In essence, Walker's attack was a forlorn hope.

Finally, as the hour approached 12:30 P.M., Walker rolled forward in his attempt to crack Salomon's line. Soon it was evident that Walker would have no more success than his fellow division commanders had had earlier in the day. The leaders in charge of Walker's brigades were courageous and well respected throughout the Texas Division and they validated that trust on this field, yet they fared no better than Churchill and Parsons. When the line advanced Waul, Randal, and Scurry were conspicuous in their presence on the battlefield as they shouted orders and provided steady guidance to their troops. Their personal leadership set an excellent example for their men and gave the Union infantrymen ideal targets for honing their marksmanship. Within minutes of the start of the engagement all three of Walker's brigade commanders were hit as a murderous fire emanated from the Union line. Randal and Scurry received mortal wounds while Waul had a serious, though not life threatening injury to his leg. The loss of these senior commanders paralyzed the Confederate attack as the leaderless brigades fell into confusion. As Walker surmised the nature of the situation, the Federals began to curl around both flanks of the Confederate division threatening to imperil its safety. Realizing his position was untenable, Walker ordered a withdrawal from the field and asked Churchill's cut up unit to give him assistance in this maneuver.[48]

With the exception of some scattered skirmishing, the Battle of Jenkins' Ferry was over. However, the ordeal for the Federals would continue for a couple more days. As the fighting subsided after the third assault, Frederick Steele rode to the front to confer with Salomon. He had left all tactical dispositions and direction of the fighting on the shoulders of Salomon. Some may argue that his appropriate place on the field was at the front rather than down at the bridge supervising the passage of the trains. While this is a reasonable judgment, Salomon's conduct of affairs was exceptional and the presence of Steele looking over the shoulder of a division commander might have caused great irritation. Further, Steele had an excellent cast of subordinates that he placed full trust in and these men justified that confidence with outstanding performance. By contrast, Kirby Smith meddled in his subordinates' business to the point of detaching individual regiments for separate attacks. Rather than coordinating the army to utilize its clear advantage in manpower, Smith accompanied small-scale brigade assaults, thus squandering a reasonable opportunity to bag Steele's army. When Steele's performance is compared to Smith's it appears that the Federal commander made a satisfactory decision in facilitating the withdrawal and allowing Salomon to fight the delaying action, which was essentially a divisional action.

Salomon received Steele cordially providing him with a succinct brief of the situation. As he concluded, Salomon suggested that perhaps now might be an appropriate time to withdraw closer to the ferry in order to contract his line into a more easily defensible perimeter. While Salomon's division had performed admirably, the soldiers were utterly worn out, hungry, and had suffered several hundred casualties over the course of the day. In addition, Salomon had several prisoners interrogated and from these he identified the presence of three separate Confederate divisions on the field. On further questioning, the ragged Rebels claimed that the army was "continually receiving reinforcements." This convinced Salomon that he must pull back since he was sure the Confederates would launch another attack when they had their forces assembled.[49]

Steele readily consented to this request and added that a deliberate defense was not necessary close to the ferry. The trains, artillery, and part of Thayer's division were already across the Saline and Salomon's stolid division could follow immediately. Salomon happily began assembling his division, but before starting he organized a small strike force to push forward to ensure the division was not attacked in the act of withdrawing. He also gathered up all the wounded — including the severely wounded General Samuel Rice — that were movable and sent them ahead of the column. Unfortunately, he could not carry all of them and assigned several surgeons and orderlies to stay behind and attend to their wounds. Meanwhile, Salomon's strike force pursued the Confederates for about a mile with only minor contact before breaking off the action. Upon their rejoining Salomon's main body, the whole division pulled back to the bridgehead. Shortly after 2:00 P.M. the last of the VII Corps crossed the pontoon bridge to the east side of the Saline and safety.[50]

The largest battle of the Camden Expedition resulted in some 700 Union casualties out of 4,000 soldiers committed from the 3rd Division and Frontier Division. This is an 18 percent casualty rate for the Federals who fought the battle primarily from defensive positions. On the other hand, estimates of Confederate casualties reveal a loss of over 1,000[51] soldiers including several general officers of some 8,000 who made the attacks. Such a high percentage of losses with reference to troops engaged attests to the ferocity of the engagement. The fight at Jenkins' Ferry was a tactical victory for the Federals who successfully brought off their entire army. In contrast, the Confederates squandered an opportunity to destroy Steele with a series of piecemeal assaults that only produced a long casualty list. But, the true repercussions of the battle echoed far beyond the field in Arkansas. Smith's decision to pursue Steele drew a sizeable Rebel force away from Louisiana and Nathaniel P. Banks' imperiled army. This gave the Army of the Gulf and the Mississippi River Squadron invaluable time to escape the grip of a frustrated and angry Richard Taylor.

Nevertheless, the Yankees were still not yet out of the woods in Arkansas or Louisiana. Steele and his thoroughly used up army were still over fifty miles from Little Rock with a huge Rebel mounted force thought to be lurking west of the Saline. Simultaneously, Banks still needed a few more days to complete a dam that would raise the Red River enough to release the trapped Federal navy. Would the Union forces in the Trans-Mississippi have enough time to effect their escape? If the scattered Federals did receive the respite they required, then sizeable Union forces would be available for use in other important theaters in the east. Only time would tell.

Notes

1. Evans, ed., *Confederate Military History*, X, 261–262.

2. *OR*, Vol. 34, Part, 556.

3. Bragg, "Chasing Steele through Jenkins Ferry," *Ouachita County Historical Quarterly* (Spring 1998), 10.

4. Blessington, *Walker's Texas Division*, 248.

5. Bragg, "Chasing Steele through Jenkins Ferry," *Ouachita County Historical Quarterly* (Spring 1998), 10.

6. Blessington, *Walker's Texas Division*, 248–249.

7. M. Jane Harris Johansson, "Peculiar Honor: A History of the 28th Texas Cavalry (Dismounted), Walker's Texas Division, 1862–1865," UMI Dissertation Services, 193.

8. *Ibid.*; and *OR*, Vol. 34, Part 1, 669, 677, and 681.

9. *OR*, Vol. 34, Part 1, 689 and 725–726; and Richards, "The Battle of Jenkins' Ferry," *AHQ* (Spring 1961), 7.

10. *OR*, Vol. 34, Part 1, 702–703 and 829.

11. *Ibid.*, 697 and 829–830.

12. *Ibid.*, 799–800; and Bragg, "Chasing Steele through Jenkins Ferry," *Ouachita County Historical Quarterly* (Spring 1998), 10.

13. Bragg, "Chasing Steele through Jenkins Ferry," *Ouachita County Historical Quarterly* (Spring 1998), 10–11; and *OR*, Vol. 34, Part 1, 799–800.

14. Bragg, "Chasing Steele through Jenkins Ferry," *Ouachita County Historical Quarterly* (Spring 1998), 11.

15. *OR*, Vol. 34, Part 1, 702–703 and 800.

16. *Ibid.*, 669, 689, 697, and 702–703; and Sperry, *History of the 33rd Iowa*, 99.

17. *OR*, Vol. 34, Part 1, 724–725 and 735–736.

18. *OR*, Vol. 34, Part 1, 809.

19. *Ibid.*, 556.

20. Arthur R. and Robert B. Buckalew, "Hillsboro's Citizen Soldier: Horatio Gates Perry Williams," *AHQ* (Spring 1972), 36–46.

21. *Ibid.*, 48; Bearss, *Steele's Retreat From Camden*, 130; and *OR*, Vol. 34, Part 1, 807–808.

22. *OR*, Vol. 34, Part 1, 800 and 808.

23. *Ibid.*, 800 and 806.

24. *Ibid.*, 800 and 809–810.

25. Crawford, *Kansas in the Sixties*, 120–123.

26. Bragg, "Chasing Steele through Jenkins Ferry," *Ouachita County Historical Quarterly* (Spring 1998), 11.

27. Sperry, *History of the 33rd Iowa*, 100 and 105; and *OR*, Vol. 34, Part 1, 703.

28. McLeod, "The Frontier Division in the Camden Expedition," 17–18; and *OR*, Vol. 34, Part 1, 690 and 698.

29. *OR*, Vol. 34, Part 1, 740–741; and Burke, *Official Military History of the Kansas Regiments*, 376.

30. Crawford, *Kansas in the Sixties*, 120; and Burke, *Official Military History of the Kansas Regiments*, 428.

31. Crawford, *Kansas in the Sixties*, 122–123; Noah Andre Trudeau, *Like Men of War*, 198; and *OR*, Vol. 34, Part 1, 735–736 and 811.

32. Crawford, *Kansas in the Sixties*, 124; Burke, *Official Military History of the Kansas Regiments*, 428; and Lonnie J. White, ed., "A Bluecoat's Account of the Camden Expedition," *AHQ* (Spring 1965), 88.

33. Crawford, *Kansas in the Sixties*, 124; and Dudley *Taylor Cornish, The Sable Arm*, 177.

34. Crawford, Kansas in the Sixties, 126–127. (Emphasis in original.) Crawford's times in this paragraph are slightly mistaken as he entered the fray closer to 10:00 A.M.

35. Cornish, *The Sable Arm*, 177.

36. *OR*, Vol. 34, Part 1, 671.

37. *Ibid.*, 697.

38. *Ibid.*, 697 and 725.

39. *Ibid.*, 698 and 725.

40. *Ibid.*, 698, 725, 730, 735, and 808; and Buckalew, "Hillsboro's Soldier-Citizen: Horatio Gates Perry Williams," *AHQ* (Spring 1972), 48–49. Darnall received a severe wound before Dengler arrived to drive the Confederate regiment back.

41. *OR*, Vol. 34, Part 1, 690.

42. Blessington, *Walker's Texas Division*, 249–250; and Walker, "The War of Secession West of the Mississippi River," 62–64.

43. Walker, "The War of Secession West of the Mississippi River," 64.

44. *Ibid.*

45. *Ibid.*; and *OR*, Vol. 34, Part 1, 817.

46. *OR*, Vol. 34, Part 1, 817; Walker, "The War of Secession West of the Mississippi River," 64–65; and Johansson, "Peculiar Honor: A History of the 28th Texas Cavalry (Dismounted)," 194–195.

47. Bearss, *Steele's Retreat From Camden*, 152; Walker, "The War of Secession West of the Mississippi River, 65; and *OR*, Vol. 34, Part 1, 817–818.

48. *Ibid.*; and Walker, "The War of Secession West of the Mississippi River," 65–66.

49. *OR*, Vol. 34, Part 1, 670 and 690.

50. *Ibid.*

51. *Ibid.*, 691, 759, and 787–788; and Burke, *Official Military History of the Kansas Regiments*, 429. Both armies' casualty reports are incomplete since Thayer, in the Union army, and Walker, in the Confederate, did not file reports.

11

Steele Loses a Campaign but Saves an Army

Although there were still a few days left before the campaign would actually conclude, in reality the six-week Camden Expedition had already ended. On the surface this minor action in 1864 appears as little more that a footnote in Civil War historiography. In reality it had an effect far out of proportion to the resources committed by the Union authorities. A full analysis of the facts in context with corresponding events in the Red River Valley and subsequent actions east of the Mississippi reveals the great opportunity that the Confederates allowed to slip from their grasp. Before an analysis of the expedition in full light however, a discussion of the final days of this exhausting campaign is in order.

The Federal army had successfully defeated three major assaults by the Confederate army at Jenkins' Ferry. Further, they brought off all their trains and artillery. Yet, the Federals were still in great danger since Fagan's 4,000 cavalry lurked somewhere between the Arkansas River and the Ouachita. Of greater danger was the debilitating effect that hunger was wreaking on man and animal. The soldiers were certainly suffering from lack of food, but the draft animals were literally starving. The horrid weather conditions compounded the problem by making an already tough march more exhausting as the army struggled through deep, sticky mud. Steele had made it north of the Saline, but could he continue the retreat any farther with desperately weak horses and mules?

On the afternoon of the 30th of April Steele sent scouts forward to determine the condition of the road between Jenkins' Ferry and Little Rock. Having deployed the scouts, Steele moved the army down the road a short distance to ensure that the force was beyond direct observation of the Rebels. As darkness began to fall, the scouts reported their findings and the information was foreboding. The road ascending out of the Saline Bottom eastward was a veritable morass of deep mud, and even when the army reached higher ground it did not promise relief from backbreaking toil. The scouts believed that "the road had become impassable for trains and artillery." If true, the draft animals could simply not pull the wagons out of the bottom. Therefore, Steele decided to abandon low priority wagons and equipment in order to use the remaining animals to double up the teams on the vehicles considered more important. In accordance with this decision, Steele issued orders designating select vehicles for destruction. He placed his trusty quartermaster, Captain Henry, in charge of the operation with instructions to destroy all excess transport. Those vehicles protected from the directive included all army headquarters wagons, ambulances, and artillery. Further, the order limited each division to only five vehicles to carry ordnance. All other wagons would be put to the torch. Henry was to commence the operation when details from the divisions reported for duty.[1]

Henry began methodically assembling the mass of transports in the early evening darkness just off the Military Road. As the order reached the division and brigade commanders, they authorized the formation of details to assist Captain Henry. After some time, all the work parties reported to the chief quartermaster and he quickly set about the business of destroying the wagons. Soon after midnight Henry had an enormous bonfire blazing in the early morning twilight. The fire drew many spectators who were fascinated by the extent of the conflagration. Private Sperry, placed on the work party, commented that the most interesting aspect of the task was rummaging through the contents of the wagons. Many of the soldiers took great delight in exchanging their tattered uniforms for the "glossy coats with shining buttons" of the officers before torching the train. After taking what they wanted, the privates set the wagons aflame. Sperry reported that "mess-chests, company-boxes, etc., made excellent fuel." Before assembling for a 4:00 A.M. start of the retreat, the soldiers used the blaze to boil their coffee and cook their "poor pretense of a breakfast."[2]

Promptly, in accordance with Steele's orders, the VII Corps mustered to commence the final leg of their journey to Little Rock. The ambulances with the wounded and the trains led the column followed by Salomon's 3rd Division. Thayer's fresher Frontier Division assumed duties as the rear guard protecting the army should Kirby Smith succeed in throwing infantry across the Saline in pursuit. Shortly after starting the Federals came upon the intersection of the Military and Pine Bluff roads. Here, Steele sent the ambulances and a small escort down the Pine Bluff Road while he, with the main body continued on to Little Rock. Steele, in sending the wounded to Pine Bluff, reasoned that this would get these poor souls to hospitals sooner since Pine Bluff was half the distance compared to a march to Little Rock. Also, Pine Bluff was closer to the Mississippi River meaning transports could evacuate these men to hospitals in the north sooner. Additionally, Steele still believed that Fagan was somewhere between him and Little Rock. Should Fagan turn up in a blocking position on the Military Road, Steele would have to fight his way through the roadblock, further delaying medical care for the wounded. Steele's judgment proved correct as the ambulances arrived in Pine Bluff that evening after an uneventful passage.[3]

Steele's fear of interference by Fagan, however, was unwarranted, as events would show. Smith had frantically attempted to move Fagan into position to stop the Federal retreat for some time after the Federals left Camden. Finally, late on April 29 one of Smith's couriers reached Fagan informing him of the situation. Fagan was some 34 miles away from Jenkins' Ferry by now and, more frustrating, Fagan was on the west side of the Saline. Therefore, the erstwhile cavalry commander was in no position to block Steele's retreat. In essence, the Union army had a free pass to Little Rock once they spanned the Saline. Fagan now belatedly flew into action issuing orders for an early start on the 30th to join Smith in the fight with Steele. Fagan furiously drove his men that day arriving at the Jiles' farmhouse around four in the afternoon. On Fagan's reporting to Smith, the disappointed commanding general instructed his subordinate to provide a brigade to reinforce Greene's troopers who were pursuing the Federals to the bridgehead. By the time the cavalry reached the near bank of the Saline, the Federals were taking up the final planks of the bridge ending any thought of pursuit.[4]

Fagan went back to Smith to plead for permission to swim the river to keep pressure on the Federals. Smith balked at this suggestion fearing it too risky to swim the flooded Saline. Already disgusted by Fagan's poor performance and the repulse of the army in battle, Smith decided to suspend operations for the day. Many in the Rebel ranks expressed deep regret that Smith allowed the Federals to withdraw unmolested. John Walker believed that had Smith authorized Fagan's request "the greater portion of Steele's army would have been captured or destroyed."[5] Blessington recorded sarcastically that apparently Smith "was satisfied with the laurels he had already won."[6]

On closer examination though, Smith's decision appears proper for several reasons. First, Smith was correct in denying Fagan's request to swim the river. The high level of the stream and swift current would certainly have resulted in unnecessary deaths from drowning. Second, the Rebels were fast becoming destitute of supplies. Finally, the Confederates were simply in no condition to pursue the Federals. The army had suffered 17 percent casualties in the fight, had no safe means of crossing the raging Saline, had no supplies on hand, and were exhausted by forced marches. In light of these factors Smith's decision seems reasonable. Therefore, Steele would enjoy an uncontested retreat in the final leg of a most frustrating campaign.

As General Salomon spent most of the 30th fending off repeated attacks by Smith's Rebels, Eugene Carr relentlessly drove his cavalry division toward Little Rock. Carr had the dual mission of reconnaissance of the Military Road and logistic relief. Carr made an early start in the pre-dawn hours and the march was uneventful until the column reached a place called Whitmore's Mill. Here, the van came in contact with elements of the 1st Missouri Cavalry Battalion. Part of Fagan's force, the Missourians had been scouting east of the Saline. The battalion had expected to link up with Fagan a day earlier but failed to find Fagan at the appointed place. At midmorning pickets from the 1st Missouri exchanged shots with Carr's troopers. The Rebel pickets, realizing the strength of the Yankee horsemen, gave ground falling back to their bivouac site. Upon reaching the mill the pickets reported to their commanding officer, Lieutenant Colonel Benjamin Elliot. Elliot sent forward two companies of cavalry to confirm the intelligence provided by the nervous pickets. Rather than attacking Carr's column, the Rebels prudently shadowed the Yankees as they continued on to Little Rock. Elliot estimated Carr's force at around 2,000 mounted men; he made a futile attempt to report this information to Fagan.[7]

The brush with the Missourians seemed to confirm in Carr's mind that Fagan, indeed, was lurking somewhere between Jenkins' Ferry and Little Rock. With added urgency Carr sought to press his men to move faster. A way to gain more speed was to abandon the division train. Carr, therefore, ordered the cavalry wagons—some 200 of them—destroyed on the spot in order to pick up the pace of the retreat. Shortly, Carr had all his transport wagons set ablaze as his troopers drove on for Little Rock. As darkness began to blanket the Arkansas landscape, the weary troopers expected to halt for the evening, but Carr had other plans. Carr knew that Steele was in desperate need of rations for the infantry and animals and decided to continue the march through the night. Undoubtedly, the decision must have caused a great deal of grumbling among the cavalrymen, but Carr's determination to succor his commander kept them in the saddle through a miserable night.[8] Though Carr's men loathed the decision, the infantry divisions would greatly appreciate Carr's sacrifice.

The Federal cavalry division reached Little Rock at 5:00 A.M. on May 1. Carr's arrival did not curtail his activity though. Within minutes of releasing his troopers for a deserved rest, Carr turned and rushed over to the garrison commander's headquarters. Brigadier General Joseph West had assumed command from Nathan Kimball only days before Carr clattered into Little Rock and had little information of the whereabouts of Steele. Upon receiving the news of Steele's dire lack of provisions, West, a man of great energy, flew into action. Carr had informed West that Steele would set a course to Pine Bluff. Therefore, West telegraphed Brigadier General Christopher Andrews at that location ordering him to organize a relief train with 30,000 rations that would meet Steele on the road. To guard against Rebel raiders, Andrews assigned the reliable Powell Clayton with two infantry regiments, a battery, and cavalry escort to carry the train through to Steele. By mid-afternoon, Andrews had the train assembled and on its way to relieve the gaunt infantry of the VII Corps.[9]

Unfortunately for the ragged Yankees in Steele's column, the commanding general had decided to stay on course for Little Rock meaning they would have to wait a little longer to obtain any food. Until then the men would have to drive on through another monotonous day of marching. At one point during the trek the army came upon a "pine swamp of four miles' width." Already inundated, the tramp of thousands of soldiers "now cut [the swamp] into almost unfathomable softness." This forced the army to corduroy more of the Arkansas lowlands to get the remaining trains and artillery through. Sperry observed that the train "still stretched out ... two or three miles" even after the details destroyed hundreds of wagons in the Saline Bottom. Many of the remaining wagons stuck in the thick mud and soldiers simply unhitched the teams burning them where they stopped. Finally, after a couple of hours in the swamp, the army moved up onto some high ground making progress somewhat easier. Only rumors of impending Rebel ambushes broke up the relentless monotony of the retreat.[10]

As the sun began to hang low in the west, Steele called a short halt. Many soldiers hoped that they would be allowed to bivouac for the night, but Steele had other ideas. Instead of rest, details set about lighting fires along the sides of the road. This meant that the commanding general intended to make a night march. Steele had already made the mistake of failing to press the retreat before Jenkins' Ferry. This had afforded Kirby Smith an opportunity to catch the Federals and deal a severe blow. Steele determined not give Smith another chance and soon had the weary soldiers moving again. "We were now almost at the limits of human powers of endurance," Sperry remembered. Many a soldier struggled to keep up with the column. Sperry claimed that some of the troops "actually slept while marching."[11] True or not, the long hard march moved the Yankees closer to relief as the sun rose on May 2.

The Federals made no stop on the morning of May 2 because the army was now out of provisions outside of coffee. Hunger began to take its toll on the men as straggling picked up and some became desperate. Andrew Sperry witnessed a man pay two dollars for a solitary piece of hardtack while another traded away a silver watch for the hard bread. The march continued onward in spite of the hunger pangs. Spirits rose in the late afternoon as the column passed the Benton Road, less than days' march from Little Rock. Within an hour the army encamped on the very ground of the first night of the expedition. "How we contrasted the two nights!" Sperry exclaimed, "and how long seemed the times between them."[12]

The sun began to set on May 2 as the exhausted soldiers milled about preparing bedrolls and boiling coffee when excitement gripped the camp. Rations had arrived from Little Rock. When Brigadier General West realized that Steele was not headed for Pine Bluff he assembled a train of his own and sent it down the Military Road. Escorted by the 54th Illinois, pickets sighted the train coming and lifted an elated shout that relief had arrived. Word raced through the bivouac as excited Yankees rejoiced at the thought of eating a full meal for the first time in weeks. Pleased with Carr and West's efforts, Steele ordered the rations distributed for immediate consumption. Grateful soldiers distributed the fare in record time and soon all enjoyed a filling dinner of "hard-tack and sow-belly." On other days the men would have complained mightily at such provisions, but tonight every soldier was pleased. On this, the last night of the expedition, the bluecoats would get a fitful rest with full stomachs.[13]

The night of May 2 was unseasonably cold, but it did not seem to matter. After 48 hours without sleep and a full meal the Union soldiers quickly fell asleep wrapped in woolen blankets despite the elements. Reveille sounded before dawn and the men wasted no time in preparing for the last few miles' march. After downing a breakfast of hardtack and coffee, the army fell in line "renewed with better hope and vigor." The pace was considerably faster than on the days previous to May 3 as the thought of rest and recuperation pushed the army to greater exertions. Then at about 10:30 A.M. the outlying fortifications of Little Rock came into view. The army called a short halt "to form better order" before reentering into the city. Then the army smartly started forward with fife and drums keeping sharp cadence as if they were a victorious army entering a conquered city. In reality the VII Corps was a beaten army lucky to make it back to Little Rock in the shape that it did. After parading past Steele's headquarters the Yankees reoccupied their old campgrounds as if they had never left.[14] In some strange way Little Rock had become a home away from home and all hands were happy to be back. The Camden Expedition was over for Steele's weary army.

The Confederates had done little more than lick their wounds following the nasty fight at Jenkins' Ferry, but there were many good reasons for this fact. First, dead and wounded Rebels and Yankees littered the field. Beleaguered southern doctors attempted to ease the suffering, but a meager supply of medicines and austere conditions made their efforts difficult. Local citizens offered their services in helping with the grisly business of gathering in the human wreckage and nursing the wounded. In spite of the help, the casualties numbering over one thousand overwhelmed the Confederate medical system.[15]

Compounding the problem of caring for the wounded was the now serious subsistence situation. The Confederate commissary department was in no better shape than their opponents in the Camden Expedition. Hunger was beginning to plague the Rebels just it had the Yankees. The Confederate quartermasters issued what they had to give after the battle amounting to a miserable ear of corn and two ounces of bacon per man, but this was entirely inadequate. It seemed unlikely that the Confederate army could move forward from Jenkins' Ferry to pursue the Federals in light of the lack of provisions. Rather than pursuit, it seemed more realistic that the Rebels would have to retreat back to Camden to obtain sufficient foodstuffs.[16]

Finally, the southern soldiers were utterly worn out after their exertions of the previous three days. During that time they had constructed an improvised bridge; marched over 70 miles in mud and rain; and fought a major battle that produced close to 20 percent casualties. The Rebels were simply used up and in "wretched condition." Rebel accounts and after action reports are rife with tales of the exhaustion of the army.[17] Before the army could resume operations of any magnitude the men had to have food and rest.

Smith was well aware of these conditions when he decided to let Steele make his way uncontested back to Little Rock. Probably the major factor weighing on this decision was the fact that he believed the Confederates had accomplished their mission. While Smith had entertained notions of sacking the entire army under Steele, the purpose of operations in Arkansas was to restore the status quo in the department. This was in consonance with the overarching Confederate strategy to maintain the territorial integrity of the nation while taking any opportunity to strike at Union vulnerabilities.[18] Steele's incursion south from Little Rock required his expulsion and offered a rare chance to land a heavy blow on an isolated Union column. Though Smith could not destroy Steele, the Confederates had certainly sent the Federals flying back to their starting point. Therefore, Smith concluded both that continuing to chase Steele was no longer necessary in light of the logistical problems and also that the Rebels had fulfilled their mission.

With the campaign won, Smith began to tidy up the rear in Louisiana and plan for the future. From the time Smith announced that he would move to Arkansas Richard Taylor hounded him with letters requesting reinforcements and criticizing

Smith's conduct of affairs. Taylor was convinced that had the infantry divisions not been detached from his army, he could have destroyed Banks and he vociferously attacked Smith on that basis in his writings. In order to restore a measure of civility, Smith agreed to send Walker's Division followed later by the Arkansas and Missouri divisions back to Louisiana as soon as they had recovered from their exertions in the recent campaign in Arkansas. Taylor still had Banks' army and Porter's fleet trapped at Alexandria as the first week of May opened. By sending Walker's Division south, Smith hoped to quiet his dissatisfied subordinate and possibly inflict a crippling defeat on the Army of the Gulf. Neither would occur. It would take over a week for Walker to reach Alexandria after he started and by then Banks and Porter had escaped. This event so angered Taylor that it caused the final break between him and Kirby Smith. The tone of Taylor's dispatches turned so venomous that Smith felt he had to relieve Taylor.[19]

Smith had really only wanted Banks to leave Louisiana of his own accord anyway. Instead, Smith, under the influence of Sterling Price, had his sights set north of the Arkansas River. On May 19 Smith's chief of staff, Brigadier General William R. Boggs, penned a dispatch to Sterling Price advising him "to accumulate large depots" in preparation for transferring "the theatre of operations" to Missouri.[20] Smith hoped that by unleashing Price north into Missouri to threaten St. Louis he could draw Federal pressure away from the Confederate army operating in Georgia. Additionally, Smith hoped to obtain recruits to fill the ranks of the ever-shrinking Rebel armies of the Trans-Mississippi.[21] Price, in contrast to Taylor, was elated by the orders to prepare for an expedition north into his home state. He had clamored for some two and a half years for the opportunity to reenter Missouri. At first, Price's approach to achieving his goal had irritated his superiors until they refused to listen to him. Since becoming commander of the District of Arkansas Price had moderated his tone. Instead of arrogantly pressing for adoption of his program, he congenially acceded to all of Smith's requests while gently suggesting that a Missouri expedition might have some utility.[22] In the end, Taylor had driven Smith away while Price inveigled his commander into seeing things his way. From the Rebel perspective the counteroffensive of the Camden Expedition was over.

At the operational level of war Camden and Red River were extraordinarily successful for the Confederates. These twin campaigns arguably had the most favorable outcome of any during the entire war for the Confederacy. The Camden Expedition, in particular, produced spectacular results against minimal losses. The Union army suffered almost 3,000 casualties, lost eight pieces of artillery, 700 supply wagons, and about 2,500 animals. While the casualties suffered do not represent a large loss, those in equipment are nothing short of catastrophic. Steele lost an astounding 70 percent of his transportation assets, virtually crippling the army's mobility for the foreseeable future. By contrast, the Confederates suffered some 2,000 casualties and only lost three guns at Jenkins' Ferry and 35 wagons burned in the Mount Elba battles. Finally, the Confederates with meager resources had handily dealt a serious blow to Federal power in the Trans-Mississippi region by sending Steele flying back to Little Rock. Kirby Smith clearly had adequate reason to claim a substantial victory.[23]

In addition to the immediate results, Confederate efforts upset the Federal timetable for spring operations in 1864. General Grant had planned to set the major Union armies in motion during the last week of April. The objective was the primary Confederate armies in the field in Virginia and Georgia. To destroy these Rebel armies, Grant wanted to use all resources –including manpower — available to the much stronger Union. But, before Grant assumed supreme command of all United States forces, Henry Halleck had already set in motion the ill-fated Red River Campaign. This represented a diversion from Grant's design, but he allowed it to continue out of respect to his predecessor.[24]

For the Red River Campaign to be a success, Grant realized that Federal forces must attack with force from more than one direction. Halleck had tapped Steele's VII Corps to provide this support for Nathaniel Banks on the Red. Steele, however, had a litany of legitimate reasons why a thrust from Little Rock was impractical. As of March 17 — five days after Banks jumped off— Steele continued to stonewall the commanding general in Washington. Grant had heard enough of excuses and summarily ordered Steele to move in support of Banks.[25] Grant also telegraphed Banks informing him that he should wrap up operations in Louisiana by April 15 in order to send A. J. Smith's two corps back to Mississippi and so the Army of the Gulf could prepare for a Mobile expedition.[26] When Banks sputtered at Mansfield, he upset the entire Union program.

Instead of capturing Shreveport by mid-April, Banks became mired in the "pine desert" of west Louisiana with the tenacious Richard Taylor. This deprived the Union armies east of the Mississippi of manpower needed to bring the enormous pressure to bear on the primary Confederate armies. The Confederates capitalized on this opportunity by shifting their forces to counter Grant's spring offensive. First, Nathan Bedford Forrest launched a major raid against Sherman's tenuous supply line out of Nashville threatening to ground his offensive against Atlanta. Simultaneously, the Rebels reinforced Johnston's Army of Tennessee with Polk's Corps from Mississippi providing that army with a major accession in strength. Next, Robert E. Lee detached a division to North Carolina under Major General Robert F. Hoke that captured the important transportation node at Plymouth. Finally, Lee sent the aggressive Lieutenant General Jubal A. Early on a raid down the Shenandoah Valley with open-ended orders to enter Maryland if the opportunity offered.[27] The Confederates, seemingly on the ropes at the start of 1864, were now surging on all fronts, especially in the Trans-Mississippi where Taylor had a large fleet and army cornered and Price had frustrated Steele's hungry corps. If they could destroy Banks and Porter, the potential existed for the ragtag Rebels in the far west to influence the war far beyond anyone's expectations.

The Confederates, however, did not exploit this opportunity to change the outcome of the war because Kirby Smith failed to recognize the potential of the situation. To understand how the Trans-Mississippi Department could have changed the war one must examine the events that took place after Banks and Porter escaped the Red River Valley. Upon leaving Louisiana Grant had the Army of the Gulf broken up to reinforce the major theaters in the east. First, A. J. Smith took the XVI and part of the XVII corps back to Mississippi to tangle with Forrest. The sudden appearance of over 10,000 Union soldiers in Mississippi in June forced the Rebel cavalryman to focus his efforts on defeating Smith rather than on destroying Sherman's supply line.[28] Had A. J. Smith been captured along the Red River, Forrest could have concentrated on breaking the Louisville & Nashville Railroad. Disruption of this line — Sherman's sole avenue of logistic support — would have forced Sherman to halt operations in Georgia for an indefinite period of time. With northern morale already sagging and a presidential election in the offing, such a turn of events would probably have had a detrimental effect on the Union cause.

Second, Grant had the 19th Corps transferred to Virginia. George Meade's Army of the Potomac had suffered horrific losses in the six weeks since the spring campaigns kicked off in May. The manpower of the XIX Corps would at least partially make up for the 50,000 casualties absorbed by Meade's army to this point. Instead of disembarking around Richmond in July, Grant diverted the XIX to Washington where the cantankerous Jubal Early was threatening to snatch the Federal capital. Since launching his raid down the Shenandoah, Early had met and defeated two Federal armies and followed up his success by investing Washington. The arrival of the XIX and VI corps—from Meade's army — in the capital blunted Early's foray. Grant then appointed General Phillip Sheridan to command the combined force in order to drive Early back up the Shenandoah and destroy his Rebel corps if possible. Sheridan relentlessly pursued Early over the next three months defeating him at Winchester and Fisher's Hill. Then in October, only a month before the national election, Sheridan virtually destroyed Early's small army at Cedar Creek forever closing the Shenandoah Valley to Confederate control.[29] The victory at Cedar Creek gave the Union war effort a huge boost, practically ensuring Lincoln's reelection. The XIX Corps played a central role in defeating Early, but if they had not escaped Louisiana in May Grant would have had to tap his already depleted Army of the Potomac for soldiers to drive Early away from Richmond.

Next, the XIII Corps formed the nucleus of the force that would close Mobile Bay to Confederate blockade runners. Grant had intended for Banks to launch an expedition to Mobile as part of his overall program for winning the war in 1864. Banks' miscues in Louisiana upset his plans, however, and allowed forces under Leonidas Polk to move away from a position covering Mobile to Georgia to reinforce Johnston. This helped even Johnston's odds in confronting Sherman in his campaign to take Atlanta. Almost as soon as the XIII Corps returned to New Orleans they began making preparations for the expedition to close Mobile. By July the XIII was in position to take the outlying forts protecting the harbor in conjunction with the navy. On August 5 Admiral David Farragut ran Forts Morgan and Gaines at the mouth of the bay as the XIII took them from the land face. Gideon Welles, Secretary of the Navy, exclaimed that "news of Farragut's having passed Forts Morgan and Gaines was received last night and sent a thrill of joy through all true hearts."[30] Indeed, the victory at Mobile was the first piece of good news from the war front that the Lincoln Administration had received for sometime. Word of the triumph had a positive effect on public morale in the North and did much to help Lincoln's reelection prospects.

Finally, elements of Thomas Kilby Smith's XVII Corps division returned to Sherman's army in Georgia while Porter's Mississippi Squadron resumed its patrols on the river from which it derived its name. While the addition of a few regiments of infantry would not make a significant accession to Sherman's troop strength, it certainly could not hurt. The return of the Mississippi Squadron, however, was critical to Union plans for success in 1864. These gunboats enforced the split between the eastern and western Confederacy preventing her from transferring troops and resources between the two halves of the struggling nation. Until July 1863 the Rebels had used their interior lines to shift forces across the great river to reinforce threatened points. The capture of Vicksburg cut off the Trans-Mississippi from the rest of the Confederacy and the Union navy ensured that they could no longer make any major transfers across the Mississippi. The capture or destruction of 19 warships in the Red would have jeopardized Federal superiority of the western rivers. This is because the innovative Rebels would certainly have salvaged the Union ships in order to challenge the remaining Union boats in the Mississippi Squadron.[31] The Confederates might have been able to wrest temporary control of a section of the river to shift forces to the east. The addition of more Rebels in the east against a loss of over 30,000 Federals would have thrown Grant's plans off track and had a detrimental effect on the Northern homefront.

Therefore, it is reasonable to make the assumption that if the Confederates under Richard Taylor had captured or destroyed the Army of the Gulf and the Mississippi Squadron it would have seriously upset Union strategy for winning the war. This is because the Rebels would have made it appear in the eyes of the northern public that the Federal armies could not subdue them. With this in mind, voters going to the polls in November might have cast ballots for George B. McClellan repudiating the Lincoln Administration's war policy. Thus, the Confederacy could win the war by not losing on the battlefield.[32] Countering the Red River Campaign offered the Confederacy such opportunities to influence the outcome of the war in their favor, but Kirby Smith failed to recognize it. What events occurred that blinded Smith to these possibilities? The Camden Expedition; the power struggle within the Confederate high command in the Trans-Mississippi; and the first rate conduct of affairs by the leaders of the VII Corps acted together to cause the Confederacy to let an excellent chance to influence the war slip from their grasp. When Frederick Steele launched the expedition it confused Smith as to where to place the preponderance of his resources to counter the twin offensives. In choosing to go after Steele, Smith tacitly allowed Banks and Porter to escape believing that Arkansas represented the greater threat to the department.

As stated in the beginning, the Camden Expedition almost did not happen at all. Steele had never fully embraced the idea of an expedition from Little Rock to Shreveport for several reasons. First and most important, the department under his command was utterly denuded of food for man and animal. This would require Steele to subsist his army by water or rail instead, but these transportation networks did not exist in southwest Arkansas. Therefore, from a logistic standpoint, a march to Shreveport was not practical. Second, Steele realized that cooperation between the two converging forces would be problematic at best. A large Confederate force interposed between the Union armies making communication difficult and allowing the Rebels to make full use of interior lines to mass against the widely separated columns. In light of these reasons, Steele attempted to squirm out of launching a full expedition, instead favoring a large cavalry raid.[33]

Ulysses Grant understood Steele's position very well, but he also saw the bigger picture. Should Banks move through the Red River Valley unsupported, the Confederates would simply mass against him stopping his offensive short of the objective, Shreveport. If Banks then became bogged down in Louisiana he could not wrap up the campaign quickly enough to return east to support Grant's grand scheme for 1864. A supporting effort from the direction of Arkansas would give the Rebels pause and afford Banks better odds to accomplish his mission in the time Grant allotted. As a result, Grant issued a blunt directive ordering Steele to begin a full-scale offensive immediately in support of Banks.[34] Grant's decision proved prescient as the Camden Expedition had the intended effect of confusing the Rebel commander, E. Kirby Smith. The confusion was supposed to result in ensuring Banks' success, but instead it saved him and his army and the Union fleet from destruction. Had Steele not advanced Banks would probably have met with a disaster.

When Banks appeared at Simmesport, Louisiana, in early March, Smith began busying himself with massing available forces in the Trans-Mississippi against the Army of the Gulf. Then, two weeks later, Sterling Price reported the thrust from his quarter of the department. As Grant expected, the move confounded Kirby Smith who began to consolidate forces at Shreveport rather then sending them forward to Taylor to contend with Banks. After several days of indecision, Smith determined, erroneously, that Frederick Steele's column was the main effort aimed at the Trans-Mississippi capital. In conjunction with this determination, Smith decided to push Banks back, frustrating his offensive, and then turn with full force on Steele.[35] This sent Taylor into a rage as he believed Smith was laying his home state open for depredations by the Federal army.

Taylor took matters into his own hands by launching a counteroffensive against Banks at Mansfield. The attack realized spectacular results as the small Confederate army under Taylor sent Banks running for cover. Taylor seemed to realize that he had an unprecedented opportunity to deal a death blow to Banks that could have effects reaching well beyond the confines of the Trans-Mississippi. Therefore, he wanted to relentlessly pursue the Army of the Gulf, which he believed was cornered in northwest Louisiana.[36] However, Smith saw the situation differently. Taylor had decisively defeated Banks who would now withdraw from Louisiana of his own accord. The discomfiture of Banks fit neatly into Smith's plans since he could now turn on Steele in Arkansas. Kirby Smith then stripped Taylor of most of his infantry and headed north to drive away Steele. As events turned out, Steele had already halted his advance by veering off course to Camden in an effort to supply his army. This raises the question: did Smith really need to go after the struggling VII Corps? Due to the precarious logistic situation in Steele's army, the answer is no. Smith, however, persisted in his determination to attack the VII Corps, which he believed represented the greatest threat to the department.

One probable reason Smith favored pursuing Steele is that he could put some distance between himself and the irritable Richard Taylor. The commander of the District of West Louisiana had relentlessly criticized and insulted Kirby Smith in a deluge of correspondence. Although a patient and polite man, Smith certainly had a breaking point with reference to how much criticism he would tolerate from Taylor. Price, on the other hand, had paid Smith the proper respect due his position, making his relationship with Smith far more cordial. As a result, Smith moved north as much to get away from Taylor as to come to grips with Steele. When Taylor offered to accompany Smith north to assist in any fighting in Arkansas, the commanding general refused stating "that his leadership was no longer needed." Taylor felt snubbed by the "curt manner" of this refusal and again brooded over his situation and perception of Smith's poor style of leadership.[37] In addition to the efforts of the Federals to divert attention from Banks, infighting between Smith and Taylor had contributed much to enabling the Army of the Gulf to escape disaster.

The Camden Expedition then had direct effects on the outcome of events in the Red River Valley, which, in turn had a vast indirect influence on the course of the war. Had this minor offensive not occurred it is highly plausible that with nothing to divert Confederate attention, the Rebels would have destroyed Nathaniel P. Banks and the Army of the Gulf along the Red River. This eventuality would have deprived the Union of over 30,000 veteran troops and a score of warships at a pivotal time for the United States. For the Confederacy to win the Civil War in 1864 it would have had to win in the minds of the northern voters by making it appear that the Federal armies could not defeat them. Confidence in the Lincoln Administration's war policy was already fragile and any serious setbacks might have convinced the public that a change of government was in order. This could have led to the election of the Democratic candidate, George B. McClellan, whom the Confederates believed would push for a negotiated peace recognizing the Confederacy.[38] Disaster in Louisiana would have facilitated this outcome since the Army of the Gulf could not have participated in the successful actions at Mobile, Atlanta, and Cedar Creek if captured.

It is a tribute to the senior leaders of the VII Corps that they were able to conduct the expedition in the manner they did in light of the serious obstacles facing them from the outset. After expressing his misgivings, Steele had reluctantly launched the expedition on Grant's personal order and, in spite of the logistic constraints, turned in a competent performance. Of equal importance is the outstanding service provided by the subordinate commanders of the corps during the expedition. In contrast to the troubled Rebel command environment, the Union leaders maintained a high level of loyalty and civility. While an undercurrent of dissension existed within the army, to a man the division commanders exhibited the utmost deference to Steele. This promoted an air of cooperation and unity of effort that enabled the hungry Federals to overcome great adversity. Carr, Thayer, and Salomon each performed in a professional and competent manner bringing their unique capabilities to bear at the appropriate time throughout the trying six weeks. Salomon, in particular, commanded brilliantly in the rear guard action at the Battle of Jenkins' Ferry saving the beleaguered corps from possible annihilation. The positive leadership environment existing in the Union Department of Arkansas played the leading role in the outcome of the Camden Expedition and directly influenced the results of the Red River Campaign.

On the Confederate side, Kirby Smith successfully implemented his Fabian defensive strategy, expelling the twin offensives and thus maintaining the integrity of his department. However, he fumbled a larger opportunity to succor the Confederate cause largely because of his defensive strategy and the poor command climate within his department. The Army of the Gulf escaped providing Ulysses Grant with a source of trained manpower to press his plans for the campaign of 1864. The arrival of the various corps at decisive points and critical times in the east made significant contributions to several victories in the summer and fall. This helped sagging morale in the North to rebound ensuring Lincoln's reelection and, more important, vindicating his war policy of total victory.

Grant's direct order forcing Steele to move, along with the poor command climate in the Trans-Mississippi high command, saved the Army of the Gulf from destruction. Steele's assessment of the possibility of success proved quite correct as his army struggled just to feed man and animal. The Union army suffered from the elements, hunger, and the enemy in its forlorn attempt to cooperate with Banks in Louisiana. Many of the participants on the Federal side believed the expedition constituted a "gigantic failure" or "terrible defeat," and, on the surface, this is the case.[39] Yet, unknown to these men their sufferings had not occurred in vain. They diverted the attention of the Confederates away from the more lucrative target, the Army of the Gulf. This made that army's escape and later contributions to winning the war possible. For this the soldiers and leaders of the VII Corps deserve great credit as their tiny force had done much to win the Civil War and preserve the Union.

═══════════════

Notes

1. *OR*, Vol. 34, Part 1, 670, and Part 3, 360.
2. Sperry, *History of the 33rd Iowa*, 109–110.
3. *OR*, Vol. 34, Part 1, 670.
4. *Ibid.*, 790, and Blessington, *Walker's Texas Division*, 253.
5. Walker, "The War of Secession West of the Mississippi River," 66.

6. Blessington, *Walker's Texas Division*, 253.

7. *OR*, Vol. 34, Part 1, 840.

8. *Ibid.*

9. *Ibid.*, Part 3, 377–379.

10. Sperry, *History of the 33rd Iowa*, 110.

11. *Ibid.*, 112.

12. *OR*, Vol. 34, Part 1, 727; and Sperry, *History of the 33rd Iowa*, 112.

13. Sperry, *History of the 33rd Iowa*, 112–113; and *OR*, Vol. 34, Part 3, 395.

14. Sperry, *History of the 33rd Iowa*, 113.

15. Bearss, *Steele's Retreat From Camden*, 175–177; Walker, "The War of Secession West of the Mississippi River," 67; and Blessington, *Walker's Texas Division*, 254.

16. Blessington, *Walker's Texas Division*, 254–255; and Walker, "The War of Secession West of the Mississippi River," 65.

17. *Ibid.*, 248; Bragg, "Chasing Steele through Jenkins' Ferry," *Ouachita County Historical Quarterly* (Spring 1998), 10; Walker, "The War of Secession West of the Mississippi River," 65; and *OR*, Vol. 34, Part 1, 782, 790, 815, 818, and 837.

18. *OR*, Vol. 34, Part 1, 530–531, and Part 3, 728, 744, 759, 761, and 801–802; and Foote, *The Civil War*, III, 102–103.

19. *OR*, Vol. 34, Part 1, 537 and 540–548, and Part 3, 802 and 810–811; and John G. Walker "Papers," University of North Carolina Southern Historical Collection. From an April 26, 1864, letter penned by Taylor's aide-de-camp to Walker highly critical of Smith's conduct of operations during the Red River Campaign.

20. *OR*, Vol. 34, Part 3, 828–829.

21. Foote, *The Civil War*, III, 576.

22. Shalhope, *Sterling Price*, 256–257.

23. *OR*, Vol. 34, Part 1, 684, 692, 712, 714, 746, 767, and 786–788. Confederate returns are estimates.

24. Grant, *Memoirs*, II, 129–140.

25. *OR*, Vol. 34, Part 1, 616.

26. *Report of the Joint Committee*, 382–385.

27. Wyeth, *That Devil Forrest*, 342–343; Foote, *The Civil War*, III, 104–115; and Vandiver, *Jubal's Raid*, 25–26.

28. Wyeth, *That Devil Forrest*, 375–380.

29. Jeffrey D. Wert, *From Winchester to Cedar Creek*, 20–29.

30. Hearn, *Mobile Bay and the Mobile Campaign*, 70–79; and Welles, *Diary of Gideon Welles*, II, 100.

31. *Report of the Joint Committee*, 244–245 and 250–253.

32. Foote, *The Civil War*, III, 101.

33. *Report of the Joint Committee*, XXXI-XXXII.

34. *OR*, Vol. 34, Part 1, 616.

35. *Ibid.*, 526 and 531–532.

36. *Ibid.*, 530 and 541–542.

37. Prushankin, "A Crisis in Command," 81; and Taylor, *Destruction and Reconstruction*, 213.

38. Long, *The Jewel of Liberty*, 265–268.

39. Crawford, *Kansas in the Sixties*, 134; and Sperry, *History of the 33rd Iowa*, 113.

Appendix 1.

Campaign Chronology[1]

Date	Event
1863	
10 August	Halleck sends dispatch to Banks informing him of need "to restore flag" to Texas soil and suggesting Red River as invasion route. Banks is cool to such an idea.
10 September	Union Army commanded by Major General Frederick Steele takes Little Rock, capital of Arkansas.
19 November	Major General John M. Schofield, commander of the Department of Missouri, expresses support for Halleck's plan to Major General Nathaniel P. Banks as a means of securing Missouri from future threats from Rebel raids.
12 December	Steele states in a letter to Schofield, his misgivings about providing support to Banks from Arkansas.
1864	
4 January	Halleck again "suggests" that Banks carry out a Red River Campaign with support from Arkansas by Steele.
23	Banks for the first time gives his support to Halleck's plan for a Red River Campaign and seeks assurances from him that adequate "cooperation" will materialized from the Navy, Sherman, and Steele in Arkansas. Steele, however, in a series of messages remains unconvinced of the merits of the proposed effort, especially the role assigned to him.
12 March	Steele requests permission from Halleck to make a "demonstration" with his cavalry rather than a full-scale expedition. At the same time, the Red River Campaign begins at Simmesport, Louisiana.
13	General Edmund Kirby Smith expresses his opinion to Major General Richard Taylor that Steele in Arkansas represents the primary threat to the Trans-Mississippi Department.
14	Major General A. J. Smith as part of the movement up the Red captures Fort DeRussy.

Date	*Event*
15 March	Lieutenant General U. S. Grant, the new Union general-in-chief, orders Steele to "move in full cooperation" with Banks' campaign in Louisiana.
17	Steele orders Brigadier General John Milton Thayer to prepare for march south in a cooperative effort to support Banks. They will link up at Arkadelphia.
18	General Edmund Kirby Smith orders Major General Sterling Price to detach his infantry to Taylor in Louisiana.
20	Sherman in a dispatch to Steele expresses his displeasure that Steele has dragged his feet on supporting Banks.
23	Steele advances from Little Rock en route to Shreveport and immediately orders issuance of half rations for the duration of the expedition. Simultaneously, Thayer leaves Fort Smith en route to Arkadelphia.
26	Steele crosses the Ouachita vicinity of Rockport after some skirmishing.
29	Steele occupies Arkadelphia after some skirmishing around the town. He awaits Thayer here for the designated link-up on April 1, but Thayer's column finds rough going in the Arkansas swamps and bottomlands and with guerillas nipping at their heels.
30	Union cavalry under Colonel Powell Clayton disperses a Confederate brigade at the battle of Mt. Elba. This action secures the Federal supply base at Pine Bluff.
2 April	Banks and Admiral David D. Porter arrive at Grand Ecore, La. Steele decides to continue march after hearing no word of Thayer's whereabouts.
4	Banks receives orders from Grant to wrap up the Red River Campaign by April 10.
5	Banks decides to diverge from river road to save time en route to Shreveport.
4–6	Steele engages Price at Elkin's Ferry attempting to cross the Little Missouri River.
7	Steele sends urgent request to his rear detachment commander at Little Rock, Brigadier General Nathan Kimball, to send a supply train to Camden. Steele's already depleted logistic situation is becoming desperate due to the delay in waiting for Thayer.
8	Banks defeated by Taylor at Mansfield marking the turning point of the Red River Campaign. Steele continues his march southward as he has no established line of communication with Banks in Louisiana. He will not receive word of Banks' setback for several days.
9	Thayer's lead elements begin arriving in the vicinity of the Little Missouri River, finally uniting Steele's forces in Arkansas. Meanwhile, Banks repulses Taylor in the Battle of Pleasant Hill, but decides to retreat back to Grand Ecore. Steele now presses Rebel cavalry hard at the Prairie D'Ane in a feint toward Washington.
10	Banks arrives at Grand Ecore while Porter's fleet encounters trouble from guerillas and rapidly lowering water levels in the Red. Smith

Date	*Event*
10 April	informs Taylor of his intent to take three infantry divisions from his Louisiana army up to Arkansas to meet Steele, over Taylor's loud objections.
11–12	Steele forces Price's cavalry back on Washington then suddenly shifts his line of march toward Camden.
13	Discovering the Federals gone from his front, Price turns in pursuit of Steele sending the bulk of his force to the rear of the column while simultaneously pushing Brigadier General Jo Shelby's brigade around the Union army to cut it off from Camden.
14	Taylor reluctantly detaches Churchill's, Parsons', and Walker's divisions north into Arkansas while he maintains a loose cordon around Banks' army at Grand Ecore. Porter is now back at Grand Ecore after struggling with low water levels in the Red. Price skirmishes with Steele but cannot slow him appreciably.
15	Shelby successfully places a line across the Federal avenue of advance, but Steele overwhelms him forcing his way into Camden. On the Red River, the pride of Porter's fleet, *Eastport*, sinks when it strikes a mine.
16	Steele receives rumors of Banks' demise in Louisiana, later confirmed by a dispatch from Banks. Steele now has no regular rations and decides to send out foraging parties to provide relief from the strained subsistence situation.
17	A large Union forage train of some 200 wagons and over 1,000 men departs Camden for farm areas west of town in search of subsistence.
18	Confederate cavalry under Brigadier General John S. Marmaduke destroys all 200 wagons and disperses the guard at Poison Springs. This exacerbates the serious supply situation. The 1st Kansas (Colored) Infantry suffers horrendous casualties as Rebels seek to "punish" Negro soldiers.
20	Confederate infantry starts arriving in Arkansas bolstering Price's forces around Camden.
21	Banks brushes aside Taylor at Grand Ecore and commences a retreat to Alexandria. Taylor pursues with a meager force in an attempt to trap Banks between the Cane and Red Rivers.
22	Steele sends 240 wagons and about 1,800 men to Pine Bluff for supplies. Vigilant Rebel cavalry observes the movement.
23	Taylor's small "army" is defeated at Monette's Ferry on the Cane River as the Federal XIXth Corps forces a crossing of the stream.
25	Confederate cavalry under Brigadier General James Fagan ambushes the supply train at Marks' Mills, once again destroying all the wagons and capturing most of the escort. In Louisiana Banks arrives at Alexandria.
26	Steele knows that his position is now untenable and seeks the opinions of his officers. All but one general agree that a retreat back to Little Rock is the only course of action left to the army. The movement begins in secret that night.

Date	*Event*
27 April	Kirby Smith orders a pursuit of Steele when his pickets discover Camden abandoned. Banks and Porter are trapped at Alexandria when the gunboats cannot pass the rapids. Taylor clamors for reinforcements from Smith to no avail.
30	Smith's army in Arkansas catches Steele at Jenkins' Ferry on the Saline River attempting to cross the stream. He launches a full-scale assault on the Federal rear, but is bloodily repulsed. Federals now destroy all remaining impediments to their retreat such as wagons and artillery that their weakened animals cannot pull. Steele successfully crosses the Saline and continues retreating to Little Rock.
3 May	Steele arrives unmolested in Little Rock ending the Camden Expedition.
4	Rebels wreak havoc in Louisiana destroying several Union gunboats at David's Ferry on the Red while attempting to communicate with Porter and Banks at Alexandria. Construction of dam begins in attempt to pass gunboats over rapids at Alexandria.
13	Porter's fleet passes falls as Banks pushes Taylor aside. Retreat continues to Simmesport.
19	Smith directs Price in a dispatch to begin preparations for an August invasion of Missouri.
14–21	After several sharp engagements the Federal Army of the Gulf crosses the Atchafalaya making good their escape from Red River Valley much to Taylor's disgust. This ends the Red River Campaign.
22	A. J. Smith's XVI and XVII Corps divisions reembark for Mississippi.
5 June	Kirby Smith relieves Taylor after a long string of insubordinate correspondence.
11 July	Elements of the XIX Corps (formerly of the Army of the Gulf) arrive in Washington, D.C., in time to repulse Jubal Early's attack on the city.
14	A. J. Smith with XVI Corps (formerly attached to the Army of the Gulf) meets Nathan Bedford Forrest at Tupelo, Mississippi, forcing Forrest back into central Mississippi. This successfully prevents Forrest from cutting Sherman's supply line to Georgia.
2–8 August	Elements of XIII Corps, Army of the Gulf, in conjunction with Admiral David Farragut take the forts protecting Mobile Bay sealing off the port for further Confederate use.
2 September	Confederates evacuate Atlanta, while Sherman, with the elements of the XVII Corps that participated in the Red River Campaign, moves into the city.
7	Price crosses the Arkansas River with over 10,000 troops thus launching the long awaited invasion of Missouri.
19	XIX Corps, now in Major General Philip Sheridan's Army, defeats Early

Date	*Event*
19 September	at Winchester, Virginia, in the Shenandoah Valley. Price crosses the Missouri state line.
22	Early suffers another setback at Fisher's Hill in the Shenandoah with the XIX Corps present.
19 October	XIX Corps once again plays a decisive role in battle as Sheridan routs Early at Cedar Creek finally wresting control of the Shenandoah from the Confederates.
23	Price meets with a resounding defeat in his invasion of Missouri at Westport. Union troops under Major General William S. Rosecrans nearly destroy Price's army and force him on a long retreat back to Arkansas. In the process, Price's army dwindles to a fifth of its original strength as men desert by the thousands.
8 November	Northern public reelects Lincoln by a large majority guaranteeing a Union victory in the Civil War. All the Federal troops that escaped from the Red River Valley have now made significant contributions to the Union cause. Their contributions were not possible except for the diversion made by the Union army in Camden Expedition, which, in effect, saved them for service on other fields.

Notes

1. Compiled from the following sources: *OR*, series 1, Vol. 34, part 1, 653–654; E. B. and Barbara Long, *The Civil War Day By Day*, 474–579; and *Report of the Joint Committee.*

Appendix 2.
Order of Battle[1]

Union
Union Department of Arkansas and VII Army Corps
Maj. Gen. Frederick Steele

Headquarters Troops (escort)
D Company, 3rd Illinois Cavalry
H Company, 15th Illinois Cavalry

Third Division
Brig. Gen. Frederick Salomon

First Brigade	*Second Brigade*	*Third Brigade*
Brig. Gen. Samuel Rice	Col. William E. McLean	Col. Adolph Englemann
50th Indiana	43rd Indiana	43rd Illinois
29th Iowa	36th Iowa	40th Iowa
33rd Iowa	77th Ohio	27th Wisconsin
9th Wisconsin		

Artillery
Vaughn's Illinois Battery
E Battery, 2nd Missouri Light
Voegele's Wisconsin Battery

Frontier Division
(Joined the march in the vicinity of Elkins Ferry)
Brig. Gen. John M. Thayer

First Brigade	*Second Brigade*	*Third Brigade (Cavalry)*
Col. John Edwards	Col. Charles W. Adams	Col. Owen Bassett
1st Arkansas	1st Kansas (Colored)	2nd Kansas
2nd Arkansas (8 Cos.)	2nd Kansas (Colored)	6th Kansas
18th Iowa	12th Kansas	14th Kansas
2nd Indiana Battery	1st Arkansas Battery	

Cavalry Division
Brig. Gen. Eugene A. Carr

First Brigade
Col. John F. Ritter
3rd Arkansas (4 Cos.)
1st Missouri (8 Cos.)
2nd Missouri
13th Illinois and 3rd Iowa
   (Detachment)

Third Brigade
Col. Daniel Anderson
1st Iowa
10th Illinois
   (Detachment)
3rd Missouri

Independent Cavalry Brigade
   (At Pine Bluff)
Col. Powell Clayton
1st Indiana Cavalry (8 Cos.)
5th Kansas Cavalry
7th Missouri Cavalry
28th Wisconsin Infantry
18th Illinois Infantry
1st Indiana Battery

Total effective Union force: approximately 11,500 men of all arms

---

CONFEDERATE

Confederate Army

General Edmund Kirby Smith, Commanding, Dept. of the Trans-Mississippi

District of Arkansas
Maj. Gen. Sterling Price

Escort: 14th Missouri Battalion

Fagan's Cavalry Division[2]
Brig. Gen. James F. Fagan

Cabell's Brigade
Brig. Gen. W. L. Cabell
1st Arkansas
2nd Arkansas
4th Arkansas
7th Arkansas
Gunter's Arkansas
   Battalion
Harrell's Arkansas Battalion
Blocher's Battery

Dockery's Brigade
Brig. Gen. Thomas Dockery
18th Arkansas
19th Arkansas
20th Arkansas
12th Arkansas
   Sharpshooters

Crawford's Brigade
Col. W. A. Crawford
3rd Arkansas
Crawford's Regiment
Wright's Arkansas Regiment
Poe's Battalion
McMurtrey's Arkansas
   Battalion
Hughey's Arkansas Battery

Marmaduke's Cavalry Division
Brig. Gen. John S. Marmaduke

Greene's Brigade
Col. Colton Greene
3rd Missouri
4th Missouri
7th Missouri
8th Missouri
10th Missouri
Harris' Missouri Battery

Shelby's Brigade
Brig. Gen. Joseph O. Shelby
1st Missouri Battalion
5th Missouri
11th Missouri
12th Missouri
Hunter's Regiment
Collins' Missouri Battery

Maxey's Cavalry Division
(Arrived from Indian Territory 7-12 April and departed on 27 April)
Brig. Gen. Samuel B. Maxey

Gano's Brigade   *Choctaw Brigade*
Col. Charles DeMorse   Col. Tandy Walker
29th Texas   1st Regiment
30th Texas   2nd Regiment
31st Texas
Welch's Company
Krumbhaar's Texas Battery

(The following infantry divisions arrived on 20 April in Arkansas and were
attached to General Price's command on 26 April 1864)

Walker's Division
Maj. Gen. John G. Walker (wounded)

Waul's Brigade   *Scurry's Brigade*   *Randal's Brigade*
Brig. Gen.   Brig. Gen. W. R. Scurry   Col. Horace Randal
  Thomas N. Waul   (killed at Jenkins' Ferry) (killed at Jenkins' Ferry)
8th Texas   3rd Texas   28th Texas Cavalry
18th Texas   16th Texas   (Dismounted)
22nd Texas   17th Texas   11th Texas
13th Texas Cavalry   19th Texas   14th Texas
  (Dismounted)   16th Texas Cavalry   Gould's Battalion
                            (Dismounted)

Arkansas Division
Brig. Gen. Thomas J. Churchill

Tappan's Brigade   *Gause's Brigade*   *Hawthorn's Brigade*[3]
Brig. Gen. James C. Tappan   Col. Lucien C. Gause
19th and 24th Arkansas (Consolidated)   26th Arkansas
27th and 38th Arkansas (Consolidated)   32nd Arkansas
33rd Arkansas   36th Arkansas

Missouri Division
Brig. Gen. Mosby M. Parsons

First Brigade   *Second Brigade*
Brig. Gen. John B. Clark   Col. S. P. Burns
8th Missouri   10th Missouri
9th Missouri   11th Missouri
Ruffner's Missouri Battery   12th Missouri
                                   16th Missouri
                                   9th Missouri Battalion Sharpshooters
                                   Lesueur's Missouri Battery

Total effective Confederate force: approximately 14,000 men

Notes

1. Compiled from the *OR,* Vol. 34, Part 1, 657–658; *B & L* Vol. 4, 368; and *Confederate Military History* Vol. 10, 273–279. Confederate field returns are incomplete for the District of Arkansas and the data contained here are based on scanning several reports from the commanders. Data concerning Confederate artillery units are almost entirely incomplete. The Arkansas and Missouri divisions' commanders kept better returns than Price's cavalry units and the order of battle is more complete.

2. Confederate units at the division and brigade levels generally took the name of their commanding officers and did not have number designations. Most of the regiments were numbered; however, in some cases these units took on the name of their commander as the designation.

3. Incomplete records in the *OR* do not permit the listing of subordinate units.

Bibliography

Bibliographical Note

One would think that since so little has been written about the Camden Expedition it would be difficult to find adequate sources. I found that this was not the case. In fact, there is a wealth of sources available for researching this forgotten operation. In this note, I would like to identify those sources I found most useful and those that are questionable in reliability; and offer a possible explanation for a yawning gap in Camden's historiography.

Without a doubt the most useful source is *War of the Rebellion: A Compilation of the Official Records of the Union and Confederate Armies*, which compiles all after action reports and correspondence of the unit commanders into Volume 34, Parts 1–3. It is an excellent repository for investigating the progress of the campaign and veracity of the participants. By far the best firsthand account is *The History of the 33rd Iowa Volunteer Infantry* by the oft-quoted Union Private Andrew Sperry. I found his record of the Camden Expedition accurate, lively, and complete. Sperry had a talent for capturing the moment and placing the reader at the center of the action he was experiencing. Without this fine chronicle, a full history of the expedition would have been far more difficult to weave together.

No full-length firsthand Confederate account exists of the expedition. Therefore, I used several reminiscences of the expedition written at different points to piece together a viewpoint from the Confederate soldier's perspective. Among the best is Dr. Junius Bragg's short article "Chasing Steele through Jenkins' Ferry" and Joseph Blessington's *Walker's Texas Division*.

There are two excellent general overviews available that provide an account from the Union and Confederate points of view. Both were written by participants some years after the war and give a fairly accurate synopsis of events. From the Union side, Wiley Britton's history *The Civil War on the Western Border* provided a fine overview of the entire operation, while the authoritative *Confederate Military History*, Volume 10 — Clement Evans, editor — gives a review from the Rebel standpoint.

Unfortunately, some chroniclers wrote highly biased treatises that, while useful in specific areas, were suspect in others. John Edwards' *Shelby and His Men* is the most prominent of these from the Confederate side. Edwards was an aide to Joseph Shelby and his biography of the cavalry commander was an unabashed attempt to inflate the considerable reputation of his chief. Yet, Edwards does provide an excellent glimpse of such incidents as the atrocities at Poison Springs and Marks' Mills. While maintaining a critical eye, one can find a great deal of excellent information from his biography. Samuel Crawford's *Kansas in the Sixties* is a subjective history on the Union side. Crawford openly expresses disdain for Frederick Steele's leadership. However, just like Edwards, Crawford offers many interesting anecdotes of the expedition and his role as commander of the 2nd Kansas (Colored) is critical to unfolding events at Jenkins' Ferry.

As rich as the Camden literature is, a gap still exists in the written history of the expedition from the perspective of the Rebels. With the exception of the *Official Records* and John Edwards's biography of Shelby, there is no Confederate account of the opening phases from a private soldier's standpoint. There is little primary Confederate source material describing the Union advance on Washington and Elkins' Ferry, or the attempt to block Steele from reaching Camden — those phases prior to the point where the Rebel infantry divisions arrived from Louisiana. We may find a possible explanation by examining the background of the Confederate units that participated in the early operations. By and large the Confederates hailed from the poorest, hardscrabble regions of the Confederacy. These men came from the backwoods of Missouri, lowlands of Arkansas and Louisiana, and open plains of the Indian Territory. Not noted for emphasis on education, these areas had a high percentage of illiterate men who were of military age. Therefore, few would have left a written account of their experiences. Perhaps this is the reason for the dearth of Rebel material from the opening stages of the Camden Expedition.

Nevertheless, I enjoyed searching for sources and reading about the unique and trying expedition. Though history has largely ignored the experiences of the men who fought its battles, Camden is no less exciting than any other action of the Civil War. Further, as I attempt to show in the text, this operation did have an important effect on the outcome of the war and is well worthy of examination by serious students of the conflict as well as by casual readers.

Unpublished Sources

Banks, Nathaniel P. Papers. Charles Ramsdell Microfilm Collection, reels 786.1, 786.7, 786.9, and 786.16, University of Texas at Austin.

Carr, Eugene Asa, Papers. United States Army Military History Institute, Carlisle Barracks, Carlisle, Pennsylvania.

Price, Sterling, Papers. Special Collections, Rice University Library. Copies of General Orders issued by Sterling Price as Commander of the Missouri State Guard.

_____. Manuscript and Special Collections Library, Duke University, Durham, North Carolina.

_____. Missouri State Historical Society. Papers and General Orders, University of Missouri, Columbia.

Smith, Edmund Kirby, Papers. Southern Historical Collection, University of North Carolina, Chapel Hill.

Steele, Frederick, Papers. Department of Special Collections, Collection number M0191, Stanford University Libraries, Stanford, California.

Taylor, Richard, Papers. Louisiana Adjutant General's Office, Jackson Barracks, New Orleans.

Thayer, John Milton, Collection. Nebraska State Historical Society, Collection number RG001 Nebraska Governors, Sub-group 14, John Thayer, Box 12, Lincoln.

Walker, John G., Papers. Southern Historical Collection, University of North Carolina, Chapel Hill.

_____. "The War of Secession West of the Mississippi River During the Years 1863-4 & 5. Mss. Myron Gwinner Collection, United States Army Military History Institute, Carlisle Barracks, Carlisle, Pennsylvania.

Published Primary Sources

Basler, Roy P., ed. *The Collected Works of Abraham Lincoln*. 9 vols. New Brunswick: Rutgers University Press, 1953.

Bee, Hamilton. "Battle of Pleasant Hill." *Southern Historical Society Papers* VIII: 184–186. 1880.

Boggs, William R. *Military Reminiscences of General Wm. R. Boggs, C. S. A.* Durham: Seeman Printery, 1913.

Buck, Nina Smith. "Blucher of the Day at Manassas." *Confederate Veteran*, VII (March 1889): 108. Reprint. Broadfoot Publishing Company, 1987–88.

Blessington, Joseph P. *The Campaigns of Walker's Texas Division*. New York: Lane, Little & Co., 1875. Reprint. Austin, Texas: State House Press, 1994.

Britton, Wiley. *Civil War on the Border* II. Ottawa, Kansas: reprint by Kansas Heritage Press, 1999.

_____. *The Union Indian Brigade in the Civil War*. Kansas City, Mo.: Franklin Hudson, 1922. Reprint, Ottawa, Kansas: Kansas Heritage Press, 1992.

Crawford, Samuel J. *Kansas in the Sixties*. Ottawa, Kansas: reprint by Kansas Heritage Press, 1994.

Crist, Lynda Lasswell, Mary Seaton Dix, and Kenneth H. Williams, eds. *The Papers of Jefferson Davis*. Ten Volumes. Baton Rouge: Louisiana State University Press, 1997.

Davis, Jefferson. *Jefferson Davis, Constitutionalist: His Letters, Papers, and Speeches*. Edited by Roland Dunbar. Volume VI, New York: Press of J. J. Little & Ives Company for the Mississippi Department of Archives and History, 1923.

Debray, Xavier. "Debray's 26th Texas Cavalry." *Southern Historical Society Papers* XIII. 153–165, 1885.

Dooley, Amanda M. *Autobiography of August Bondi: 1833–1907*. Bethesda, Maryland: University Publications of America, 1993. On microfiche at the Combined Arms Research Library, Fort Leavenworth, Kansas.

Dorsey, Sarah A. *Recollections of Henry Watkins Allen, Brigadier-General, Confederate States Army, Ex-Governor of Louisiana*. New York: M. Doolady, 1866.

Douglas, H. T. "The Trans-Mississippi Department." *Confederate Veteran*, XXV (April 1917): 153-155. Reprint, Broadfoot Publishing Company, 1987-88.

Drake, F. M. "Campaign of General Steele." *War Sketches and Incidents from Iowa Commandery of the Military Order of the Loyal Legion of the United States*, Vol. 1. Des Moines: 1893.

Edwards, John N. *Shelby and His Men or the War in the West*. Cincinnati: Miami Printing and Publishing Company, 1867.

Elliot, M. A., ed. *The Garden of Memory: Stories of the Civil War as Told by Veterans and Daughters of the Confederacy*. Camden, Arkansas: The Hurley Co., 1976.

Evans, Clement, ed. *Confederate Military History: Louisiana and Arkansas*, X. Atlanta: Confederate Publishing Co., 1899.

Fountain, Sarah M., ed. "Letters of War." *Ouachita County Historical Quarterly*, Vol. 27/No. 2 (Winter 1995): 15–35. Excerpts from *Sisters, Seeds and Cedars*.

Grant, U. S. *Personal Memoirs of U. S. Grant*. Edited by E. B. Long. Cleveland: World Publishing, 1952. Reprint with an introduction by William S. McFeely, New York: Da Capo Press, 1982.

Hay, John, and John Nicolay. *Abraham Lincoln: A History*. 10 vols. New York: The Century Co., 1909.

Hazewell, C. C. "The Twentieth Presidential Election." *Atlantic Monthly*, 14 (November 1864): 633–641.

Heartsill, W. W. *Fourteen Hundred and 91 Days in the Confederate Army*. Edited by Bell I. Wiley. Jackson, Tennessee: McCowat-Mercer Press, 1953.

Hinton, Richard J. *Rebel Invasion of Missouri and Kansas and the Campaign of the Army of the Border, Against General Sterling Price in October and November, 1864*. Chicago: Church and Goodman, 1864. Microfilmed by the Combined Arms Research Library, Fort Leavenworth, Kansas.

Johnson, Robert U., and Clarence C. Buell, eds. *Battles and Leaders of the Civil War*. 4 vols. New York: 1887. Reprint, New Jersey: Castle Company, 1989.

Jones, J. B. *A Rebel War Clerk's Diary*. 2 vols. Philadelphia: Lippincott & Co., 1866. Reprint, edited by Earl Schenck Miers in one volume, New York: Sagamore Press, Inc., 1958.

Kean, Robert Garlick Hill. *Inside the Confederate Government: The Diary of Robert Garlick Hill Kean*. Edited by Edward Younger. New York: Oxford University Press, 1957.

Liddell, St. John R. *Liddell's Record*. Edited by Nathaniel C. Hughes. Dayton: Morningside, 1985.

Lothrop, Charles. *A History of the First Iowa Cavalry Volunteers, from Its Organization in 1861 to Its Muster Out of United States Service in 1866*. Lyons, Iowa: Beers & Eaton, 1890.

Lowell, James Russell. "The Next General Election." *North American Review*, 99 (October 1864): 557–72.

Official Military History of Kansas Regiments During the War for Suppression of the Great Rebellion. Joshiah B. McAfee, compiler. Leavenworth, Kansas: 1870.

Porter, David Dixon. *Incidents and Anecdotes of the Civil War*. New York: D. Appleton and Company, 1885. Reprint, Harrisburg, Pennsylvania: The Archive Society, 1997

_____. *The Naval History of the Civil War*. New York: Sherman Publishing Company, 1886. Reprint, Harrisburg, Pennsylvania: The Archive Society, 1998.

Quaife, Milo Milton, ed. *The Diary of James K. Polk: During His Presidency, 1845–1849*. With an introduction by Andrew Cunningham McLaughlin. Chicago: A. C. McClurg & Co., 1910.

"The Red River Campaign." *Ouachita County Historical Quarterly*, Vol. 31/No. 3 (Spring 2000): 9–28. Excerpt from *Harper's Pictorial History of the Civil War*.

Red River Expedition: Extracts from: United States Congress: Joint Committee on the Conduct of the War: Report of the Joint Committee on the Conduct of the War, 1863–1865; The Thirty-Eighth Congress, Second Session. Millwood, New York: Kraus Reprint Co., 1977.

Ryan, Frank T. "The Kentucky Campaign and Battle of Richmond." *Confederate Veteran*, XXVI (April 1918): 158–160. Reprint, Broadfoot Publishing Company, 1987–1988.

Scott, Winfield. *Memoirs of Lieutenant General Scott, LL.D*. Two vols. New York: Sheldon & Co., Publishers, 1864.

Shaw, William T. "The Red River Campaign." *Confederate Veteran*, XXV (March 1917): 116–118. Reprint, Broadfoot Publishing Company, 1987–1988.

Sherman, William T. *Memoirs of General W. T. Sherman*. 2 vols. New York: D. Appelton and Company, 1875. Reprint, Harrisburg, Pennsylvania: The Archive Society, 1997.

Sliger, J. E. "How General Taylor Fought the Battle of Mansfield, La." *Confederate Veteran*, XXXI (December 1923): 456–458. Reprint, Broadfoot Publishing Company, 1987–1988.

Sperry, A. F. *History of the 33rd Iowa Infantry Volunteer Regiment 1863–6*. Edited by Gregory J. W. and Cathy Kunzinger Urwin. Fayetteville: University of Arkansas Press, 1999.

Stinson, Virginia M. "The Yankees in Camden." *Ouachita County Historical Quarterly*, Vol. 25/No. 3 (Spring 1994): 25–28.

Stuart, A. A. *Iowa Colonels and Regiments: Being a History of Iowa Regiments In the War of the Rebellion; and Containing a Description of the Battles in Which They Fought*. Des Moines: Mills & Co., 1865.

Taylor, Richard. *Destruction and Reconstruction: Personal Experiences of the Late War*. New York: Appelton and Company, 1879. Reprint with an introduction by Edwin C. Bearss. New York: Bantam Books, 1992. This reprint does not follow the same pagination of the original text.

Twelfth Kansas Infantry Association. *Regimental Roster*. Bethesda, Maryland: University Publications of America, 1993. On microfiche at the Combined Arms Research Library, Fort Leavenworth, Kansas.

United States War Department. *Official Records of the Union and Confederate Navies in the War of the Rebellion*. 31 vols. Washington, D.C.: Government Printing Office, 1894–1927.

_____. *The War of the Rebellion: A Compilation of the Official Records of the Union and Confederate Armies*. 127 vols. Washington, D.C.: Government Printing Office, 1880–1901.

Welles, Gideon. *The Diary of Gideon Welles, Secretary of Navy Under Lincoln and Johnson*. 3 vols. Boston: Houghton Mifflin, 1911.

White, Lonnie J., ed. "A Bluecoat's Account of the Camden Expedition." *Arkansas Historical Quarterly*, Vol. 24 (Spring 1965), 82–89.

Wilcox, Cadmus. *History of the Mexican War*. Washington, D.C.: The Church News Publishing Co., 1892.

Zorn, Roman J., ed. "Campaigning in Southern Arkansas: A Memoir By C. T. Anderson." *Arkansas Historical Quarterly*, Vol. 8 (Autumn 1949): 240–244.

Secondary Sources

Abel, Annie Heloise. *The American Indian as Participant in the Civil War*, II. Cleveland: The Arthur Clark Company, 1919.

Anders, Curt. *Disaster in Damp Sand: The Red River Expedition*. Indianapolis: Guild Press of Indiana, 1997.

Atkinson, Edward. "The Battle of Marks' Mill." *Arkansas Historical Quarterly*, Vol. XX (Winter 1955): 381–384.

Atkinson, J. H. "The Action at Prairie De Ann." *Arkansas Historical Quarterly*, Vol. XIX (Spring 1960): 40–50.

Bailey, Anne J. "The Abandoned Western Theater: Confederate National Policy Toward the Trans-Mississippi Region." *Journal of Confederate History*, V (1990): 35–54.

_____. *Arkansas in the Civil War*. Fayetteville: University of Arkansas Press, 1998.

_____. "Edmund Kirby Smith." *Confederate General*. Ed. William C. Davis. V: 162–171. Harrisburg: National Historical Society, 1991.

Bearss, Edwin C. "The Battle of Poison Springs." *Ouachita County Historical Quarterly*, Vol. 25/No. 3 (Spring 1994): 13–24.

_____. *The Battle of Wilson's Creek*. Cassville, Missouri: Wilson's Creek National Battlefield Foundation, 1992.

_____. *Steele's Retreat from Camden and the Battle of Jenkins' Ferry*. Little Rock: Pioneer Press, 1961.

_____. *The Vicksburg Campaign*. 3 Vols. Dayton, Ohio: Morningside House, Inc., 1985.

Black, Robert C. III. *The Railroads of the Confederacy*. Chapel Hill: University of North Carolina Press, 1952. Reprint with new foreword by Gary W. Gallagher, 1998.

Boritt, Gabor S., ed. *Jefferson Davis's Generals*. New York: Oxford University Press, 1999.

Bragg, Jefferson D. *Louisiana in the Confederacy*. Baton Rouge: Louisiana State University Press, 1941.

Brooksher, William R. *War Along the Bayous: The 1864 Red River Campaign in Louisiana*. Washington and London: Brassey's, 1998.

Buckalew, Arthur R., and Robert B. Buckalew. "Hillsboro's Soldier-Citizen: Horatio Gates Perry Williams." *Arkansas Historical Quarterly*, Vol. 31 (Spring 1972), 36–57.

Castel, Albert. *Decision in the West: The Atlanta Campaign of 1864*. Lawrence: University of Kansas Press, 1992.

_____. *General Sterling Price and the Civil War in the West*. Baton Rouge: Louisiana State University Press, 1968; paperback edition, 1993.

Cathey, Henry. "Extracts from the Memoirs of William Franklin Avera." *Arkansas Historical Quarterly*, Vol. XXII (Winter 1963), 99.

Catton, Bruce. *Grant Takes Command*. Boston: Little, Brown, 1968.

_____. *Never Call Retreat*. New York: Doubleday, 1965.

Comtois, Pierre. "Red River Campaign: Collision at Sabine Crossroads." *Military History*, Vol. 14 (October 1997), 54–61.

Connelley, William E. *Doniphan's Expedition and the Conquest of New Mexico and California*. Kansas City: Bryant & Douglas Book and Stationery Co., 1907.

Connelly, Thomas L. *Army of the Heartland: The Army of Tennessee, 1863–1865*. Baton Rouge: Louisiana State University Press, 1967; reprint 1993.

Cooper, William J., Jr. *Jefferson Davis, American*. New York: Alfred A Knopf, Division of Random House Publishing, 2000.

Cornish, Dudley T. *The Sable Arm: Negro Troops in the Union Army, 1861–1865*. New York: W. W. Norton & Co., 1966.

Cozzens, Peter. *The Darkest Days of the War: The Battles of Iuka and Corinth*. Chapel Hill: University of North Carolina Press, 1997.

Daniel, Larry J. *Shiloh: The Battle That Changed the Civil War*. New York: Simon & Schuster, 1997.

Dawson, Joseph G. III. "American Civil-Military Relations and Military Government: The Service of Colonel Alexander Doniphan in the Mexican War." *Armed Forces and Society*, Vol. 22 (Summer 1996), 555–573.

Donald, David H., ed. *Why the North Won the Civil War: Six Authoritative Views on the Economic, Military, Diplomatic, Social, and Political Reasons Behind the Confederacy's Defeat*. New York: Simon & Schuster, 1996.

Dougan, Michael B. *Confederate Arkansas*. Tuscaloosa: University of Alabama Press, 1976; reprint 1991.

_____. "Life in Confederate Arkansas." *Arkansas Historical Quarterly*, Vol. XXXI (Spring 1971), 15–31.

Eisenhower, John S. D. *So Far from God: The U. S. War with Mexico 1846–1848*. New York: Random House, 1989.

"The Federal Occupation of Camden as Set Forth In the Diary of a Union Officer." *Arkansas Historical Quarterly*, Vol. IX (Autumn 1950), 214–219.

Fisher, Mike. "The Camden Expedition." M.A. thesis: Kansas State College of Pittsburg, 1975.

Foote, Shelby. *The Civil War: A Narrative*. Volume III, *Red River to Appomattox*. New York: Random House, 1974.

"The Forgotten March: The Red River Campaign." Produced by James Kilcoyne, Henry Maggio, and Daniel Graves, 35 mins. The Museum of Historic Natchitoches, 1994. Videocassette.

Forsyth, Michael J. *The Red River Campaign of 1864 and the Loss by the Confederacy of the Civil War*. Jefferson, North Carolina: McFarland, 2002.

Gabel, Christopher R. *Railroad Generalship: Foundations of Civil War Strategy*. Fort Leavenworth, Kansas: U. S. Army Command and General Staff College, 1997.

Glatthaar, Joseph T. *Partners in Command: The Relationships Between Leaders and the Civil War*. New York: The Free Press, 1994.

Harrington, Fred H. *Fighting Politician: Major General N. P. Banks*. Philadelphia: University of Pennsylvania Press, 1948.

Hearn, Chester G. *Admiral David Dixon Porter*. Annapolis: Naval Institute Press, 1996.

_____. *Mobile Bay and the Mobile Campaign*. Jefferson, North Carolina: McFarland, 1993.

Henry, Robert S. *"First with the Most" Forrest*. New York: Mallard Press, 1991.

Hollandsworth, James G. *Pretense of Glory: The Life of General Nathaniel P. Banks*. Baton Rouge: Louisiana State University Press, 1998.

Horn, Stanley F. *The Army of Tennessee*. Norman: University of Oklahoma Press, 1952.

Hudson, James J., ed. "From Paraclifta to Marks' Mill: The Civil War Correspondence of Lieutenant Robert C. Gilliam." *Arkansas Historical Quarterly*, Vol. XVII (Autumn 1958), 272–280.

Jackson, Donald Dale. *Twenty Million Yankees: The Northern Home Front*. Civil War Series. Alexandria, Virginia: Time-Life Books, 1985.

Johansson, M. Jane Harris. "Peculiar Honor: A History of the 28th Texas Cavalry (Dismounted), Walker's Texas Division, 1862–1865." Ann Arbor, Michigan: Doctoral dissertation reprinted by UMI Dissertation Services, 1995.

Johnson, Ludwell. *Red River Campaign: Politics and Cotton in the Civil War*. Kent, Ohio: Kent State University Press, 1993.

Josephy, Alvin M., Jr. *War on the Frontier: The Trans-Mississippi West*. Alexandria, Virginia: Time-Life Books, 1986.

Kerby, Robert L. *Kirby Smith's Confederacy: The Trans-Mississippi South, 1863–1865*. Tuscaloosa: University of Alabama Press, 1991.

Kinchen, Oscar A. *Confederate Operations in Canada and the North: A Little Known Phase of the American Civil War*. Quincy, Massachusetts: Christopher Publishing House, 1970.

Lester, Robert E., ed. *Civil War Unit Histories: Regimental Histories and Personal Narratives. Part 4. The Union — Midwest and West*. Bethesda, Maryland: University Publications of America, 1993.

Lewis, Lloyd. *Captain Sam Grant*. Boston: Little, Brown and Company, 1950.

Long, David E. *The Jewel of Liberty: Abraham Lincoln's Re-election and the End of Slavery*. Mechanicsburg, Pennsylvania: Stackpole Books, 1994.

Long, E. B., and Barbara Long. *The Civil War Day by Day: An Almanac 1861–1865*. With foreword by Bruce Catton. New York: Doubleday, 1971; reprint in paperback, New York: Da Capo Press, 1991.

McDonough, James L. *Shiloh: In Hell Before Night*. Knoxville: University of Tennessee Press, 1977.

McLeod, Edward S. "The Frontier Division in the Camden Expedition." Thesis, University of Northern Iowa Special Collections Library, 1912.

McPherson, James M. *Battle Cry of Freedom: The Civil War Era*. New York: Oxford University Press, 1988.

Military Analysis of the Civil War: An Anthology by the Editors of Military Affairs. Introduction by T. Harry Williams: Millwood, New York: KTO Press, 1977.

Monachello, Anthony. "Missouri in the Balance: Struggle for St. Louis." *America's Civil War*, Vol. 11 (March 1998), 44–51.

Nelson, Larry E. *Bullets, Ballots, and Rhetoric: Confederate Policy for the United States Presidential Contest of 1864*. University: University of Alabama Press, 1980.

O'Flaherty, Daniel. *General Jo Shelby: Undefeated Rebel*. Chapel Hill: University of North Carolina Press, 1954.

Palmer, Patricia J. *Frederick Steele: Forgotten General*. Stanford: Stanford University Libraries, 1971.

Parks, Joseph H. *General Edmund Kirby Smith C. S. A.* Baton Rouge: Louisiana State University, 1954 and 1982.

Parrish, T. Michael. *Richard Taylor: Soldier Prince of Dixie*. Chapel Hill: University of North Carolina Press, 1992.

Prushankin, Jeffery S. "A Crisis in Command: Richard Taylor and Edmund Kirby Smith in Confederate Louisiana During the Red River Campaign." M.A. thesis, Falvey Memorial Library, Villanova University, 1996.

Rea, Ralph R. *Sterling Price: The Lee of the West*. Little Rock: Pioneer Press, 1959.

Reeves, Bob. "Fort Lookout." *Ouachita County Historical Quarterly*, Vol. 30/No. 1 (Fall 1998): 12–20.

Richards, Ira Don. "The Battle of Jenkins' Ferry." *Arkansas Historical Quarterly*, Vol. 20 (Spring 1961), 3–16.

_____. "The Battle of Poison Spring." *Arkansas Historical Quarterly*, Vol. 18 (Winter 1959), 338–349.

_____. "The Camden Expedition, March 23-May 3, 1864." M.A. thesis, University of Arkansas, 1958.

_____. "The Engagement at Marks' Mills." *Arkansas Historical Quarterly*, Vol. 19 (Spring 1960), 51–60.

Shalhope, Robert E. *Sterling Price: Portrait of a Southerner*. Columbia: University of Missouri Press, 1971.

Shea, William L. "The Camden Fortifications." *Arkansas Historical Quarterly*, Vol. 41 (Winter 1982), 318–326.

_____, and Earl J. Hess. *Pea Ridge: Civil War Campaign in the West*. Chapel Hill: University of North Carolina Press, 1992.

Trudeau, Noah André. *Like Men of War: Black Troops in the Civil War 1862–1865*. New York: Little, Brown, 1998.

United States. Army. *Field Manual 3–0, Operations*. Washington, D.C.: U. S. Government Printing Office, 2001.

_____. _____. *Student Text 101–5, Command and Staff Decision Processes*. Fort Leavenworth, Kansas: Command and General Staff College, 1995.

Vandiver, Frank E. *Jubal's Raid: General Early's Famous Attack on Washington in 1864*. New York: McGraw-Hill, 1960; reprint, Lincoln: University of Nebraska Press, 1992.

Warner, Ezra J. *Generals in Blue: Lives of the Union Commanders*. Baton Rouge: Louisiana State University Press, 1964; reprint 1992.

_____. *Generals in Gray: Lives of the Confederate Commanders*. Baton Rouge: Louisiana State University Press, 1959; reprint 1992.

Waugh, John C. *Reelecting Lincoln*. New York: Crown, 1997.

Welsh, Jack M.D. *Medical Histories of Confederate Generals*. Kent, Ohio: Kent State University Press, 1995.

_____. *Medical Histories of Union Generals*. Kent, Ohio: Kent State University Press, 1995.

Wert, Jeffry D. *From Winchester to Cedar Creek*. South Mountain Press, 1987; reprint with new material, Mechanicsburg, Pennsylvania: Stackpole Books, 1997.

Wiley, Bell I. *The Life of Johnny Reb: The Common Soldier of the Confederacy*. New York: Bobbs-Merrill, 1943.

Wills, Brian Steel. *A Battle from the Start: The Life of Nathan Bedford Forrest*. New York: HarperCollins, 1992.

Winschel, Terrence J. *Triumph and Defeat: The Vicksburg Campaign*. Mason City, Iowa: Savas Publishing Company, 1999.

Winters, John D. *The Civil War in Louisiana*. Baton Rouge: Louisiana State University Press, 1963.

Woodworth, Steven E. *Jefferson Davis and His Generals: The Failure of Confederate Command in the West*. Lawrence: University of Kansas Press, 1990.

Wyeth, John Allan. *That Devil Forrest: A Life of General Nathan Bedford Forrest*. Reprint, with a new foreword by Albert Castel. Baton Rouge: Louisiana State University Press, 1989.

Index

Numbers in boldface refer to pages with photographs